CAMBRIDGE LANGUAGE TEACHING LIBRARY

A series covering central issues in language teaching and learning, by authors who have expert knowledge in their field.

In this series:

Language test construction
and evaluation

Language Test Construction and Evaluation

J. Charles Alderson,
Caroline Clapham and
Dianne Wall

CAMBRIDGE
UNIVERSITY PRESS

CAMBRIDGE UNIVERSITY PRESS
Cambridge, New York, Melbourne, Madrid, Cape Town, Singapore, São Paulo

Cambridge University Press
The Edinburgh Building, Cambridge CB2 2RU, UK

www.cambridge.org
Information on this title: www.cambridge.org/9780521478298

First published 1995
9th printing 2005

A catalogue record for this publication is available from the British Library

ISBN-13 978-0-521-47829-8 paperback
ISBN-10 0-521-47829-4 paperback

Transferred to digital printing 2006

To Simon and Lucy, Phoebe and Tom

Contents

1 Origins and overview

This book is written for teachers of any language who are responsible for drawing up tests of language ability and for other professionals who may not be actively involved in teaching but who have some need to construct or evaluate language tests or examinations, or to use the information that such tests provide. (Since the distinction between a *test* and an *examination* is so vague, we use the terms interchangeably in this book.) Although our examples are mostly taken from the field of English as a Foreign Language, the principles and practice we describe apply to the testing of any language, and this book is certainly relevant to teachers and testers of any second or foreign language as well as to teachers and testers of first languages.

Those who are teaching may have to design placement tests for new incoming students, they may need to construct end-of-term or mid-year achievement tests for different levels within an institution, or they may be responsible for the production of major achievement test batteries at the end of a relatively long period of study.

Those who are not teaching but need to know how to produce tests include officials working for examination boards or authorities, and educational evaluators, who need valid and reliable measures of achievement.

Others who may need to design language tests include postgraduate students, researchers and academic applied linguists, all of whom need tests as part of their research. The test may be a means of eliciting linguistic data which is the object of their study, or it may be intended to provide information on linguistic proficiency for purposes of comparison with some other linguistic variable.

But in addition to those who need to construct tests, there are those who wish to understand how tests are and should be constructed, in order better to understand the assessment process, or in order to select from among a range of available tests one instrument suitable for their own contexts. Such people are often uncertain how to evaluate the claims that different examining authorities make for their own instruments. By understanding what constitutes good testing practice and becoming aware of current practices, such readers should be enabled to make more informed choices to suit their purposes.

In this book, we describe the process of test construction, from the drafting of the initial test specifications through to the reporting of test scores and the devising of new tests in the light of developments and feedback. The book is intended to describe and illustrate best practice in test development, and the principles of test design, construction and administration that underpin such best practice.

The book is divided into eleven chapters, each dealing with one stage of the test construction process. Chapter 2 deals with the drawing up of the specifications on which the test is based. Chapter 3 describes the process of writing individual test items, their assembly into test papers and the moderation or editing which all tests should undergo. Chapter 4 discusses the importance of trialling the draft test and describes how tests should be analysed at this stage. Chapter 5 describes the training of markers and test administrators, whilst Chapter 6 shows how to monitor examiner reliability. Chapter 7 deals with issues associated with the setting of standards of performance and the reporting of results, whilst Chapter 8 describes further aspects of the process of test validation. Chapter 9 describes how reports on the performance of the test as a whole should be written and presented, and Chapter 10 discusses how tests can be developed and improved in the light of feedback and further research. The final chapter discusses the issue of standards in language testing and describes the current State of the Art.

Doubtless, this brief sketch of the content of the book sounds daunting: the test construction process is fairly complex and demanding. However, we have attempted to render our account user-friendly by various means. Each chapter opens with a brief statement of the questions that will be addressed and concludes with a checklist of the main issues that have been dealt with which can be consulted by busy teachers, exam board officials, researchers and test evaluators.

Our descriptions of the principles and procedures involved in language testing do not presuppose any knowledge of testing or of statistics. Indeed, we aim to provide readers with the minimum technical knowledge they will need to construct and analyse their own tests or to evaluate those of others. However, this is not a textbook on psychometrics: many good textbooks already exist, and the reader who becomes interested in this aspect of language testing is encouraged to consult the volumes listed at the end of this chapter. However, the reader should note that many books on educational measurement do not confine themselves to language testing, and they frequently assume a degree of numeracy or a familiarity with statistical concepts that our experience tells us most people involved in language testing do not possess. Our hope, though, is that having read this volume, such people will indeed be ready to read further.

Something we do not do in this book is to describe language testing techniques in detail. This is partly because this topic is already addressed to some extent by a number of single volumes, for example, Oller 1979; Heaton 1988; Hughes 1990; Weir 1990; Cohen 1994. However, more importantly for us, we believe that it is not possible to do justice to this topic within the covers of one volume. In order to select test techniques and design good test items, a language tester needs a knowledge of applied linguistics, language teaching and language learning which cannot adequately be conveyed in a 'How-To' book, much less in the same volume as the discussion of testing principles and procedures. For the present we refer readers to the above language testing textbooks if what they need is a brief exemplification of test techniques.

Throughout the book we complement our discussion of the principles of test design with examples of how EFL examination boards in the United Kingdom implement these in practice. The second half of each chapter provides an illustration of how what we describe in the first part of each chapter is actually put into practice by examination boards in the UK.

Our aim is not to advocate that all tests should be constructed in the way UK examination boards do so: far from it. Rather, we wish to provide concrete examples that should help our readers understand the theory. We intend that this illustration should be relevant to all our readers and not just to exam board officials, although we believe that such officials will find it instructive to see the procedures and practices of other examination boards. Although the examples in this book are clearly located in a particular context – the UK – we know from experience that similar practices are followed elsewhere, and we firmly believe that language testers anywhere in the world will find aspects of the practice in a particular setting of relevance to their own context. The principles are universal, even if the practice varies.

We have discovered, from conducting workshops around the world with budding language testers, that anyone interested in learning about test construction, be it a placement test, an achievement test or a proficiency test, can learn from the experience of others. We present the data on current practice in the UK critically: we discuss strengths and weaknesses, and make suggestions for change if best practice is to be realised. The reader can perhaps take heart that even examination boards do not always do things perfectly; we all have things to learn from relating principles to practice.

We gathered this information in a variety of ways which we describe below, but first we digress to describe why this volume came to be written. All three authors had experienced considerable frustration at not having available any account of how examination boards construct language tests. We have all three taught language testing on MA courses, in-service courses for practising teachers, and in workshops around the world for different audiences. We have had considerable experience of working with UK examination boards as item writers, members of editing committees, examiners, test validators and testing researchers. We are all acquainted with language testing theory and the principles of test design. Yet nowhere had we found an adequate description of how examinations are constructed in order to implement the principles.

Our first attempt systematically to collect information about UK examination boards began in 1986, when we were invited to carry out a research project that was to make recommendations for quality control procedures in new English language examinations in Sri Lanka. We held a series of interviews with representatives of various EFL examining boards in order to find out how they conducted tests of writing and speaking. These interviews resulted in a number of reports whose content was subsequently agreed with respondents. The reports were circulated internally at Lancaster and made available to visitors and students, but were never published, and did not in any case cover all the bodies engaged in EFL examining in the UK.

One of the authors of this book was invited by Karl Krahnke and Charles Stansfield to contribute as co-editor to the TESOL publication *Reviews of English Language Proficiency Tests*. Part of the work involved commissioning reviews of twelve UK EFL examinations. These reviews were subsequently sent to the respective examination boards for comment. They were then amended where necessary and published in Alderson et al. 1987. Many of the reviewers made similar points about both the strengths and weaknesses of UK exams, some of which were contested by the examination boards. Of the twelve UK tests reviewed, the reviewers criticised nine for failing to provide sufficient evidence of reliability and validity, and in only two cases did the reviewers express satisfaction with the data provided. Alderson included in this TESOL publication *An Overview of ESL/EFL Testing in Britain*, which explained British traditions to readers from other countries. In this overview he stated:

> Due to the constant need to produce new examinations and the lack of
> emphasis by exam boards on the need for empirical rather than
> judgemental validation, these examinations are rarely, if ever, tried out
> on pupils or subjected to the statistical analyses of typical test
> production procedures. Examination boards do not see the need to
> pretest and validate their instruments, nor conduct post-hoc analyses of
> their tests' performance. Although the objective items in the tests are

usually pretested, the statistics are rarely published.
(Alderson et al. 1987)

This overview was subsequently updated for a chapter in Douglas 1990 on UK EFL examining. In order to gather up-to-date information, Alderson sent a copy of the original overview to UK examination boards and asked whether it was still substantially correct or whether any amendments were necessary. Few boards responded, but those that did said that things had not changed.

The Lancaster Language Testing Research Group next decided to survey the boards. For this purpose, we referred to the Appendix in Carroll and West 1989, the report of the English Speaking Union (ESU)'s Framework Project. In addition, we decided to include in our survey the Schools Examination and Assessment Council (SEAC, formerly SEC, the Secondary Examinations Council), a body set up by the Government and charged with the responsibility of establishing criteria for judging educational examinations and of determining the validity of such exams.

Our survey was in three parts. First, in December 1989 we wrote letters to each of the examining authorities listed, and to SEAC. These letters contained the three following open-ended questions, which sought to elicit the boards' own views of their standards and the procedures they used to establish reliability and validity:

1. Do you have a set of standards to which you adhere?
2. What procedures do you follow for estimating test reliability?
3. What procedures do you follow to ensure test validity?

We presented the results of this first phase of our research to a meeting of the Association of British ESOL Examining Boards (ABEEB) in November 1990.

Secondly, we circulated a questionnaire to the same examination boards in December 1990. A summary of the responses to this questionnaire forms part of the second half of each chapter of this book. A written version of the results was circulated to the responding examination boards for their comments in May 1991, and discussions were held about the study. We subsequently gave each board the opportunity to update its response, on the grounds that much development had taken place during the intervening months, and we received very detailed responses to this from the University of Cambridge Local Examinations Syndicate (UCLES) in particular.

Thirdly, we also received a large amount of printed material associated with the various examinations from the boards, and we have analysed these in some detail: we present summaries of and examples from this analysis where appropriate in each chapter. It may be of interest to the reader, however, to know which documents we received. They are listed, together with the names of the boards and the examinations they produce, in Appendix 1.

A summary of some of the main results from Phase Two of the survey has already appeared in Alderson and Buck 1993, but this book contains more detail than that paper, and updates much of the information in it. It is, of course, possible there may have been changes in the procedures followed by some boards since we completed our research. We hope that we have not misrepresented any examining body, but would welcome any corrections, additions or other modifications that might be necessary. Since most examination boards preferred to remain anonymous when the results of the survey were published, we only name those boards which gave us permission to do so, or where we are quoting from publicly available literature.

This book has very much benefited from the knowledge gained as a result of the survey. We hope that our readers will benefit equally from being able to read an account of current practice alongside a description of the principles of language testing, and the procedures we believe to be appropriate for test construction.

More important than the details of the practice of individual examination boards are the principles that should underlie language testing practice, and that is why each chapter contains a detailed treatment of these principles. That is also why each chapter ends with a section that lists the questions an evaluator might ask of any test, or a checklist of things that test designers or evaluators need to pay attention to.

The overarching principles that should govern test design are *validity* and *reliability,* and we make constant reference to these throughout the book. Validity is the extent to which a test measures what it is intended to measure: it relates to the uses made of test scores and the ways in which test scores are interpreted, and is therefore always relative to test purpose. Although the only chapter in the book with a reference to validity in its title is Chapter 8, the concept of validity is central to all the chapters. Reliability is the extent to which test scores are consistent: if candidates took the test again tomorrow after taking it today, would they get the same result (assuming no change in their ability)? Reliability is a property of the test as a measuring instrument, but is also relative to the candidates taking the test: a test may be reliable with one population, but not with another. Again, although reliability is only mentioned in one chapter title (Chapter 6), it is a concept which runs through the book.

We attempt to define the specialist testing terminology when we first use it, and so we will not enter into further definitions at this point.

However, we have supplied a glossary of important terms in testing, for the reader's reference. We are also aware that most readers will not be familiar with the abbreviations and acronyms often used in EFL testing, and in particular those that are used to denote the UK examination boards. We have therefore also supplied a comprehensive list of such terms at the end of the book.

The research reported in this book is the result of many months of collaboration amongst members of the Lancaster Language Testing Research Group and visiting researchers. We are very grateful to the following for their assistance, encouragement and criticisms: Joan Allwright, Gary Buck, Nicki McLeod, Frank Bonkowski, Rosalie Banko, Marian Tyacke, Matilde Scaramucci and Pal Heltai. We would also like to thank the various examination boards, the British Council, and Educational Testing Service, New Jersey, for their help.

Bibliography

Alderson, J.C. and G. Buck. 1993. Standards in Testing: A Survey of the Practice of UK Examination Boards in EFL Testing. *Language Testing* 10(1): 1–26.

Alderson, J.C., K. Krahnke and C. Stansfield (eds.). 1987. *Reviews of English Language Proficiency Tests.* Washington, DC: TESOL.

Anastasi, A. 1988. *Psychological Testing.* London: Macmillan.

Carroll, B.J. and R. West. 1989. *ESU Framework: Performance Scales for English Language Examinations.* London: Longman.

Cohen, A. 1994. *Assessing Language Ability in the Classroom.* 2nd edition. Rowley, Mass.: Newbury House/Heinle and Heinle.

Crocker, L. and J. Algina. 1986. *Introduction to Classical and Modern Test Theory.* Chicago, Ill.: Holt Rinehart Winston.

Douglas, D. (ed.). 1990. *English Language Testing in U.S. Colleges and Universities.* Washington, DC: NAFSA.

Ebel, R.L. 1979. *Essentials of Educational Measurement.* 3rd edition. Englewood Cliffs, NJ: Prentice-Hall.

Ebel, R.L. and D.A. Frisbie. 1991. *Essentials of Educational Measurement.* 5th edition. Englewood Cliffs, NJ: Prentice-Hall.

Guilford, J.P. and B. Fruchter. 1978. *Fundamental Statistics in Psychology and Education.* Tokyo: McGraw Hill.

Hambleton, R.K., H. Swaminathan and H.J. Rogers. 1991. *Fundamentals of Item Response Theory.* Newbury Park, Calif.: Sage Publications.

Heaton, J.B. 1988. *Writing English Language Tests.* 2nd edition. London: Longman.

Henning, G. 1987. *A Guide to Language Testing.* Cambridge, Mass.: Newbury House.

Hughes, A. 1990. *Testing for Language Teachers*. Cambridge: Cambridge University Press.

Ingram, E. 1977. Basic Concepts in Testing. In J.P.B. Allen and A. Davies (eds.), *Testing and Experimental Methods*. Oxford: Oxford University Press.

Lord, F.M. 1980. *Applications of Item Response Theory to Practical Testing Problems*. Hillsdale, NJ: Lawrence Erlbaum.

Oller, J.W. 1979. *Language Tests at School*. London: Longman.

Popham, W.J. 1990. *Modern Educational Measurement: A Practitioner's Perspective*. 2nd edition. Boston, Mass.: Allyn and Bacon.

Weir, C.J. 1990. *Communicative Language Testing*. Englewood Cliffs, NJ: Prentice-Hall Regent.

2 Test specifications

The questions that this chapter seeks to answer in detail are: What are test specifications? Who needs test specifications? What should test specifications look like? How can we draw up test specifications? What do current EFL examinations prepare in the way of specifications?

2.1 What are test specifications?

A test's specifications provide the official statement about what the test tests and how it tests it. The specifications are the blueprint to be followed by test and item writers, and they are also essential in the establishment of the test's construct validity.

Deriving from a test's specifications is the test syllabus. Although some UK examination boards use *specifications* and *syllabus* interchangeably, we see a difference between them. A test specification is a detailed document, and is often for internal purposes only. It is sometimes confidential to the examining body. The syllabus is a public document, often much simplified, which indicates to test users what the test will contain. Whereas the test specification is for the test developers and those who need to evaluate whether a test has met its aim, the syllabus is directed more to teachers and students who wish to prepare for the test, to people who need to make decisions on the basis of test scores, and to publishers who wish to produce materials related to the test.

The development and publication of test specifications and syllabuses is, therefore, a central and crucial part of the test construction and evaluation process. This chapter will describe the sorts of things that test specifications and syllabuses ought to contain, and will consider the documents that are currently available for UK EFL tests.

2.2 Who needs test specifications?

As has already been suggested, test specifications are needed by a range of different people. First and foremost, they are needed by those who produce the test itself. Test constructors need to have clear statements about who the test is aimed at, what its purpose is, what content is to be covered, what methods are to be used, how many papers or sections there are, how long the test takes, and so on. In addition, the specifications will need to be available to those responsible for editing and moderating the work of individual item writers or teams. Such editors may operate in a committee or they may be individual chief examiners or board officials. (See Chapter 3 for further discussion of the editing process.) In smaller institutions, they may simply be fellow teachers who have a responsibility for vetting a test before it is used. The specifications should be consulted when items and tests are reviewed, and therefore need to be clearly written so that they can be referred to easily during debate. For test developers, the specifications document will need to be as detailed as possible, and may even be of a confidential nature, especially if the test is a 'high-stakes' test.

Test specifications are also needed by those responsible for or interested in establishing the test's validity (that is, whether the test tests what it is supposed to test). These people may not be the test constructors, but outsiders or other independent individuals whose needs may be somewhat different from those of the item writers or editors. It may be less important for validators to have 'practical' information, for example, about the length of the test and its sections, and more important to know the theoretical justification for the content: what theories of language and proficiency underpin the test, and *why* the test is the way it is.

Test users also need descriptions of a test's content, and different sorts of users may need somewhat different descriptions. For example, teachers who will be responsible for the learners placed in their classes by a test need to know what the test scores mean: what the particular learners know, what they can do, what they need to learn. Although the interpretation of test scores is partly a function of how scores are calculated and reported (see Chapter 7), an understanding of what scores mean clearly also relates to what the test is testing, and therefore to some form of the specifications.

Teachers who wish to enter their students for some public examination need to know which test will be most appropriate for their learners in relation to the course of instruction that they have been following. They need information which will help them to decide which test to choose from the many available. Again, some form of the specifications will help here – probably the simplified version known as the syllabus.

Admissions officers who have to make a decision on the basis of test scores will also need some description of a test to help them decide whether the test is valid for the particular decisions to be taken: for university admissions purposes, a test that does not measure academic-related language skills is likely to be less valid than one that does.

Finally, test specifications are a valuable source of information for publishers wishing to produce textbooks related to the test: textbook writers will wish to ensure that the practice tests they produce, for example, are of an appropriate level of difficulty, with appropriate content, topics, tasks and so on.

All these users of test specifications may have differing needs, and writers of specifications need to bear the audience in mind when producing or revising their specifications. What is suitable for one audience may be quite unsuitable for another.

2.3 What should test specifications look like?

Since specifications will vary according to audience, this section is divided according to the different groups of people needing specifications. However, as the principal user is probably the test writer/editor, the first section is the longest and encompasses much that might be relevant for other users.

2.3.1 Specifications for test writers

Test writers need guidance on practical matters that will assist test construction. They need answers to a wide range of questions. The answers to these questions may also be used to categorise an item, text or test bank so that once items have been written and pretested, they can be classified according to one or more of the following dimensions, and stored until required.

1. What is the *purpose* of the test? Tests tend to fall into one of the following broad categories: placement, progress, achievement, proficiency, and diagnostic.

   Placement tests are designed to assess students' level of language ability so that they can be placed in the appropriate course or class. Such tests may be based on aspects of the syllabus taught at the institution concerned, or may be based on unrelated material. In some language centres students are placed according to their rank in the test results so that, for example, the students with the top eight scores might go into the top class. In other centres the students' ability in different skills such as reading and writing may need to be identified. In such a centre a student could conceivably be placed in the top reading class, but in the bottom writing class, or some other combination. In yet other centres the placement test may have the purpose of deciding whether students need any further tuition at all. For example, many universities give overseas students tests at the start of an academic year to discover whether they need tuition in the language or skill used at the university.

Progress tests are given at various stages throughout a language course to see what the students have learnt.

Achievement tests are similar, but tend to be given at the end of the course. The content of both progress and achievement tests is generally based on the course syllabus or the course textbook.

Proficiency tests, on the other hand, are not based on a particular language programme. They are designed to test the ability of students with different language training backgrounds. Some proficiency tests, such as many of those produced by the UK examination boards, are intended to show whether students have reached a given level of general language ability. Others are designed to show whether students have sufficient ability to be able to use a language in some specific area such as medicine, tourism or academic study. Such tests are often called Specific Purposes (SP) tests, and their content is generally based on a *needs analysis* of the kinds of language that are required for the given purpose. For example, a proficiency test for air traffic controllers would be based on the linguistic skills needed in the control tower.

Diagnostic tests seek to identify those areas in which a student needs further help. These tests can be fairly general, and show, for example, whether a student needs particular help with one of the four main language skills; or they can be more specific, seeking perhaps to identify weaknesses in a student's use of grammar. These more specific diagnostic tests are not easy to design since it is difficult to diagnose precisely strengths and weaknesses in the complexities of language ability. For this reason there are very few purely diagnostic tests. However, achievement and proficiency tests are themselves frequently used, albeit unsystematically, for diagnostic purposes.

2. What sort of *learner* will be taking the test – age, sex, level of proficiency/stage of learning, first language, cultural background, country of origin, level and nature of education, reason for taking

the test, likely personal and, if applicable, professional interests, likely levels of background (world) knowledge?

3. How many *sections/papers* should the test have, how long should they be and how will they be differentiated – one three-hour exam, five separate two-hour papers, three 45 minute sections, reading tested separately from grammar, listening and writing integrated into one paper, and so on?

4. What *target language situation* is envisaged for the test, and is this to be simulated in some way in the test content and method?

5. What *text types* should be chosen – written and/or spoken? What should be the sources of these, the supposed audience, the topics, the degree of authenticity? How difficult or long should they be? What functions should be embodied in the texts – persuasion, definition, summarising, etc.? How complex should the language be?

6. What *language skills* should be tested? Are enabling/micro skills specified, and should items be designed to test these individually or in some integrated fashion? Are distinctions made between items testing main idea, specific detail, inference?

7. What *language elements* should be tested? Is there a list of grammatical structures/features to be included? Is the lexis specified in some way – frequency lists etc.? Are notions and functions, speech acts or pragmatic features specified?

8. What sort of *tasks* are required – discrete point, integrative, simulated 'authentic', objectively assessable?

9. How many *items* are required for each section? What is the relative weight for each item – equal weighting, extra weighting for more difficult items?

10. What test *methods* are to be used – multiple choice, gap filling, matching, transformation, short answer question, picture description, role play with cue cards, essay, structured writing?

11. What *rubrics* are to be used as instructions for candidates? Will examples be required to help candidates know what is expected? Should the criteria by which candidates will be assessed be included in the rubric?

12. Which *criteria* will be used for assessment by markers? How important is accuracy, appropriacy, spelling, length of utterance/script, etc.?

Some of the above questions inevitably partially cover the same ground: for example 'text type', 'nature of text' and 'complexity of text' all overlap. However, it is nevertheless helpful to address them from a variety of angles. Complete taxonomies for specifications are beyond the scope of this chapter, and in any case it is impossible, given the nature of language and the variety of different tests that can be envisaged, to be exhaustive. A very useful taxonomy that readers might consider, however, is that developed by Lyle Bachman in *Fundamental Considerations in Language Testing* (1990). This is described more fully in the next section, but in order to give the reader an idea of what specifications for test writers might contain, there follows a fictional example of the specifications for a reading test. (For an example of some more detailed specifications for an academic reading test, see Davidson and Lynch 1993.)

TEST OF FRENCH FOR POSTGRADUATE STUDIES

Specifications for the Reading Test

General Statement of Purpose

The Test of French for Postgraduate Studies is a test battery designed to assess the French language proficiency of students who do not have French as their first language and who hope to undertake postgraduate study at universities and colleges where French is the medium of instruction.

The aim of the battery is to select students who have sufficient French to be able to benefit from an advanced course of academic study, and to identify those linguistic areas in which they might need help.

The focus of the test battery is on French for Academic Purposes.

The Test Battery

The battery consists of four tests:

Reading	60 minutes
Writing	60 minutes
Listening	30 minutes
Speaking	15 minutes

Separate scores are reported for the four tests. There is a different set of specifications for each of the four tests.

Reading Test

Time allowed: One hour

Test focus: The level of reading required for this test should be in the region of levels 5 to 7 of the English Speaking Union (ESU) Yardstick Scale.

Candidates will have to demonstrate their ability to read textbooks, learned articles and other sources of information relevant to academic education. Candidates will be expected to show that they can use the following reading skills:

a) skimming
b) scanning
c) getting the gist
d) distinguishing the main ideas from supporting detail
e) distinguishing fact from opinion
f) distinguishing statement from example
g) deducing implicit ideas and information
h) deducing the use of unfamiliar words from context
i) understanding relations within the sentence
j) understanding relations across sentences and paragraphs
k) understanding the communicative function of sentences and paragraphs

Source of texts: Academic books, papers, reviews, newspaper articles relating to academic subjects. The texts should not be highly discipline-specific, and should not disadvantage students who are not familiar with the topics. All passages should be understandable by educated readers in all disciplines. A glossary of technical terms should be provided where necessary.

There should be four reading passages, each of which should be based on a different academic discipline. Two of the texts should be from the life and physical sciences, and two from the social sciences. As far as possible the four texts should exemplify different genres. For example, one text might consist of an introduction to an academic paper, and the other three might consist of a review, a description of some results and a discussion.

The texts should be generally interesting, but not distressing. Recent disasters and tragedies should be avoided.

Passages should be based on authentic texts, but may receive minor modifications such as abridgement and the correction of grammatical errors.

The length of the passages together should total 2,500 to 3,000 words.

Test tasks: Each test question should sample one or more of the reading abilities listed above. Test writers should try to achieve a balance so that one or two skills are not over tested at the expense of the others.

Item types: The Reading Test should contain between 40 and 50 items – approximately 12 items for each reading passage. Each reading passage and its items will form one sub-test. Each item will be worth one mark. Items may be open-ended, but they must be objectively markable. Item writers should provide a comprehensive answer key with their draft test.
Item writers should use a variety of item types. These may include the following:

> identifying appropriate headings
> matching
> labelling or completing diagrams, tables, charts, etc.
> copying words from the text
> information transfer
> short answer questions
> gap filling
> sorting events or procedures into order

Item writers may use other types of test item, but they should ensure that such items are objectively markable.

Rubrics: There is a standard introduction to the Reading Test which appears on the front of each Reading Test question paper. Item writers, however, should provide their own instructions and an example for each set of questions. The language of the instructions should be no higher than Level 4 of the ESU Yardstick Scale.

2.3.2 Specifications for test validators

Every test has a theory behind it: some abstract belief of what language is, what language proficiency consists of, what language learning involves and what language users do with language. This theory may be more or less explicit. Most test constructors would be surprised to hear that they have such a theory, but this does not mean that it is not there, only that it is implicit rather than articulated in metalanguage. Every test is an operationalisation of some beliefs about language, whether the constructor refers to an explicit model or merely relies upon 'intuition'.

Every theory contains *constructs* (or psychological concepts), which are its principal components and the relationship between these components. For example, some theories of reading state that there are many different constructs involved in reading (skimming, scanning, etc.) and that the constructs are different from one another. Construct validation involves assessing how well a test measures the constructs. For validation purposes, then, test specifications need to make the theoretical framework which underlies the test explicit, and to spell out relationships among its constructs, as well as the relationship between the theory and the purpose for which the test is designed.

The Bachman model mentioned above is one such theoretical framework, which was developed for the purpose of test analysis. It was used by Bachman et al. 1988, for example, to compare tests produced by the University of Cambridge Local Examinations Syndicate (UCLES) and Educational Testing Service (ETS), but it could equally be used as part of the test construction/validation process. The taxonomy is divided into two major sections: communicative language ability and test method facets. The model below shows how each section consists of a number of components.

Bachman's Frameworks of Communicative Language Ability and Test Method Facets

A. COMMUNICATIVE LANGUAGE ABILITY

1. ORGANISATIONAL COMPETENCE

Grammatical Competence
Vocabulary, Morphology, Syntax, Phonology/Graphology
Textual Competence
Cohesion, Rhetorical organisation

2. PRAGMATIC COMPETENCE

Illocutionary Competence
Ideational functions, Manipulative functions, Heuristic functions, Imaginative functions
Sociolinguistic Competence
Sensitivity to differences in dialect or variety, Sensitivity to differences in register, Sensitivity to naturalness, Ability to

interpret cultural references and figures of speech

(Bachman 1990: Chapter 4)

B. TEST METHOD FACETS

1. FACETS OF THE TESTING ENVIRONMENT

Familiarity of the Place and Equipment
Personnel
Time of Testing
Physical Conditions

2. FACETS OF THE TEST RUBRIC

Test Organisation
Salience of parts, Sequence of parts, Relative importance of parts
Time Allocation
Instructions
Language (native, target), Channel (aural, visual), Specification of procedures and tasks, Explicitness of criteria for correctness

3. FACETS OF THE INPUT

Format
Channel of presentation, Mode of presentation (receptive), Form of presentation (language, non-language, both), Vehicle of presentation ('live', 'canned', both), Language of presentation (native, target, both), Identification of problem (specific, general), Degree of speededness
Nature of Language
Length, Propositional content (frequency and specialisation of vocabulary, degree of contextualisation, distribution of new information, type of information, topic, genre), Organisational characteristics (grammar, cohesion, rhetorical organisation), Pragmatic characteristics (illocutionary force, sociolinguistic characteristics)

4. FACETS OF THE EXPECTED RESPONSE

Format
Channel, Mode, Type of response, Form of response, Language of response
Nature of Language
Length, Propositional content (vocabulary, degree of

contextualisation, distribution of new information, type of information, topic, genre), Organisational characteristics (grammar, cohesion, rhetorical organisation), Pragmatic characteristics (illocutionary force, sociolinguistic characteristics)

Restrictions on Response

Channel, Format, Organisational characteristics, Propositional and illocutionary characteristics, Time or length of response

5. RELATIONSHIP BETWEEN INPUT AND RESPONSE

Reciprocal
Nonreciprocal
Adaptive

(Bachman 1990: 119)

Other models on which test specifications have been based in recent years include *The Council of Europe Threshold Skills,* and Munby's *Communication Needs Processor* (1978), which informed the design and validation of both the Test of English for Educational Purposes (TEEP) by the Associated Examining Board (AEB) and the UCLES/British Council English Language Testing Service (ELTS) test. Other less explicitly articulated models of communicative competence are behind the design if not the validation of tests like the former Royal Society of Arts (RSA) Examination in the Communicative Use of English as a Foreign Language (CUEFL).

The content of test specifications for test validators will obviously depend upon the theoretical framework being used, and will not therefore be dealt with at length here. Nevertheless, the reader should note that much of the content outlined in the previous section would also be included in validation specifications. In particular, information should be offered on what abilities are being measured, and the interrelationships of these abilities, what test methods are to be used and how these methods influence (or not) the measurement of the abilities, and what criteria are used for assessment. Of less relevance to this sort of specification is perhaps the matter of test length, timing, item exemplification, text length, and possibly even difficulty: in short, matters that guide item writers in producing items but which are not known to have a significant effect on the measurement of ability. It should, however, be emphasised at this point that language test researchers are still uncertain as to which variables do affect construct validity and which do not, and the most useful, if not the most practical, advice is that validation specifications should be more, rather than less, complete.

A discussion of the value of any particular model or theory is well beyond the scope of this book, and is properly the domain of books dealing with language, language learning and language use. Nevertheless, any adequate treatment of test design must include reference to relevant theories. For example, *Fundamental Considerations in Language Testing* (Bachman 1990) is essentially a discussion of a model of language, and John Oller's *Language Tests at School* (1979) contains an extended treatment of his theory of a grammar of pragmatic expectancy which provides the rationale for the types of tests he advocates. Sadly, however, too many textbooks for language testers contain little or no discussion of the constructs which are supposedly being tested by the tests and test/item types that are discussed. Yet it is impossible to design, for example, a reading test without some statement of what reading is and what abilities are to be measured by an adequate test of reading. Such a statement, therefore, should also form part of test specifications.

2.3.3   Specifications for test users

Test specifications which are aimed at test users (which we will call *user specifications* for the sake of this discussion, and which include the notion of syllabus presented in Section 1 above) are intended to give users a clear view of what the test measures, and what the test should be used for. They should warn against specific, likely or known misuses.

A typical example of misuse is the attempt to measure students' language progress by giving them the same proficiency test before and after their course. Proficiency tests are such crude measures that if the interval is three months or less there may well be no improvement in the students' scores, and some students' scores may even drop. To avoid such misuse, the specifications should accurately represent the characteristics, usefulness and limitations of the test, and describe the population for which the test is appropriate.

Such user specifications should provide representative examples of item types, or, better, complete tests, including all instructions. They should provide a description of a typical performance at each significant grade or level of the test and, where possible and relevant, a description of what a candidate achieving a pass or a given grade can be expected to be able to do in the real world. In addition to examples of items or tests, it is particularly helpful to teachers but probably also to learners if examples can be provided of candidates' performances on typical or previous items/tests, and a description of how the criteria used to assess those performances apply to the examples.

For many examinations it may also be helpful to provide users with a description of what course of study or what test preparation would be particularly appropriate prior to taking the examination.

It is clearly important that candidates are given adequate information to enable them to know exactly what the test will look like: how long it will be, how difficult it is, what the test methods will be, and any other information that will familiarise them with the test in advance of taking it. The intention of such specifications for candidates should be to ensure that as far as possible, and as far as is consistent with test security, candidates are given enough information to enable them to perform to the best of their ability.

2.4 How can we draw up test specifications?

The purpose for which the test will be used is the normal starting point for designing test specifications. This should be stated as fully as possible. For example:

> Test A is used at the end of the second year of a three-year Bachelor of Education degree course for intending teachers of English as a Foreign Language. It assesses whether students have sufficient competence in English to proceed to teaching practice in the final year of study. Students who fail the test will have an opportunity to re-sit a parallel version two months later. If they subsequently fail, they will have to repeat the second year English course. Although the test relates to the English taught in the first two years, it is a proficiency test, not a measure of achievement, and is not intended to reflect the syllabus.

or:

> Test B is a placement test, designed to place students applying for language courses at the Alliance Française into classes appropriate to their language level.

or:

> Test C is intended to diagnose strengths and weaknesses of fourth year secondary school pupils in German grammar.

From the above examples, it should be clear that the test's purpose will influence its content. Test A will probably need to include measures of abilities that are relevant to the student teachers' use of English in English classes during their teaching practice. Test B may attempt to sample from the syllabus, or achievement tests, of each course level within the Alliance Française. Test C will need to refer to a model of German grammar, a list of structures that students need to know at this level, and probably to typical problems students have and errors they produce.

Having determined the purpose and the target population, test designers will then need to identify a framework within which the test might be constructed. This may be a linguistic theory – a view of language in the case of proficiency tests or a definition of the components of aptitude in the case of aptitude tests – or it may be considered necessary first to engage in an analysis of target language situations and use, and the performance which the test is intended to predict. In this case, designers may decide to undertake analyses of the likely jobs/tasks which learners may have to carry out in the future, and they may have to undertake or consult analyses of their linguistic needs.

Needs analyses typically involve gathering information on what language will be needed by test candidates in relation to the test's purpose. This might involve direct observation of people in target language use situations, to determine the range of variables relevant to language use. It may involve questionnaires or interviews with language users, or the consultation of relevant literature or of experts on the type of communication involved. An example of the sorts of variables that might be involved have been listed by Munby in his Communication Needs Processor (Munby 1978), and these include:

Participant	age, sex, nationality, domicile
Purposive domain	type of ESP involved, and purposes to which it is to be put
Setting	e.g. place of work, quiet or noisy environment, familiar or unfamiliar surroundings
Interaction	participant's role, i.e. position at work, people with whom he/she will interact, role and social relationships
Instrumentality	medium, mode and channel of communication, e.g. spoken or written communication, monologue or dialogue, textbook or radio report
Dialect	e.g. British or American English
Target Level	required level of English
Communicative Event	e.g. at a macro level: serving customers in restaurant, attending university lectures, and at a micro level, taking a customer's order, introducing a different point of view
Communicative Key	'the tone, manner and spirit in which an act is done' (Hymes 1972).

The literature on English for Specific Purposes (ESP) (see, for example, Hutchinson and Waters 1987; Robinson 1980; Swales 1985) is useful for test developers who need to conduct some form of needs analysis before they can begin to draw up their specifications. Note that both TEEP and ELTS were initially developed using some form of Munby-style needs analysis.

Needs analyses usually result in a large taxonomy of variables that influence the language that will be needed in the target situation. From this taxonomy, test developers have to sample tasks, texts, settings and so on, in order to arrive at a manageable test design. However, the ELTS Revision Project which was responsible for developing the International English Language Testing System (IELTS) test, successor to the original ELTS, proceeded somewhat differently. Once the main problems with ELTS had been identified (see Criper and Davies 1988), the revision project undertook an extensive data-gathering exercise in which a variety of test users such as administrators, teachers and university officials were asked how they thought the ELTS test should be revised. At the same time the literature relating to English for Academic Purposes (EAP) proficiency testing was reviewed, and eminent applied linguists were asked for their views on the nature of language proficiency and how it should be tested in IELTS. Teams of item writers were then asked to consider the data that had been collected and to produce draft specifications and test items for the different test components. These drafts were shown to language testers and teachers, and also to university lecturers in a wide range of academic disciplines. The lecturers were asked whether the draft specifications and sample texts and tasks were suitable for students in their disciplines, and whether other text types and tasks should be included. The item writers then revised the test battery and its specifications to take account of all the comments. By proceeding in this way the revision project members were able to build on existing needs analysis research, and to carry out a content validation of the draft test (see Alderson and Clapham 1992a and 1992b, and Clapham and Alderson forthcoming). For a discussion of how to develop ESP test specifications, and the relationship between needs analyses, test specifications and informants, see Alderson 1988b.

The development of an achievement test is in theory an easier task, since the language to be tested has been defined, at least in principle, by the syllabus upon which the test will be based. The problem for designers of achievement tests is to ensure that they adequately sample either the syllabus or the textbook in terms of content and method.

Hughes 1988 has argued that while he agrees with the general distinction made between proficiency and end of course achievement tests, he does not agree that different procedures should be followed for deciding their content. He argues that such achievement tests should be based on course *objectives*, rather than course *content*, and would therefore be similar or even identical to proficiency tests based on those same objectives.

At the end of this chapter there is a checklist containing the possible points to be covered in a set of specifications. This checklist is presented in a linear fashion, but usually the design of a test and its specifications is cyclical, with early drafts and examples being constantly revised to take account of feedback from trials and advisers.

2.5   Survey of EFL Examinations Boards: Questionnaire and Documentation

In this section we describe the EFL examinations boards' approach to test specifications: how they draw them up and what the specifications contain. We shall report the answers to the questionnaire and we shall also, as far as possible, refer to the documents the boards sent us. (See Chapter 1 for details of how this survey was conducted.) This is not always easy, because the boards use different methods and different terminology. For example, few of them use the expression *specifications*: some refer to *syllabuses*, some to *regulations* and some to *handbooks*, and the meaning of each of these terms differs from board to board. In addition, some of the boards' procedures are confidential or are not well publicised. Nor do most of the boards say for whom their publications are intended, so we are not able to consider the documents' intended audiences.

Our report on the boards' responses to this section of the questionnaire is longer than those in later chapters. This reflects the detail of the responses: not only did the boards give their fullest answers to those questions relating to test specifications, but the documents they sent contained a wide variety of information on such aspects of the exams as their aims and syllabuses.

Since UCLES filled in separate questionnaires for each of their EFL exams, it is difficult to combine their results with those from the other boards, where answers sometimes referred to one exam and sometimes to more than one. In addition, subject officers of four of the UCLES exams answered separate questionnaires for individual papers within those exams. The UCLES answers have therefore been somewhat conflated. In Table 2.1, which gives the breakdown of all the boards' answers to Questions 6 to 10, the UCLES figures represent the majority of the answers. If, for example, out of the five papers in an exam, three subject officers said Yes to a question and two said No, the answer is reported as Yes. (For details of the wording of each sub-question, see below, and for a copy of the whole questionnaire, see Appendix 2.)

QUESTIONS 6 TO 7(d): *Does your board publish a description of the content of the examinations(s); does this include a statement of its purpose, and a description of the sort of student for whom it is intended?*

TABLE 2.1 THE EXAMINATIONS BOARDS' ANSWERS

	11 exam boards		8 UCLES exams		
Question	*Yes*	*No*	*N/A*	*Yes*	*No*
6. Publish description	11	0	0	8	0
7. Does this include:					
a) purpose	11	0	0	8	0
b) which students	11	0	0	8	0
c) level of difficulty	11	0	0	8	0
d) typical performance	10	1	0	5	3
e) ability in 'real world'	9	1	1	4	4
f) course of study	2	7	1	1	7
g) content of exam					
structures	6	3	0	2	6
vocabulary	5	4	0	2	6
language functions	6	3	0	2	6
topics	6	3	0	3	5
text length	6	2	1	5	2
question types	9	0	0	8	0
question weighting	8	1	0	3	5
timing of papers	9	0	0	8	0
timing of sections	6	3	0	1	7
h) criteria for evaluation	9	1	0	2	6
i) derivation of scores	4	6	0	2	5
j) past papers	8	0	2	6	0
k) past student performance	2	5	2	7	1
8. Needs analysis	7	1	0	4	3
9. Guidance to item writers	7	1	2	8	0

As can be seen from Table 2.1, everyone said Yes to Questions 6 to 7(c). All the boards published descriptions of their examinations, and each description included a statement of the purpose of the exam, a description of the sort of student for whom it was intended and a description of its level of difficulty. A study of the published documents showed that the level of detail, however, varied from board to board. Here are a few examples:

STATEMENT OF PURPOSE

In its syllabus, the Joint Matriculation Board (JMB) gives one of the fullest descriptions of the purpose of an exam:

> The objective of the examination is to test the skills identified ... in a context as close as possible to that likely to be encountered in an undergraduate course. The test is considered particularly suitable for candidates who wish to undertake studies in the areas of science, engineering, business studies and the social sciences. The test is not seen as a sufficient or appropriate qualification in English for those who wish to pursue literary studies, preparation for which should involve a more comprehensive study of the English language than is required for the purposes of this examination.
>
> (Syllabus for UETESOL, JMB 1991)

The London Chamber of Commerce and Industry (LCCI) exams also have clear definitions of purpose:

> The aim of the examination is to test a high level ability to understand, write and variously process the general and special varieties of English used in business, and the ability to use appropriate formats.
>
> A successful candidate will have demonstrated the ability to write mature, fluent, accurate and idiomatic English on behalf of an employer, choosing technical terms, tone, form and content appropriate to the requirements of a particular situation.
>
> (English for Business, Third Level, Regulations, syllabuses and timetables of examinations, London Chamber of Commerce and Industry Examinations Board 1991)

Boards with examinations which are not EAP or ESP in orientation tend to describe the purpose of their exams in terms of the language skills required. For example:

> *Aim*
> The aim of the examination is to test the ability of the candidates to understand and produce the type of factual, impersonal language and related cognitive skills that are the medium of education across the curriculum and of normal day to day transactions.
>
> (Tests in English Language Skills, CENTRA, 1992)

and similarly:

> The principal aim is to find out how well the student understands 'educated' spoken English, within the limits of each Grade, and how well he or she can speak it.
>
> (Syllabus, Grade Examinations in Spoken English for Speakers of Other Languages, Trinity College, London 1990)

TARGET STUDENTS

Of course the purpose of the exam, and the students for whom it is intended, often overlap. The JMB extract above shows this, as do the extracts below:

> This certificate is designed for experienced and mature candidates who, in the course of their work or social activities, have to inform and instruct through the medium of English. Candidates should have reached bilingual competence in their fields of experience, and they should therefore be able to communicate with authority and hold the attention of their listeners, and should demonstrate their ability to lead and control discussion and to impart information at a professional level, with sensitivity to listeners' difficulties with the subject matter.
>
> (The Certificate in English as an Acquired Language, English Speaking Board (ESB) 1990)

and similarly:

> *Candidates*
> Those taking the test are envisaged to be young people or adults who are attending an English course either in the UK or abroad. Candidates can be learning English as part of their school or college curriculum or learning English for use outside the classroom.
>
> The examinations are designed for learners who require external certification of their progress in English and they are particularly suitable for those who are attending a course over some time and require a series of graded tests which provide 'rungs up the ladder' of proficiency.
>
> (A Guide for Teachers, Examinations in English for Speakers of Other Languages, Pitman Examinations Institute 1988)

Trinity College describes the students for whom the test is not suitable, rather than those for whom it is:

> Entry for the spoken English examinations is not open to those who speak English as a native language, nor to any candidate below seven years of age. It is recommended that adults should not enter below Grade Three and that candidates younger than fourteen should not enter for Grades Eleven and Twelve; otherwise there are no restrictions on entry.

Some boards never specifically describe the target students, presumably expecting that the description of the content and level of the exam will make it clear.

LEVEL OF DIFFICULTY

Several boards define the language levels of their exams by referring to the Council of Europe stages. For example:

> Both examinations are based on the *Waystage* level laid down by the Council of Europe. Less formally, this can be described as 'Survival' level: a key objective of the test is to determine whether a candidate can survive in an English speaking environment. The examinations are suitable for 'Lower Intermediate' students who have studied about 300–400 hours of English.
>
> (New Edition of Rationale, Regulations and Syllabuses, the Oxford-ARELS Examinations).

The Trinity College grades are compared to both the Council of Europe levels and the English Speaking Union's nine levels. UCLES charts the levels of its examinations against the ESU nine point band scale, but uses its own descriptors. So, for example, the First Certificate in English (FCE) is considered to be Level 5, which is described as 'Independent User', and the Certificate in Proficiency in English (CPE) is Level 7 'Good User'. Two of the levels are also compared to the Council of Europe levels; Level Three is called 'Waystage Level User' and Level 4 is 'Threshold Level User' (A Brief Guide to EFL Examinations and TEFL Schemes, UCLES). Pitmans do not compare the levels of their exams with any outside criteria, but use their own descriptors. For example:

> *Levels*
> Basic: the candidate can operate in English only to communicate basic needs in short, often inaccurately and inappropriately worded messages. The candidate can understand such things as labels, simple signs, street names, prices, etc., but really does not have sufficient language to cope with normal day to day, real life communication.
>
> (A Guide for Teachers, ESOL, Pitman Examinations Institute 1988)

Some of the boards never explicitly describe the levels of their exams, presumably expecting that the descriptions of the test contents will make this level clear.

QUESTION (7d): *A description of a typical performance at each grade level or score*

The Oxford-ARELS Regulations give descriptions of what successful students should be able to do. For example, at Pass level at the Preliminary Stage of the Oxford exam, a candidate among other things:

> has the basic survival skills in writing and reading English;

has the ability to communicate clearly in writing (even though a
number of errors may be made, and knowledge of structure and
vocabulary may be limited);

can understand and abstract the relevant material from authentic non-
literary texts (e.g. instructions, regulations, forms) and respond
appropriately.

(Rationale, Regulations and Syllabuses, New Edition, The Oxford-ARELS
Examinations in English as a Foreign Language)

Trinity College has a description of what a candidate is able to do at
each of the 12 levels. Here, for example, are Grades 1 and 12:

Grade 1
The candidate uses a few words or phrases such as common greetings,
and the names of common objects, and common actions. Some
communication is possible with assistance.

Grade 12
The candidate uses a full range of language with proficiency
approaching that of his own mother tongue. He copes well with
demanding and complex language situations. Occasional minor lapses
in accuracy, fluency, appropriateness and organisation do not affect
communication. There are only rare uncertainties in conveying or
comprehending the content of the message.

(Syllabus of Grade Examinations in Spoken English for Speakers of Other
Languages, Trinity College, London 1990)

The UCLES IELTS test reports students' scores at nine levels, each of
which has a performance descriptor. For example, a candidate with an
overall band level of 7 is described as:

Good User. Has operational command of the language, though with
occasional unsystematic inaccuracies and inappropriacies.
Misunderstandings may occur in unfamiliar situations. Handles
complex detailed argumentation well.

(An Introduction to IELTS, The British Council, UCLES, International
Development Program of Australian Universities and Colleges)

As is the case with 'difficulty level' above, levels of typical students
appear to be considered implicit in the overall test descriptions. In most
of the boards' publications they are not specifically described, and have
to be inferred from the test descriptions.

QUESTION 7(e): *A description of what a candidate achieving a pass or any given grade or level can be expected to be able to do 'in the real world'*

With the trend towards the use of authentic tasks and situations in language tests, many boards might argue that performance in the test mirrors performance in the 'real world'. Certainly the descriptors presented above refer to the real world rather than just to the testing environment. None of the boards distinguishes between test performance and the real world.

QUESTION 7(f): *A description of a/the course of study which students might be expected to follow prior to taking the examination*

On the whole, the examinations boards do not expect their candidates to have followed particular courses of study. One board said in its reply to the questionnaire, 'We devise schemes, i.e. exemplar content, *not* courses', and another said that the fact that courses were not described was intentional.

However, the Oxford-ARELS Regulations recommend two text-books.

QUESTION 7(g): *A description of the content of the examination with respect to: (i) structures, vocabulary, language functions*

The amount of detail concerning macro- and micro- language skills depends to a large extent on the level of the exam. Of the UCLES exams, only the Preliminary English Test (PET) provides lists of vocabulary, syntax and language functions.

The syllabus for Grade 1 of the Trinity College exams includes a list of typical commands or requests:

Touch
Point to
Hold up
Show me
Give me
Put it (them) here (there)

and a list of typical questions, and the names of adjectives of colour and size. Grade 2 includes:

The present continuous, as in *What am I (are you/we/they, is he/she/it) doing?*
The present habitual, etc.

and says:

Vocabulary: candidates should be familiar with about a hundred common words other than those mentioned above. A large vocabulary is *not* expected.

(Syllabus of Grade Examinations in Spoken English for Speakers of Other Languages, Trinity College, London 1990)

The ESB's Oral Assessments in Spoken English as an Acquired Language are much less specific. For the three foundation stages, candidates:

will be expected to recognise and produce names of common objects (e.g. clothes, furniture), and should show from the beginning that they are aware of basic word order patterns of English (e.g. adjective noun phrase, preposition noun phrase; subject-verb-object).

(Oral Assessments in English as an Acquired Language, ESB 1990)

One board says that lists 'exist for examiners, but are not published intentionally'. Another says that some guidance is given, but that a 'detailed description [is] not seen as appropriate for communicative exams'. It was difficult for us to see the logic behind this statement.

QUESTION 7(g): *A description of the content of the examination with respect to: (ii) topics and text length*

ARELS and Oxford do not include a prescribed set of topics for their exams, but they do list topics that have been covered in past exams. For example, the Oxford Preliminary Level syllabus lists the following topics which have been used for the 'Write About' question:

Reasons for moving house
Best day in your life
A typical working day
Your first day at school
A frightening experience
The end of a friendship.

In the ESB oral exams the candidates select their own topics for approximately half of each exam. For example, they prepare talks in advance and choose reading passages to read aloud. In the Certificate in English as an Acquired Language there is also a Comprehension section in which candidates are expected to respond to questions and opinions on a passage of topical interest read to them by the examiner.

Passages will be selected for their topicality and general interest and, where appropriate, will be relevant to the candidates' national and cultural backgrounds.

(The Certificate in English as an Acquired Language, ESB 1990)

The two LCCI exams which test English for Business Purposes do not specifically list any topics, but these can to a certain extent be deduced from the description of the tasks and source materials. For example, one of four tasks in English for Business, Third Level is:

> A comprehension task in which candidates will be asked to show understanding of a passage for a defined purpose. This might be a press article, an extract from a business journal, company report, circular letter, tender, or some other form of business reading matter, with which candidates are familiar at this stage.
>
> (Regulations, syllabuses and timetables of examinations, LCCI 1991)

Although six of the boards and five of the UCLES exam officers said that text lengths were given, they were not described in most of the boards' publications that we received. However, the ESB specified the maximum length of time allowed for passages which were to be read out, and CENTRA reported the number of words for each text.

QUESTION 7(g): *A description of the content of the examination with respect to: (iii) question types, weighting of questions, timing of each paper, timing of subsections of each paper*

As can be seen from Table 2.1, all the boards who answered these questions said they did describe the question types to be included in their exams, and they did specify how long each exam would last, but there was more variation in provision of information about weighting and timing of sections. Some, such as ARELS, publish the percentage of marks allocated to each section:

Preliminary Level
Section 1   Social English   (20% of marks)
Section 2   Aural Comprehension   (50% of marks)
Section 3   Extended Speaking   (30% of marks)

(New Edition of Rationale, Regulations and Syllabuses, the Oxford-ARELS Examinations in English as a Foreign Language)

QUESTION 7(h): *A description of the criteria which will be used to evaluate students' performance*

Although most of the examination boards said they published the criteria by which students' performance would be evaluated, this information was only available in a few of the documents sent to us. The JMB described its criteria for assessing the two writing tasks:

Criteria For Assessment
The higher mark allocation for Part B reflects its greater organisational and interpretational demands.

Answers of about 300 words will be required. As candidates are required to develop a logical piece of writing which interprets the information provided, it is clearly important that they avoid any attempt to describe extensively all the information provided. Candidates should be able to compare and contrast, show cause and effect relationships, draw conclusions, make hypotheses and produce other such patterns of discourse. They should be able to paragraph their writing and use a variety of means to create coherence at the inter sentential and inter paragraph level. They should be able to produce sentences of a complexity consistent with the formal register.

Candidates will be expected to write grammatical prose with due regard to word order, subject/verb agreement and appropriate use of tense and voice.

(Syllabus for UETESOL, JMB 1991)

This does list the criteria, but does not explain how these ideas are transformed into marks. Nor does the following LCCI extract:

2. Marks will be awarded differentially for content, tone, style, layout, correctness and communicative impact, according to the nature of the various tasks.

4. There should be no doubt that, for all foreseeable business purposes, candidates can perceive and convey meaning in its written English forms, both quickly and accurately.

Their English should be sufficiently accurate, specialised and idiomatic for them to detect subtleties of detail and meaning in English material presented to them, and to express such subtleties when they write. Candidates will be required to exercise their judgement on matters of appropriacy and adequacy. They should be able to grasp a total situation from fragments presented to them and respond linguistically in a way that would benefit their business.

(Regulations, syllabuses and timetables of examinations, English for Business, 3rd Level, LCCI 1991)

The answers to this question clearly overlap with those to Question 7(d) which asked whether boards gave descriptions of a typical performance at each grade level. One of the examples cited under Question 7(d) above was from Trinity College, which introduces each of its twelve oral tests with a brief paragraph describing the level of the successful candidate at that grade.

What is not clear is whether examiners use any of the above examples as actual marking criteria, or whether they are for reporting purposes only. IELTS has a set of overall band levels which are reported to the students, but which are different from the sets of criteria used to mark candidates' written and spoken work. It is not clear why some boards keep their marking criteria confidential since test users would benefit from knowing exactly what the criteria are.

An examination board that does publish its marking criteria is the Oxford Delegacy, which produces a document called *Marking Criteria and Samples*. This presents the marking criteria for each of the writing questions, for example:

Marking Question 1

Bracket 1 (26 to 30 marks)	Well-manipulated, appropriate style. Well-addressed to the task. Good, appropriate range of vocabulary and good control of structure. Any errors should be completely unobtrusive. A really competent performance.
Bracket 2 (20 to 25 marks)	Few errors, really sound control. Well-addressed to the task. Good, appropriate range of vocabulary. Awareness of suitable style, not necessarily fully in control. OR Extremely accurate, but lacking range, necessary complexity or style.

(Marking Criteria and Samples, Higher Level Paper 1, The Oxford Examination in English as a Foreign Language)

The document explains the system of marking each of the writing questions and makes a few comments on students' performance on the questions. It also prints some sample writing tasks, and facsimiles of a range of students' answers to the questions. Each sample has been assigned a mark, and each mark is accompanied by an explanation.

This is a very useful document for both students and teachers. For this paper, at least, students can be well prepared before they enter the examination hall.

UCLES also provides sample scripts and marks for some of its exams. In a volume called *English as a Foreign Language: General Handbook* (UCLES 1987) some of the EFL exams are described. It includes sample papers and, for the subjective writing sections of FCE and CPE, marking criteria, facsimiles of students' answers and marks with explanations.

QUESTION 7(i): *A description of how final scores or grades are derived*

This is partially discussed under 7(g) above, and will be discussed in more detail in Chapter 7.

QUESTION 8: *Has any form of 'needs analysis' been conducted to help the board decide upon the purpose, content, method, level, etc. of the examination?*

The boards' interpretation of the term *needs analysis* varied widely. The AEB referred to Weir's Ph.D. thesis (Weir 1983), which contains a detailed analysis of the needs of students in academic settings; one board attached some reports; and one mentioned a research report which was used as the basis for test revision. Three boards referred either by name or by implication to market research, and two said that teachers and others provided feedback which informed revisions to syllabuses or exams. One board said that its syllabuses were reviewed annually but did not indicate how it decided what to modify each year.

QUESTION 9: *Are item or test writers given any further information or guidance?*

Almost all the boards said that further guidance was given to item writers. However, one said it was not, and two said the question was inapplicable. Of these two, one was referring to the AEB TEEP test where further versions of the test are not being written, and the other was a board which carries out oral examining. The board which said No to the question implied that further guidance to test writers was unnecessary because the test was an oral one. It is not clear why the latter two boards felt that further guidance to item writers was not relevant to their tests, unless they meant to emphasise that it is up to the oral examiners rather than the item writers to decide what questions to ask. If this is in fact the case, then we would expect the oral examiners to receive guidance on how to select the next questions or tasks. This was not addressed by either board.

Most of the boards did not give details of their guidelines to item writers, but two provided item writers' handbooks, and one or two others provided brief explanations:

> Round table setting meetings with the Chief Examiner
> Items written with guidance and 'vetted' at the meeting

> The Chief Examiners provide detailed setting procedures for question setters.

> They attend moderating meetings before they become setters. They work in teams of three – one setter for each paper – with the guidance of a more experienced setter. They have two meetings as a team to research the company material and plan tasks (UCLES).

Only one board gave extensive information, including a copy of a sample letter sent to item writers. Although publishing the letter would breach the anonymity condition stipulated by the board, the following information can be given:

> Item and test writers over the years have received information and

guidance in various ways:

through weekend courses and conferences for markers and item writers, at which exam content was discussed, analysed and new approaches and test types discussed;

through meetings of active item writers at which draft items were passed round, discussed and modified for inclusion in future examinations;

through a detailed letter sent to any potential item writers who show an interest in contributing to the exams;

through specific comments and notes on draft materials submitted by item writers to [the Board official].

QUESTION 10: *When students register for your examination, what information are they given about the test's purpose and content?*

Nine of the non-UCLES boards said that it was the examination centres that provided students with details of the exams. Typical answers from the boards were:

Information is available to students from the centres through which they register; alternatively any student may receive the same information by applying directly to us.

and:

It is the responsibility of examination centres to provide full information about the test's purpose and content.

However, one said that the relevant syllabus and guidelines were provided for each student.

Of the UCLES responses, two referred to the examination centres; two said that regulations, specifications, practice tests and past tests were available; and one mentioned a short leaflet.

Many of the responses to the questionnaire give the impression that the boards leave the centres free to decide how many of the boards' numerous documents about their exams are given to the candidates. It is possible, of course, that the centres give students everything available, but if they do not, this is cause for some concern, since if some students receive the publications and others do not, the students will be at varying stages of unpreparedness when they take the exams, and the ensuing results will be unreliable. Boards should make a point of ensuring that students receive as much information about their exams as possible, and that all examination centres should give all students the same amount of information.

2.6   Discussion

As we said in the introduction to this section, the boards vary widely in their approach to the drawing up of specifications and in the openness with which they report the rationale, contents and marking schemes that underlie their tests. This variation in the openness of the reporting needs further comment. It is certainly the case that some aspects of the contents of an exam may need to be confidential, especially if there is only one secure version of it; however, in many cases there does not seem to be any case for confidentiality. The more students know about the contents and aims of a test, the more likely they are to be able to do themselves justice in the examination hall. Similarly the more teachers know about the test, the easier it will be for them firstly to decide whether the test is appropriate for their students and secondly to prepare students for it. A knowledge, for example, of the specifications written for item writers, a detailed understanding of the criteria used for marking, and a familiarity with the examiners' views of students' sample answers would be invaluable for all test users and would increase the reliability of the tests.

It should be noted that the information available from boards does not usually clearly identify its audience, certainly not along the lines we propose in Section 3 above. The boards should consider who is to receive which information before revising it to suit its intended audience.

Finally, the *Standards for Educational and Psychological Testing* (see Chapter 11) contain considerable detail about how tests should be developed. For example, Standard 3.2 says:

> The specifications used in constructing items ... and in designing the test instrument as a whole should be stated clearly. The definition of a universe or domain that is used for constructing or selecting items should be described.

(page 25)

and Standard 3.3 says:

> Domain definitions and the test specifications should be sufficiently clear so that knowledgeable experts can judge the relation of items to the domains they represent.

(page 26)

The *Code of Fair Testing Practices in Education* (see Chapter 11) says that test developers should:

> Define what each test measures and what the test should be used for.

Describe the population(s) for which the test is appropriate ...
(Statement 1).
Describe the process of test development. Explain how the content and
skills to be tested were selected. (Statement 4)

It appears that the current practice of UK examination boards does not
always meet such standards.

2.7 Checklist

Since specifications vary according to their uses, not all the points in the
following checklist will need to be covered in all specifications. Above
all, specifications writers must first decide who their audience is, and
provide the appropriate information.

Test specifications should include all or most of the following:

The test's purpose
Description of the test taker
Test level
Construct (theoretical framework for test)
Description of suitable language course or textbook
Number of sections/papers
Time for each section/paper
Weighting for each section/paper
Target language situation
Text-types
Text length
Language skills to be tested
Language elements to be tested
Test tasks
Test methods
Rubrics
Criteria for marking
Descriptions of typical performance at each level
Description of what candidates at each level can do in the real
world
Sample papers
Samples of students' performance on tasks

Bibliography

Alderson, J.C. 1988b. New Procedures for Validating Proficiency Tests of ESP? Theory and Practice. *Language Testing* 5(2): 220–232.

Alderson, J.C. and C.M. Clapham. 1992a. Applied Linguistics and Language Testing: a Case Study of the ELTS Test. *Applied Linguistics* 13: 149–167.

Alderson, J.C. and C.M. Clapham. 1992b. *Examining the ELTS Test: An Account of the First Stage of the ELTS Revision Project.* IELTS Research Report 2. Cambridge: The British Council, University of Cambridge Local Examinations Syndicate and International Development Program of Australian Universities and Colleges.

Bachman, L.F. 1990. *Fundamental Considerations in Language Testing.* Oxford: Oxford University Press.

Bachman, L.F., A. Kunnan, S. Vanniariajan and B. Lynch. 1988. Task and Ability Analysis as a Basis for Examining Content and Construct Comparability in Two EFL Proficiency Test Batteries. *Language Testing* 5: 128–160.

Clapham, C.M. and J.C. Alderson (forthcoming). *Constructing and Trialling the IELTS Test.* IELTS Research Report 3. Cambridge: The British Council, University of Cambridge Local Examinations Syndicate and International Development Program of Australian Universities and Colleges.

Criper, C. and A. Davies. 1988. *ELTS Validation Project Report,* Research Report 1(i), London and Cambridge: The British Council and the University of Cambridge Local Examinations Syndicate.

Davidson, F. and B. Lynch. 1993. Criterion-Referenced Language Test Development. A Prologomenon. In A. Huhta, K. Sajavaara and S. Takala (eds.), *Language Testing: New Openings.* Institute for Educational Research, University of Jyvaskyla, Finland.

Hughes, A. 1988. Achievement and Proficiency: The Missing Link. In A. Hughes (ed.), *Testing for University Study*, ELT Documents 127. London: Modern English Publications.

Hutchinson, T. and A. Waters. 1987. *English for Specific Purposes: A Learner Centred Approach.* Cambridge: Cambridge University Press.

Hymes, D.H. 1972. On Communicative Competence. In J.B. Pride and J. Holmes, (eds.), *Sociolinguistics.* Harmondsworth: Penguin.

Munby, J. 1978. *Communicative Syllabus Design.* Cambridge: Cambridge University Press.

Oller, J. 1979. *Language Tests at School.* London: Longman.

Robinson, P. 1980. *ESP (English for Specific Purposes).* Oxford: Pergamon.

Swales, J. 1985. *Episodes in ESP.* Oxford: Pergamon.

Weir, C.J. 1983. *Identifying the Language Problems of Overseas Students in Tertiary Education in the United Kingdom.* Ph.D. thesis, University of London

3 Item writing and moderation

In this chapter we shall be discussing what is involved in writing good test items. We shall describe some of the pitfalls to avoid and the procedures to follow that will help ensure that many obvious mistakes are caught before the test is pretested. We shall attempt to answer the following questions: What makes a good item writer – are they born or can they be trained? Where do you start when writing an item? What methods are most suitable for testing particular abilities? When people disagree about the quality of a test item, how can we resolve the disagreement? What principles and guidelines should we follow when writing test items? What is the role of the moderating committee, and how do such committees best work?

3.1 Qualifications for item writing

The purpose and content of the test will to some extent determine who will make the best item writers. It is helpful if those who write the items have recent experience teaching students who are similar to those taking the test, as the teachers' experience will provide insights into what such students find easy and difficult, what interests them, their cultural background, and so on. For example, if the test is one of Writing for Academic Purposes, then a person with experience of doing academic writing, teaching academic writing, and assessing students who submit pieces of academic writing is likely to produce a better test of academic writing than somebody without such experience. For achievement tests, it is clearly important that those who write the test know what it is reasonable to expect students to have covered at that particular stage in learning and also how far students have actually progressed through the curriculum. Thus it is likely that good item writers will be experienced teachers of similar students or relevant subject areas, who have the necessary formal professional qualifications expected of teachers in the particular context where the test is being developed.

However, such people will not necessarily be good item writers.

Having relevant experience does not guarantee either the insights into the nature of the task that are necessary in order to write good tasks, or the creativity and imagination needed to write good items. Creativity, sensitivity, insight, imagination: all these are qualities of item writers that are difficult to define and difficult to identify in prospective item writers, but very obviously missing in poor item writers.

Some tests are written by professional item writers, who either work full-time for a testing institution, or who work as freelance test writers for a range of institutions. Such writers should ideally combine the experience and qualifications of a relevant teacher with the qualities of a perceptive item writer. Some such paragons do exist and they produce exceptionally good items, but it has to be said that they are rare.

One of the advantages of employing a professional item writer is that such a person is more likely to be able to reproduce items from one testing occasion to the next: parallel tests are notoriously difficult to write, and the understanding of how test items work that professional writers develop is an important ingredient in the production of consistent tests. However, such professional item writers are likely to be less sensitive to the audience being tested, to changes in the curriculum or its implementation, to varying levels of the school or test population, and to other features of the testing context. Doubtless the best solution is to have item-writing teams consisting of professional item writers and suitably experienced teachers.

3.2 Tests versus exercises

When asking, 'What makes a good test writer?', one might just as well ask, 'What makes a good textbook writer?' The design of a test item is very similar to the design of a learning exercise, where learners are presented with a task or data which they have to cope with in order to develop insights or understanding, and, through feedback (from a teacher, from peers, from introspection and self observation), to develop a capacity to change behaviour and thoughts. Similarly, all test items ask learners to cope with tasks and with data, but in this case it is in order to produce behaviour or language which will give evidence of ability. A test item consists of a method of eliciting behaviour or language, together with a system whereby that behaviour or language can be judged.

We believe, then, that there is no important difference between writing a test item and writing a learning task or exercise. Thus whatever qualities are needed by the designer of an exercise are also needed by test writers. Perhaps more importantly, the sources of inspiration for exercises can also be used for test writing: test writers, in other words, can and should be as imaginative as possible when thinking about their item types, and one very useful source of ideas is textbooks and other learning materials.

It is interesting that, in our experience, teachers are very reluctant to show outsiders the tests they have written, yet they are usually willing to reveal the sorts of exercises they have developed for classroom use. This may well be because a mystique surrounds test writing in a way that does not apply to exercise writing: tests are thought to be inherently difficult to write. Certainly our experience is that outsiders tend to be much more critical of test items than ever they are of learning exercises, and this can have an inhibiting effect on the test writers.

This reluctance to show one's test items to others may not be due only to the belief that writing tests is difficult. It may also be due to one important difference between tests and exercises that does indeed make test writing more difficult. The fact is that when learners take a test, they do so alone: they receive no assistance from peers or from teachers. Any such assistance would be termed 'cheating'! However, when they do exercises, learners typically expect to receive help from teachers or peers, or at least to feel able to seek help if they need it. Thus, the main difference between a test and an exercise is that with exercises learners get support: with tests, they do not. The effect of this difference is that test items have to be clearer than exercises. The instructions have to be as simple and unambiguous as possible, and the tasks must be familiar to all so that all candidates are measured according to their ability, and not according to their knowledge of what is expected by the test task. Test items, then, have to stand alone in a way that exercises do not. Teachers can compensate for unclear exercises by paraphrasing them, giving examples, or demonstrations, or even simply by skipping those exercises that learners do not understand or are not interested in. The student taking a test has no such possibility, and the test writer therefore has an obligation to ensure that all items are unambiguous. Interestingly, we talk of the validity of a test item: it is very unusual to talk of the validity of an exercise. Yet the concept is applicable to a discussion of learning tasks: tasks that do not enable learners to learn or practise what they are supposed to are invalid. Tests differ from exercises in that they are expected to be valid (and reliable), whereas learning exercises are generally not.

3.3 Where to start?

Item writers have to begin their writing task with the test's specifications (see Chapter 2). This may seem an obvious point, but it is surprising how many writers try to begin item writing by looking at past papers rather than at the specifications. This recourse to past papers is probably due to the fact that many tests lack proper test specifications. There are two problems with trying to replicate or build upon past papers. Firstly, one has to infer test objectives and purposes which are often not readily inferable: objectives and statements of content are implicit in a past paper, and only explicit, usually, in the specifications. Secondly, specifications are much more wide-ranging than a past paper. Any test is of necessity only a sample of what it might have contained. Building a test on previous tests therefore restricts the item writer to what has already been tested. It is normal practice to vary test content, and often test method, for each new test that is written unless there is a requirement to produce a narrowly parallel test, which is certainly not the case for achievement tests and is normally not the case for proficiency tests. Thus it is essential to refer to test specifications in order to ensure as wide a sampling of the potential content and methods as possible.

What to do after consulting the test specifications will depend upon what sort of test one is constructing. If the test is one of language elements – lexis, grammar, and so on in discrete point format – the next step will probably be to consult past papers or some inventory of the content of previous tests in order to avoid the danger of too much duplication of content across tests. Whilst just looking at the content of previous papers can be useful, it is better systematically to classify previous content. Ideally, the test developers will keep a record of the content of all their tests.

Consulting such an inventory will also be a useful second step for item writers who are devising text-based tests, for example of reading and listening, but also possibly of speaking and writing. The record should show what sorts of texts have already been used, and the specifications will indicate the genres, sources, difficulties and so on (see Chapter 2) that are appropriate for the test in question.

For many tests, the item writer's next task is to find appropriate texts. In this case, 'appropriate' means not only texts that match the specifications, but also texts that look as if they will yield suitable items. Not all texts lend themselves to item development, and item writers are well advised to spend some time searching for texts that have promise. Finding suitable texts can be such a problem that item writers often maintain their own 'bank' of texts that can be used in some future test, and which they are constantly supplementing from their everyday reading. It is sometimes a good idea – and insisted upon by some test developers – to get the approval of the editing or moderating committee for the texts before moving on to develop items or tasks based on them. This is simply expedient: spending time developing items on texts that will ultimately be rejected is both inefficient and depressing.

3.4 Item types

It is important to realise that the method used for testing a language ability may itself affect the student's score. This is called *the method effect*, and its influence should be reduced as much as possible. We are not interested in knowing whether a candidate is good at multiple-choice tests, or can do cloze tests better than other candidates, or finds oral descriptions of a series of pictures particularly difficult. We are interested in finding out about the candidate's grammatical knowledge, or reading ability, or speaking skill. We do not yet know much about test method effect, but as more research looks at how students actually respond to particular test methods, we will begin to understand this effect, or better, these effects, more fully.

Considerable research has, however, been done into some test methods: the cloze technique, and the C-test, for example (see pages 55 and 56). A vast amount of research has been conducted using cloze tests as one of the variables, but rather less has been done to look at what cloze tests measure. What is clear, however, is that different cloze tests measure different things, that is, a test produced by the application of the cloze technique to a text may or may not measure the same thing as a different cloze test on the very same text. This variation appears to be unpredictable and may depend upon which individual words have been deleted. In short, you cannot know in advance what a given cloze test will measure without validating the test in the normal way (see Chapter 8). This means that the method effect of the cloze technique is likely to be quite complex. Nevertheless, there is some evidence that when they take cloze tests, many candidates read in a different way from usual: they read the short amount of context just before the blank, but fail to read the context after the blank. We would argue that this is because of the technique: the existence of blanks at regular intervals tends to induce a form of 'short-text' reading, and many cloze test takers show a lack of attention to the meaning of the wider context that is not shown by their normal reading, when they are indeed context-sensitive.

Similarly, there is evidence that students taking multiple-choice tests can learn strategies for taking such tests that 'artificially' inflate their scores: techniques for guessing the correct answer, for eliminating implausible distractors, for avoiding two options that are similar in meaning, for selecting an option that is notably longer than the other distractors, and so on (see Allan 1992 for an interesting account of a test of test-wiseness, developed in order to identify students who have developed such strategies). There is also evidence from anecdotal accounts of multiple-choice test takers that the test method tends to encourage students to consider alternatives they would not otherwise have considered (see also the discussion of multiple-choice questions in Oller 1979): thus the technique tricks the unwary into making incorrect interpretations they might not otherwise have made.

In addition, it is likely that particular test methods will lend themselves to testing some abilities, and not be so good at testing others. An extreme example is that multiple-choice tests are not suitable for testing a candidate's ability to pronounce a language correctly. Despite suggestions in Lado 1961 and beliefs in Japan to the contrary, Buck 1989 showed clearly that multiple-choice tests of pronunciation do not correlate at all with candidates' abilities to pronounce English phonemes correctly. A less extreme example might be the multiple-choice technique for testing reading ability: it may be easier to control the thought processes of readers with multiple-choice techniques than it is with short-answer-type questions (since the test writer can devise distractors to get candidates to think in certain ways), and this control may be desirable for the testing of inferencing in a foreign language.

Unfortunately, our understanding of the test method effect is still so rudimentary that it is not possible to recommend particular methods for testing particular language abilities. This is perhaps the Holy Grail of language testing.

In the absence of such recommendations, the best advice that can be offered to item writers is: ensure that you use more than one test method for testing any ability. A useful discipline is to devise a test item to cover some desired ability or objective, then to devise another item testing the same ability using a different method or item type. This may lead to increased insight into what certain item types are testing, and ought to lead to a greater understanding of the possibilities of different item types.

In general, the more different methods a test employs, the more confidence we can have that the test is not biased towards one particular method or to one particular sort of learner. In addition, if a series of tests is being developed over a number of years (for example, end-of-year tests in an institution), we recommend that test developers deliberately vary the methods used so that no one method predominates and becomes predictable (see also Chapter 10). Although we know surprisingly little about how tests affect teaching (see Alderson and Wall 1993 and Wall and Alderson 1993 for a discussion of the issue of washback), it is likely that 'keeping learners guessing' by varying test methods year by year will reduce the predictability of the test's format, and possibly the learning of test-taking strategies for particular test methods.

3.5   Problems with particular item types

In the meantime, even if they do not know the effects of different test methods, item writers need to be aware of the known pitfalls of particular test methods and to learn how to avoid the commonest mistakes in designing certain sorts of test items. Heaton 1988 gives advice on the constructing of different types of test item and how to avoid writing poor items, and there are several publications which give examples of different test types (see, for example, Valette 1977; Hughes 1989 and Weir 1988). We shall not go into test types in any great detail here, therefore, but will just describe some of the most common problems associated with them, starting with objective test types and progressing to more subjective ones.

3.5.1   General problems

There are some problems which apply to all test types, and perhaps the most fundamental is the question of what an item is actually testing. It is very easy with many sorts of test items to test something which is not intended. This item, for example, is supposed to test spelling:

Rearrange the following letters to make English words:

RUFTI	RSOEH	MSAPT
TOLSO	RIEWT	PAHYP

The item *may* be testing spelling, but it is also testing intelligence, ability to do anagrams and, at a pinch, vocabulary. To succeed with this task it may be more important to be able to make the mental leap required, than to be able to spell.

It is very common, unfortunately, especially in high-level proficiency tests, for intelligence to be tested as well as or instead of language. Similarly, background knowledge is frequently tested instead of reading or listening comprehension. Two examples of such items will be discussed in Section 3.5.2 below.

Another fundamental point is that if one mark is being given for each item, then each item should be independent of the others. Success on one item should not depend on success on another. For example, if it is only possible to answer the second item in a reading comprehension test after correctly answering the first, then a candidate who fails Item 1 will automatically fail Item 2, and will lose two marks rather than one. Some test writers do integrate test items so that success on later items depends on success with earlier ones, but this may lead to problems. This will be discussed in Section 3.5.4 below.

The final point in this general section is that the instructions for all items must be clear. Often students fail a test or an item not because their language is poor, but because they do not understand what they are meant to do. If possible, the language used should be simpler than that in the items themselves, and in some cases the instructions should be written in the candidates' first language. Each new set of items should be preceded by a worked example.

3.5.2 Multiple-choice

The most important requirement of a multiple-choice item is that the 'correct' answer must be genuinely correct. (See Peirce 1992 for interesting comments on this and other problems in the construction of multiple-choice tests of reading.) Although this seems obvious, it is quite possible, especially in reading or listening comprehension tasks, to write an answer that many colleagues would disagree with. Such dubious answers are particularly common in inferencing questions. Every 'correct' answer must therefore be checked with colleagues to avoid problems such as this:

Which is the odd one out?

A	rabbit
B	hare
C	bunny
D	deer

The test writer might have planned that D was the odd one out, but good language learners might have chosen C because 'bunny' is in 'baby-language'.

The other requirement is that item writers must ensure that if the answer key gives just one correct answer, then there is only one correct answer. We are all familiar with items where more than one of the alternatives is correct. Frequently item writers become fixated on a single answer, and cannot see that one or more of the alternatives are also acceptable. They can only discover this by showing their items to other people.

The following item was written strictly according to the rules given in a beginner's textbook. However, when native speakers were asked which was the correct answer they disagreed with the answer key.

'Why hasn't your mother come?'
'Well, she said she _____ leave the baby.'

       A   can't
       B   won't
       C   couldn't
       D   mayn't

According to the textbook, C is the correct answer, because of the rules of reported speech. However, many of the native speakers on whom the item was pretested said that A and B were perfectly acceptable, especially in spoken English. In our experience, too rigorous an adherence to what is taught in a textbook may lead to items where there is more than one acceptable answer.

Each wrong alternative should be attractive to at least some of the students. If an alternative is never chosen, then it is wasting everyone's time and might as well not be there. Generally it is a good idea to have at least four alternative answers, so that the chance of a student guessing an answer is only 25%, but if it is impossible to think of a third attractive wrong answer, then it is sensible to have only three alternatives for some items.

Where necessary, multiple-choice items should be presented in context. Often the item writer has a particular context in mind which is not at all obvious to the test takers, and if the context is not given, these students may get the item wrong although they are capable of the language performance required. The presentation of context will often reduce the possibilities of ambiguity, for example:

Select the option closest in meaning to the word underlined:

Come back <u>soon</u>.

       A   shortly
       B   later
       C   today
       D   tomorrow

The lack of context makes it unclear whether B is really wrong. It would be clearer as follows:

Fill in the blank with the most suitable option:

Visitor: Thank you very much for such a wonderful visit.
Hostess: We were so glad you could come. Come back _____ .

A	soon
B	later
C	today
D	tomorrow

This new version also corrects another weakness. In the original version, the correct answer, A, does not fit easily into the stem sentence, as in many contexts it is not common to say 'Come back shortly'. This might worry some of the better students and they might therefore choose a wrong answer. Since there is no direct synonym for 'soon' which would fit into the stem, and since finding synonyms is in any case perhaps unnecessary at this level of English learning, the new version is more appropriate.

The correct alternative should not look so different from the distractors that it stands out from the rest. It should not be noticeably longer or shorter, nor be written in a different style. Heaton 1988: 32 gives the following example when describing poor multiple-choice items:

Select the option closest in meaning to the word underlined:

He began to <u>choke</u> while he was eating the fish.

A	die
B	cough and vomit
C	be unable to breathe because of something in his windpipe
D	grow very angry

There are several problems with this item. The most obvious one is that the correct answer, C, is immediately identifiable because it is so much longer than the other alternatives. It looks like a dictionary definition, and any candidate in doubt about the answer would be likely to choose it.

Secondly, distractor B is related to 'choke' semantically, and would therefore be a plausible option for some learners – after all, what does 'closest in meaning' mean? To ensure that B is less 'close in meaning' than the correct answer, the item writer has been forced to provide a 'dictionary definition' so that C is recognisably 'closest in meaning' to the stimulus.

Thirdly, without more context we cannot know for certain whether the man is choking on his food or is very angry. The fact that the sentence is, 'He began to choke while he was eating the fish', rather than the more natural 'He began to choke on a fish bone' or 'He choked on a fish bone' implies that perhaps he was growing angry instead. Otherwise, why did the sentence say, '... while he was eating'? It is almost as if this is a trick question, and it might confuse the most able students. If the sentence was set in context, the alternatives would be less ambiguous.

Another requirement with multiple-choice questions is that each option should fit equally well into the stem. Heaton 1988: 29 cites the following item where the correct answer, C, does not fit into the stem, because the indefinite article 'a' cannot be used before a word beginning with a vowel:

Someone who designs houses is a _____ .
 A designer   B builder   C architect   D plumber

As we mentioned in Section 3.5.1, some items do not test what they are intended to test. This most frequently occurs in comprehension tests, where items may turn out to be testing background knowledge. It is unfortunately easy to write items which can be answered without any reference to the reading or listening passage. For example:

(After a text on memory)
Memorising is easier when the material to be learned is:
          A   in a foreign language
          B   already partly known
          C   unfamiliar but easy
          D   of no special interest

Even if we do not see the reading passage, it is clear that this is a poor item. Common sense and experience tell us that A is not true, that D is very unlikely, and that B is probably the correct answer. The only alternative which appears to depend on the text for interpretation is C since 'unfamiliar' and 'easy' are both ambiguous.

Such examples are common, even when items have gone through editing procedures. Here is another example from a large national examination, in which five items could be answered without reading the text:

(After a text about trees)
Who gets food from trees?
          A   Only man
          B   Only animals
          C   Man and animals

Whatever the text says, it is surely common knowledge that both humans and animals get food from trees.

This problem of items being independent of the reading or listening passage is not confined to multiple-choice items. It applies to other objective-type questions, and may also apply to short-answer questions. To make sure that comprehension items are not answerable without reference to the text, item editors should always try answering new comprehension items before they look at or listen to the related text.

A final difficulty that item writers may encounter relates to multiple-choice editing tasks. Students may be given a task in which they are asked to identify the error in a sentence, for example:

A   B   C

In spite of the rain/the children's teacher/would not allow them/

D   E

stay indoors/during playtime.

Here either C or D is the correct answer, depending on whether the students think the error is one of omission or commission. Either of these sentences is correct:

... the children's teacher would not let them stay ...
... the children's teacher would not allow them to stay ...

It is probably sensible to avoid sentences where the error may be one of omission.

3.5.3 Other objective-type items

DICHOTOMOUS ITEMS

True/False or Yes/No items are generally unsatisfactory, as there is a 50% possibility of getting any item right by chance alone. In order to learn anything about a student's ability, it is necessary to have a large number of such items in order to discount the effects of chance. Some item writers reduce the possibility of correct guessing by including a third category such as 'not given' or 'does not say'. This can be useful in a reading comprehension test, but in listening comprehension, especially where the text is only played once, it can be demanding and can lead to student confusion.

MATCHING

By 'matching' we mean items where students are given a list of possible answers which they have to match with some other list of words, phrases, sentences, paragraphs or visual clues. In the following example, the students have to match the four words on the left with those on the right in order to make other English words. For example, 'car' and 'pet', make 'carpet'.

1	car	A	room
2	cup	B	pet
3	bed	C	dress
4	night	D	board

The disadvantage with this item is that once three of the items have been accurately matched, the fourth pair is correct by default. It is good practice, therefore, to give more alternatives than the matching task requires. The above example would be improved if the students were given a choice of six or seven words in the right hand column.

Note also that it is important in such tasks to make sure that each item in the first column only matches one item in the second.

INFORMATION TRANSFER

Information transfer is used most in reading and listening comprehension tasks. Candidates usually have to transfer material from the text on to a chart, table, form or map. These tasks often resemble real-life activities and are therefore much used in test batteries which try to include authentic tasks. Sometimes the answers consist of just names and numbers, and can be marked objectively. Sometimes they take the form of phrases and short sentences and have to be marked more subjectively. The problems with these latter items are similar to those described in the section below on short-answer questions.

One of the main problems with information transfer questions is that the task can be very complicated. Sometimes the candidates spend so much time working out what should go where in a table that they do not manage to solve what is linguistically an easy problem.

Another problem is that the task may be culturally or cognitively biased. For example, the candidate might be asked to listen to a description of someone's journey through a town and to mark the route on a map. However, students who are unfamiliar with maps or are not good at map-reading are at a disadvantage with tasks of this sort.

ORDERING TASKS

In an ordering task candidates are asked to put a group of words, phrases, sentences or paragraphs in order. Such tasks are typically used to test simple or complex grammar, reference and cohesion, or reading comprehension. Almost all ordering tasks are difficult to construct because it is not easy to provide words or phrases which only make sense in one order. For example, the following question can be answered in at least two ways:

Put the following words in order to complete the sentence:

She gave _____ .

book   her   yesterday   mother   the   to

Even more difficult to construct are items where sentences or paragraphs have to be rearranged. For example:

The following sentences and phrases come from a paragraph in an adventure story. Put them in the correct order. Write the letter of each in the space on the right.

Sentence D comes first in the correct order, so D has been written beside the number 1.

A	it was called 'The Last Waltz'	1 <u>D</u>
B	the street was in total darkness	2 __
C	because it was one he and Richard had learnt at school	3 __
D	Peter looked outside	4 __
E	he recognised the tune	5 __
F	and it seemed deserted	6 __
G	he thought he heard someone whistling	7 __

There are at least two ways of ordering this paragraph. The answer key gives 1:D, 2:G, 3:E, 4:C, 5:A, 6:B, 7:F, but 1:D, 2:B, 3:F, 4:G, 5:E, 6:C, 7:A is also acceptable. In this case it is possible to improve the item by adding 'but' to the beginning of phrase G so that the line reads 'but he thought he heard someone whistling'. This makes the second of the two answers the only acceptable one. However, even if it is possible to prepare an item in which the components can only be ordered in one way, it is not always clear what is being tested, and there is always the problem of marking the answers. Say one student makes two mistakes in ordering early in the sequence, but then orders everything else correctly. Should this person get the same mark as someone who has all the ordering wrong? It seems unfair to mark the two the same, but once you start to give different marks for different ordering errors the marking becomes unmanageably complex. Such items are therefore frequently just marked wholly right or wholly wrong, but in that case the amount of effort involved both in constructing and in answering the item may not be considered to be worth it, especially if only one mark is given for the correct version.

EDITING

Editing tests often consist of sentences or passages in which errors have been introduced which the candidate has to identify. These can take the form of multiple-choice questions, as in Section 3.5.2 above, or can be more open. A common method is to ask students to identify one error in each line of a text, either by marking the text, or by writing a correction beside each appropriate line. The main difficulty with this kind of item is to make sure that there is only one mistake per line.

Some test writers have tried to make the task more realistic by not necessarily having only one error per line, but by asking students to list all the errors while not telling them how many there are. This means that the students may waste much time scouring the text for possible errors, since they can never be satisfied that they have found everything. It also means that the marking is difficult, since if the students miss an early error, or write down a non-existent one, the answers will not line up with the official answer key. At the very least, students should be told how many errors there are. (This applies to most tasks where candidates have to produce a list of some kind.)

GAP-FILLING

'Gap-filling' refers here to tests in which the candidate is given a short passage in which some words or phrases have been deleted. The candidate's task is to restore the missing words. The deletions have been specially selected by the test writer to test chosen aspects of language such as grammar or reading comprehension.

Gap-filling tasks are sometimes based on authentic texts and sometimes on specially written passages. In both cases the major difficulty is to make sure that each gap leads students to write the expected word. Ideally there should only be one correct answer for each gap, but this is generally difficult to achieve. The answer key is therefore likely to have more than one answer for some spaces. For reliability of marking, it is important to reduce the number of alternative answers to the minimum and to ensure that there are no other possible answers which are not listed in the answer key.

Another problem is that candidates may not be able to think of an answer, not because they have poor language but because the word simply does not spring to mind. Here again, this cannot be anticipated by the item writers because they have read the text in its entirety and the missing word therefore seems obvious. Once again it is essential that the test be tried out on colleagues and then pretested.

If many of the gaps are not easily restored, or if marking proves to be a problem, a banked gap-filling task may be the answer. This is a sort of matching task. Each of the missing words or phrases is included in a list which is presented on the same page as the gap-filling text. There are more words in this list than there are gaps in the text, and the candidate's task is to select the correct word for each gap. There should be only one possible answer for each gap, but candidates should be told that any word in the word list may fit in more than one gap. The words should be listed in alphabetical order.

(It is always important to tell students whether each gap is to be filled by one or by more than one word.)If more than one word is acceptable, the marking becomes more difficult. If only one word is allowed, then, for clarity's sake, contractions such as 'we'll' should be avoided, and so should hyphenated words.

Sometimes a sentence or phrase is equally good with or without the deleted word. For example:

> It so happened that the man _____ I was following turned out to be extremely fit.

Such items can confuse the students and should be avoided.

CLOZE

Cloze here refers only to tests in which words are deleted mechanically. Each nth word is deleted regardless of what the function of that word is. So, for example, every sixth word might be removed.

As was implied earlier in this chapter, one problem with nth word deletion tasks is that the choice of the first deletion can have an effect on the validity of the test, since once that first word is deleted, all the other deletions automatically follow. Experiments comparing tests based on the same text, but with different initial gaps, and therefore different spaces throughout the passage, have shown that the tests vary in both validity and reliability (Alderson 1978, 1979 and Klein-Braley 1981). Some versions of the test may, for example, have a high proportion of function words deleted, which may be fairly easy for competent language users to restore, and which may distinguish between students of different levels of ability, whereas other versions may have lost a high proportion of content words which may prove to be irretrievable even for native speakers.

Another disadvantage is that an nth word deletion cloze test is not easily amended. If, when it is pretested, some gaps are impossible to complete, how can the test be altered? If the tester decides to reinstate the difficult word and delete another one nearby, then the principle of nth word deletion is being flouted, and if the text is rewritten to make the nth word gap more answerable, the text becomes less authentic.

Marking cloze tests can be difficult since there may be many possible answers for any one gap, and there is often disagreement as to what answers are acceptable. To produce a comprehensive answer key may require wide pretesting of the test and then lengthy discussions on the appropriacy of different answers. All this will be time-consuming. To avoid this, some testers only accept the exact word that was used in the original text. This naturally leads to lower final scores but does not usually change the students' ranks. However, since it is counter-intuitive to mark someone wrong because they write, say, 'close the door' instead of 'shut the door', it is more common to accept any appropriate answer.

Finally, unless the aim of the cloze test is to test overall language proficiency, as advocated by Oller 1979, such tests may be a wasteful way of testing. Few of the items in any one passage may test the aspects of language with which the tester is concerned. We therefore recommend that, on the whole, test writers construct gap-filling tasks in preference to cloze tests, so that they can delete selected words or phrases in order to test the linguistic features in which they are interested.

C-TEST

C-tests also involve mechanical deletion, but this time it is every second word which is mutilated, and half of each mutilated word remains in the text in order to give the candidate a clue as to what is missing.

C-tests suffer from the same disadvantages as cloze and gap-filling tasks, although the fact that the first few letters of a missing word are given in a C-test text will reduce the number of possible answers for any one gap. Even when the first half of each missing word is provided, though, it is still possible for some answers to be almost unanswerable.

Each blank in the test below must be filled by the second half of a word. If the whole word has an EVEN number of letters, then EXACTLY HALF are missing:

to = t......; that = th......; throws = thr......

If the whole word has an UNEVEN number of letters, ONE MORE THAN HALF are missing:

the = t......; their = th......; letters = let......

Have you heard about a camera that can peer into the ground and 'see' a buried city? Or another th...... can he...... scientists est...... when a vol...... will er......? Still ano...... that c...... show h...... deeply a bu...... has go...... into fl......?

The first problem here is that the instructions are too complicated. The task can seem less daunting if the instructions simply tell the candidates that the number of missing letters is shown in each gap. The first gaps in the above example, would then look like this:

Or another th.. can he.. scientists est..... when

The second problem is that the final sentence does not provide enough clues for educated native speakers to be able to complete 'bu......' and 'fl......'. This may only be discovered when the test is pretested.

DICTATION

Dictation can only be fair to students if it is presented in the same way to them all, and this generally means having the material on tape, so that not only is it presented in an identical way to all candidates, but the speed of delivery and positioning of pauses can be tested in advance. If the use of a tape recording is impossible, the people who deliver the dictation must be very thoroughly trained.

Dictation can be objectively marked if candidates are asked to write down the original text verbatim, and if the examiner has a system for deciding how marks should be allotted. However, such systems are difficult to devise. For example, if the marking instructions say, 'Deduct one point for each misspelt word and two points for each word that is missing or is not the same as in the original', it is not always clear whether a word is misspelt or just wrong. The same problem occurs even if the marker is told to ignore spelling mistakes.

The other problem with this method of marking dictation is that it is both time-consuming and boring to mark. This means not only that the marking will be expensive but that the markers are likely to make frequent errors. Some test writers avoid this problem by giving a partial dictation in which the candidates are given a copy of the text they are to hear in which words, phrases or sentences have been deleted. The candidates are asked to fill in the gaps as they listen to the text being read.

Some dictation tests do not ask students to write down the words verbatim, but to write down the main points, as a sort of note-taking task. For example, the students might have the programme for a course of study read aloud to them, and might be asked to note down the information they would need if they were following this course. Such a dictation comprises a more authentic listening task than most traditional dictations, but gives rise to problems in marking such as those discussed in the next section.

SHORT-ANSWER QUESTIONS

By 'short-answer questions' we mean items that are open-ended, where the candidates have to think up the answer for themselves. The answers may range from a word or phrase to one or two sentences.

The most important point perhaps to remember when designing

short-answer questions is that the candidates must know what is expected of them. For example, in the following example, it is not at all clear what is wanted:

Rewrite the following sentence, starting with the words provided. The new sentence must be as close as possible to the original.

It was John who saved my life.
If it _____ .

To an item writer who was used to teaching transformations, this would no doubt be a straightforward item, but when it was pretested, most of the students had no idea what they were supposed to write. The task would have been clearer like this:

It was John who saved my life.
If it _____, I would have died.

Sometimes, on the other hand, students think they know what they are supposed to do, when they do not. For example, the following item was supposed to test students' use of the present perfect:

Write two sentences containing 'since'.

Among the students' answers were the following:

Since it is the end of term I am going on holiday.
Since it was raining they stayed at home.

The answers were quite reasonable, but they did not contain the present perfect. If an item writer requires the present perfect, that must be made clear in the instructions. For example:

Complete the following sentence, using the correct form of the verb 'to be':

I _____ here since yesterday.

This could otherwise be tested in a multiple-choice format:

Complete the following sentence.

I _____ here since yesterday.
         A   am
         B   was
         C   will be
         D   have been

Reading and listening comprehension can be tested using short-answer questions. The answers can be revealing, as they often show textual misunderstandings which would never have occurred to the test writer. However, the marking of such items is often very difficult since there are frequently many ways of saying the same thing, and many acceptable alternative answers, some of which may not have been anticipated by the item writer. Once again the items must be thoroughly pretested.

3.5.4   *Subjectively marked tests*

COMPOSITIONS AND ESSAYS

At first sight, writing the prompts for written compositions seems very easy – much easier, for example, than writing multiple-choice questions. All one seems to have to do is write a topic and leave the student to compose an answer. The following kind of prompt is very common:

'Travel broadens the mind.' (J. Smith) Discuss.

There are many disadvantages with this task. One is the problem of terminology. Candidates may not be familiar with the conventions behind the technical use of the word 'discuss', and so will not know what is expected. Test writers must make sure that terms such as 'discuss', and 'illustrate your answer' are understood by all candidates.

The instructions lack information that the candidates need if they are to be able to do justice to themselves.

Candidates need to know how long the essay should be and whether marks will be deducted if it is too short.

They need to know for whom this essay is to be written, so that they can decide whether it should be in a colloquial style as might be used in a letter, or in an academic style similar to that used in a school essay. In the above example, as long as the students are familiar with this technical use of 'discuss', they will know that the essay is to be written in a formal style. Some prompts, however, are less clear.

They need to know how the essay is to be marked. Are the markers looking for fluency or accuracy? Are marks awarded for the structure of the essay, and the ability to present a good argument, or solely for the use of grammar and vocabulary? Candidates need to know all these things in order to decide whether to use easy, well-known structures so as not to be penalised for errors, or whether to take risks because extra marks are awarded for the use of complex and creative language. (The marking of writing tasks of this kind is discussed in Chapter 5.)

Candidates would have a better idea of how to approach this

question if it was presented in the following way:

Write a formal essay for your English teacher saying whether you agree with the saying, 'Travel broadens the mind'.

You should write about 200 to 250 words.
Marks will be given for:
1   structure of the essay, e.g. the use of paragraphs (20%)
2   appropriacy of style (20%)
3   clarity of argument (20%)
4   range of grammar and vocabulary (20%)
5   accuracy of grammar and vocabulary (20%).

A further problem with many writing tasks is that they expect students to have a wide general knowledge. For example:

Describe the legal system in your country.

If the students are not well informed about their legal system, and many will not be, they may not have enough to say to be able to exhibit their level of English proficiency.

Some writing tasks ask students to use creative skills which they may not have. For example:

You are lost in a blizzard. Describe how you try to find your way home.

Other tasks expect students to write interestingly about a subject which might be irrelevant or boring. For example:

Discuss the advantages and disadvantages of living at home during your time at college.

To prevent some of these problems it is better to give students some information before they start writing so that they do not have to be creative. They may be given a short piece of text which sets the scene or provides background information, but it is important that this is short and easy to read so that the candidate does not waste valuable time reading rather than writing, and so that poor readers are not penalised. Some prompts limit the amount of reading required by using a graph or a picture or a series of pictures. In this case it is essential that the graph is easy to understand and that the pictures are clear.

Many tasks, of course, are not as formal as essays and compositions. When a student is asked to write an informal letter or note, it is important that the task should be a natural one. It is not, therefore, advisable to ask candidates to write letters or notes to friends or relations, since they would usually write to such people in their own language. It may be necessary for the item writer to invent a scenario which would require the candidate to write in the foreign language. For example, the candidate might be asked to write to a friend from abroad, or to leave a note for a landlady.

SUMMARIES

Summaries are used most often to test reading or listening comprehension and writing skills. In some recent tests they have been used for an integrated test of comprehension and writing. Writing summaries may closely replicate many real-life activities, but there are two major problems.

If the candidate writes a poor summary in which some of the main points in the original text are missing, it may be impossible to know whether this is because of poor comprehension or poor writing skills. This does not matter if a single test score is reported for, say, 'summarising a report' and if it is clear that this score is for a combination of reading and writing skills, but it is not reasonable to give the candidate two scores, one for reading and one for writing.

Marking a summary is not easy. Some examiners just give one mark for each main point that the student has written down, regardless of grammar and style. This sounds straightforward but it is not. Identifying the main points in a text is itself so subjective that the examiners may not agree as to what the main points are. The problem is intensified if the marking includes some scheme where, say, main points each get two marks, and subsidiary points get one. If the marking scheme also tries to account for features such as accuracy, fluency and appropriacy, the marking becomes unduly complex.

Some examiners resolve this problem by presenting the original text alongside a summary of it in which key words and expressions are missing. The candidates then have to fill in the missing words in the summary. A well-designed summary task of this kind is a very efficient way of testing reading comprehension, but because there are usually many possible alternative answers for each gap, marking can be difficult, especially if the test is a large-scale one. To avoid this, some examiners ask the candidates only to use the *exact* word from the original text. This should work, but unfortunately there are always some students who do not follow this instruction and enter appropriate, but not exact, answers in the spaces. If these students get low scores although their comprehension of the text is good, then the test cannot be said to be testing reading comprehension.

A good way of avoiding this problem is to provide a bank of possible words and phrases, as in 'banked gap-filling' above. Such tests are difficult to write, and need much pretesting, but can eventually work well and are easier to mark.

ORAL INTERVIEWS

It is sometimes felt that giving someone an oral interview is a quick and painless way of assessing that person's proficiency in the language. Many people think, for example, that if they have a brief chat with a new arrival at a college they will quickly be able to assess the level of that student's language. However, this is not the case. The conversation may turn on superficial topics which may require only a limited vocabulary and which will not stretch the student's ability to use complex structures. This is not the place to discuss oral interviews in detail, but it should be emphasised that the interview needs to be carefully structured so that the aspects of the test which are considered important are covered with each student, and each student is tested in a similar way. It is not fair to the students if some of them are only required to make simple but appropriate comments, while other equally good ones are forced to use complex language which betrays their inadequacies. Interviewers also need to be trained to put candidates at their ease, to get a genuine conversation going without saying much themselves, to manage to appear interested in each interview and to know how to ask questions which will elicit the language required. Chapter 5 briefly discusses the training of oral interviewers.

INFORMATION-GAP ACTIVITIES

Sometimes one, two or more students are given information-gap tasks to complete. For example, two students might be given slightly different pictures and, without seeing each other's, might be asked to work out what the differences are between them. Or a student might be asked to put questions to the interviewer in order to solve some problem. Such tasks can be enjoyable for the candidates, but they are difficult to construct and have a tendency to elicit only a limited range of language. For example, the questioner may be able to get away with using the perfectly acceptable, 'How about ... ?', for many of the questions. In addition this sort of task can be biased. For example, maps are used in many information-gap tasks, but, as we described above, not all candidates may be familiar with maps. All information-gap tasks should be rigorously pretested.

3.6 Test Editing/Moderating Committees

As we have repeatedly emphasised, no one person can possibly produce a good test, or even a good item, without advice. Being close to the item, as its designer, the item writer 'knows' what the item is intended to test, and will find it difficult to see that it might in fact be testing either something quite different, or something in addition to what is intended. Knowing what the 'correct' answer is means that the item writer has quite a different view of how students will or should process the item from somebody who does not know what the 'correct' answer is.

It is therefore absolutely crucial in all test development, for whatever purpose, at whatever level of learner ability and however trivial the consequences of failure on the test might be, that some person or persons other than the individual item writer look closely at each item, respond to the item as a student would, reflect upon what abilities are required for successful completion of the item/task, and then compare what he or she thinks the item is testing with what the item writer claims it tests. This form of item review should ideally take place at an early stage in the construction process and need not be a formal matter involving a whole committee. (The best items are subject to a number of such informal reviews before they reach their final draft stage.)

Once items have been edited into this draft stage, they should then be assembled into a draft test paper/subtest, for the consideration of a formal committee. This committee should include experienced item writers (but not normally those who have produced the items being edited), teachers who are experienced in teaching towards the test or in teaching the target group of learners, and possibly other testing experts, or even subject experts if some form of specific purpose test is being prepared.

The task of this committee is to consider each item and the test as a whole for the degree of match with the test specifications, likely level of difficulty, possible unforeseen problems, ambiguities in the wording of items and of instructions, problems of layout, match between texts and questions, and overall balance of the subtest or paper.

It is especially important that members of this editing committee do not simply read the test and its items: they must take each item as if they were students. This means that, for example, for items testing writing skills they must attempt the actual writing task, or for listening items they must hear the tape and try to answer the questions. For listening tests in particular it is important that committee members do not simply read the tapescript and treat it as a reading comprehension exercise; their taking of the test must replicate the experience of the test takers as closely as possible, and must therefore be done with a tape recording if one is required by the test.

This, of course, means that committee members will need to have devoted sufficient time to taking the test in advance of the editing meeting – a fact often forgotten by institutions who have on their editing committees busy people who may be unable or not inclined to spend the detailed time they should on taking the test.

The conduct of the committee meeting is of considerable importance. Sufficient time must be set aside for an adequate discussion of each item. In our experience, too many editing meetings spend an inordinate amount of time on the first two or three items, run out of time for the remaining items, and rush through the last three quarters of the test at a breakneck speed just to get through the agenda. In addition, in our experience, committees are much more effective before lunch than after it, and all too many committee members seem to need to leave meetings early in order to catch trains home or go on to other meetings.

An effective editing committee will have a firm chairperson who will ensure that ample time is allocated to the meeting, that no more than is necessary is spent on each item, that each member's views are heard and considered (provided that they are reasoned and reasonable), and that clear decisions are taken by the committee and recorded by the secretary or institutional official.

In addition, it is very important that one person is made responsible for ensuring that the recommendations of the committee are not only recorded but also acted upon and implemented in a revised test, which is then subjected to some form of confirmatory vetting before the test is pretested (see Chapter 4).

Although these precautions may seem excessively bureaucratic, it is our experience that when they are not taken, the resulting test is often at least as flawed as it was before the editing committee meeting.

3.7 Survey of EFL Examination Boards: Questionnaire

One board answered 'Not applicable – oral assessment' to all but two of the questions relating to item writing. To avoid repetition, therefore, this board's responses have been omitted from this chapter. It should, of course, be pointed out that oral assessment does require careful consideration (see page 62) since the nature of the task and the criteria for scoring are important components of test design.

QUESTION 9: *Are item or test writers given any further information or guidance? ('Further' means 'in addition to the specifications and sample examination papers referred to earlier in the questionnaire'.)*

Most boards said they did give item writers further information, but they gave few details. One board said that 'round-table' setting meetings were chaired by the Chief Examiner, and that items were written with guidance and 'vetted' at the meeting. Another said that the Chief Examiners provided detailed setting procedures for question setters, and one said the guidance was 'mostly verbal in committee and accompanying minutes'. Two of the UCLES respondents said that each item writer received 'Notes for guidance', and the subject officer for the Certificate in English for International Business and Trade (CEIBT) said, 'They attend moderating meetings before they become setters. They work in teams of three – one setter for each paper – with the guidance of a more experienced setter. They have two meetings as a team to research the company material and plan tasks.'

Only one board gave extensive information, including a copy of a sample letter sent to item writers (see Chapter 2, page 35 for details).

QUESTION 11: *What criteria are used in the appointment of item/test writers?*

The boards varied in their requirements. Five said item writers must have appropriate qualifications, of which one specified university and one EFL/ESL qualifications. Six asked for relevant teaching and examining experience or experience in the relevant subject area, while four expected the item writers to be practising teachers accustomed to preparing their students for the relevant exam. One asked for a strong commitment to a communicative approach to teaching and assessment, and one said that a writer's acceptability would depend upon performance at the item-writing meeting.

QUESTION 12: *For what period are item/test writers appointed?*

There was a variety of responses, ranging from four boards which appointed their item writers annually, to one which did not appoint writers for a specific period and said that the current writers had been 'producing examinations materials for the last fifteen years, experience which ensures continuity and stability'. Two boards did not appoint writers for a given number of years but for a given number of papers.

QUESTION 13: *How far in advance of the date of the exam's administration are item writers first asked to produce their items?*

Five boards asked their writers to produce their items about two years before the test's administration, and three aimed for about one year. Of the other boards replying, one said item writing was an 'ongoing activity'; one said, 'There is not necessarily a direct link between commissioning and final examination'; and one said, 'Writers submit material on an ad hoc basis, building up a bank of potential items. They are paid for items used on publication. There are no deadlines and no pressures on writers.' The UCLES responses varied from 'three years' to 'twelve to eighteen months'.

QUESTION 14: *How long are item writers given to produce the first draft of an item?*

Eight boards gave actual time intervals: these ranged from six weeks to twelve months. Two boards had a flexible approach, with one saying, 'Depends on item and writer' and the other saying, 'Very flexible, by mutual consent'. UCLES' time limits ranged from six weeks to six months.

QUESTION 15: *Once a first draft has been produced by an individual setter, what then happens to it?*

Almost all the boards sent draft papers to be checked by a Chief Examiner or a moderator, and then generally a moderating committee. The only exception was one board which banked items for incorporation in later draft papers which would be held until the appropriate revision stage.

The actual vetting procedures varied from board to board. One example is the following procedure:

> First draft is put together by [Exam Officer] who has to ensure exam is fair, of right level, and in accordance with the syllabus rationale. Items may have been trialled by [Exam Officer] on secure students to assess levels of language and task difficulty. Copies of first draft are sent to i) directors of boards and ii) chief examiner for this level; two further senior marking team leaders from a list of twelve. These people study the draft, try it out if possible on secure candidates, make suggestions for change where necessary and send a detailed report to [Exam Officer].

QUESTION 16: *Does a committee meet at any point to discuss each paper/test?*

All but two boards said Yes. One of the two boards which did not have a regular committee had 'ad hoc committees to discuss specific aspects of the examinations, changes to procedures, modifications to criteria, etc. The procedure for moderating is done by post'.

If Yes, what is this committee called?

The most common title was Moderation/Moderating Committee/

Board. Other titles were Vetting Panel, Standing Advisory Committee, EFL Revision Committee, Editing Committee, Test Construction Team and Preparatory Subcommittee.

QUESTION 17: *What qualifies people to be members of this committee?*

The composition of this committee varied. In two cases it consisted of examiners and moderators, and in a third case it also included exam setters and markers, and practising teachers. One committee also included board administrators, and another included industrialists who had made 'an outstanding contribution to the board's examining work'. The UCLES committees generally consisted of the chief examiner, the subject officer, item writers and other EFL experts. Other boards' committees consisted of experienced subject specialist teachers and/or teachers actively preparing candidates for the examinations, or moderators or materials writers.

QUESTION 18: *How long does a committee take to discuss/edit a complete examination?*

Here again the answers varied. One board said it was impossible to answer this question, and another said 'as long as required'. Two said the time varied from one day to a week or several weeks. Some were able to be slightly more specific. One said 'at least one day of formal meeting and pre- and post-postal/phone stages' and one said 'the editing/vetting process takes a minimum of three weeks, usually four or five'. Three were more specific still: 'approx. 3 hours per paper', '4 papers in one working day', and 'usually 3 days for 15 components'. One board gave more details of the procedure: 'members comment on the question papers in writing in advance of the meeting; this takes at least one day. The Chief Examiners then reply to their comments. The Preparatory Sub Committee meeting lasts one full day'.

QUESTION 19: *What steps if any are taken to ensure that the draft examination follows the syllabus (if one exists)?*

Half the boards instruct their item writers to follow the syllabus and trust them to do so. The other half give initial instructions, but also carry out subsequent checks, the responsibility for these checks resting on a) three members of the vetting panel, b) the moderators, c) the chief examiner and various directors and moderators, and d) a 'reviser' who comments on the papers and their adherence to the syllabus. UCLES seemed to mirror the other boards in that for some exams item writers were given the syllabus and were expected to follow it, and in others the test papers were checked against the syllabus by the subject officer or by, for example, the 'Chair, EFL officer, independent vetter'.

QUESTION 20: *What typically happens to the draft examination after the above committee has deliberated?*

The most informative way to report the answers to this question is to list examples of the different procedures:

1. Manuscript to printer, artwork commissioned, tapes recorded; proofs circulated to Chief Examiners and Moderator, worked through by scrutineer; final proof passed for press with print order.

2. Items approved subject to agreed amendments. Preparation and proof-reading of 'vetted' copy. Return to Chief/Senior Examiner for a final check and approval to ensure that examination has been prepared in accordance with vetted and agreed copy.

3. Once an agreed version of a paper has been completed it is (computer) typed and submitted for printing. All members of the revision committee see the first proof and are given the chance to make alterations (major and minor).

4. [Exam Officer] revises draft in light of reports from five senior examiners and arranges for production. During recording, actors comment on clarity and naturalness of language. Final text and copy of tape sent to Director who arranges printing of exam texts and copying of master tape.

5. Chair of paper and subject officer put together two parallel versions.

3.8 Survey of EFL Examination Boards: Documentation

The only documents which expanded on the answers given in the questionnaire related to the construction of test items. City and Guilds sent us two of their booklets, *Setting Multiple-Choice Tests* (1984), and *Setting and Moderating Written Question Papers (Other than Multiple-Choice)* (undated). The former gives helpful ideas on how to construct multiple-choice questions, cites a wide range of examples and advises writers about some of the potential pitfalls. The latter gives advice about rubrics and the layout of non-multiple-choice questions, and accompanies recommendations on how to design good items with examples of poor and improved questions.

Pitman sent us copies of their 'Blueprints' for each level of their English for Speakers of Other Languages (ESOL) exams. These are guidelines for item writers, and not only describe the kind and level of language to be tested but also give instructions about text types and advice about how to write good items.

3.9 Discussion

As can be seen from the answers to the above questions, most of the examination boards treat the item writing-process seriously. They give item writers ample time to produce future papers, and carry out thorough checks on the draft papers.

The one area which does not always get sufficient attention relates to coverage of the syllabus. Although almost all the boards tell their item writers that their test papers must cover the syllabus, only half the boards check that the papers actually do. Since some areas of a syllabus are always easier to test than others, item writers sometimes find they are unable or unwilling to test the more difficult aspects, and, because of this, the content of some test papers may be unbalanced. We feel, therefore, that it is essential to check draft papers to see that the syllabus has been covered adequately.

3.10 Checklist

1. In order to understand what a test item is doing, it is essential that you respond to the item as a test taker. Simply 'eyeballing' the item is quite insufficient.

2. Taking your own items is important but inadequate – you 'know' what you think the item requires. Therefore, get others who have not written the item to take it, as a test taker would.

3. Nobody writes good test items alone. Even professional test writers need the insight of other people into what they have produced. Therefore, get other people (plural!) to take (i.e. respond to, not just look at) your items.

4. Don't be too defensive about your items: be prepared to change or drop them if others see them as too problematic. We all – really, all – write bad items.

5. Get respondents to say why they gave the answer they did, and if possible to say how they went about answering the item.

6. Again, if at all possible, get your respondents to say/write what

they think the item is testing, independently of anything you may think it is testing. In other words, do not tell them what you think it is testing and then ask them to agree! Also, ask respondents to say what they think the main purpose of the item is, and what level of student it is suitable for.

7. All tests should be edited or moderated by people who have not written them. This editing committee should have available the responses of your respondents at some point in their deliberations. Items that have provoked unexpected responses from respondents must be revised.

8. If there is a defined test population, get respondents or editors to estimate roughly what proportion of the test population will get the item correct.

9. Match what most or all respondents agree the item is testing against what the test writer says it is testing. Resolve disagreements.

10. Match the agreement in 9 above against the test specifications or the syllabus.

11. Look at the syllabus or specifications and ask yourself if anything significant is missing from your test. If so, is this justifiable?

12. Ask yourself if the test method will be familiar to students. If not, change the method, or ensure that the instructions are clear. Ask yourself if another test method might be more suitable to your purpose, or clearer/easier for candidates.

13. Ask yourself what the item/collection of items will tell you about the learners' abilities. If the test/item results disagree with your opinion of the students, which will you believe – the test or yourself?

14. What are the chances of the students getting the same result if they took the test again the next day?

15. Pretest the test on students who are as similar as possible to the target students. Examine their responses and ask yourself:

   i) Are there any unexpected responses? If so, are any of them unexpectedly correct? If yes, add them to the mark scheme or change the item.

   ii) How many students found an item easy? Is it too difficult or too easy?

   iii) Which students got the item right – the stronger students or the weaker ones? In theory, the stronger ones ought to do better on each item, but in practice the item may contain a trick, an obscurity, two correct answers, or some such problem.

16. Get respondents or students to take reading and listening comprehension items without the associated (written or spoken) text. Can they still get the item right? If yes, it's probably not testing comprehension of the text.

17. With listening comprehension items, ensure that respondents actually listen to the text (rather than read it) when they respond to the item. Reading the text is easier than listening – they can do it in their own time, pause and re-read, and so on.

18. Is the language of the item easier than the language of the text? If not, you are also testing understanding of the items.

19. In multiple-choice questions, are some distractors possible – in some standard variety of the language; with a different interpretation of context; with different stress and/or intonation? Is the correct answer obvious because of length or degree of detail?

20. Have all possible/plausible answers been foreseen in the answer key?

21. Is the item contextualised? Is the context sufficient to rule out other alternative interpretations or possible ambiguities?

22. Is the item likely to be biased against or in favour of students of a particular gender/culture/background knowledge/interest?

23. How life-like is the item? Does the item look like something that students might have to do with language in the real world? For example, with writing tasks, do students have a purpose for writing and someone to write it to?

24. Would it be desirable to present the instructions, or indeed the test items, in the mother tongue?

25. How will the performance of the candidate be judged? Are the marking criteria or the correct or expected responses specified? Are they specifiable, or must you wait until you have a few sample performances before you can finalise your mark scheme?

Bibliography

Alderson, J.C. 1978. *A Study of the Cloze Procedure with Native and Non-Native Speakers of English*. Unpublished Ph.D. thesis, Edinburgh University.

Alderson, J.C. 1979. The Cloze Procedure and Proficiency in English as a Foreign Language. *TESOL Quarterly* 13 (2): 219–227. (reprinted in J.W. Oller, 1983. (ed.), *Issues in Language Testing Research*. Rowley, Mass.: Newbury House.

Alderson, J.C. and D. Wall. 1993. Does Washback Exist? *Applied Linguistics* 14: 115–129.

Allan, A. 1992. Development and Validation of a Scale to Measure Test-Wiseness in EFL/ESL Reading Test Takers. *Language Testing* 9: 101–123.

Buck, G. 1989. Written Tests of Pronunciation: Do They Work? *English Language Teaching Journal* 41: 50–56.

Heaton, J.B. 1988. *Writing English Language Tests*, 2nd edition. London: Longman.

Hughes, A. 1989. *Testing for Language Teachers*. Cambridge: Cambridge University Press.

Klein-Braley, C. 1981. *Empirical Investigation of Cloze Tests*. Doctoral Dissertation, University of Duisburg.

Lado, R. 1961. *Language Testing*. New York: McGraw Hill.

Oller, J.W. 1979. *Language Tests at School*. London: Longman.

Peirce, B.N. 1992. Demystifying the TOEFL Reading Test. *TESOL Quarterly*. 26: 665–689.

Valette, R.M. 1977. *Modern Language Testing*, 2nd edition. New York: Harcourt Brace Jovanovich.

Wall, D. and J.C. Alderson. 1993. Examining Washback. *Language Testing* 10: 41–69.

Weir, C.J. 1988. *Communicative Language Testing*. University of Exeter.

4 Pretesting and analysis

This chapter addresses the issue of the pretesting and analysis of test items. We discuss the reasons for pretesting, the nature of the processes involved and the differences between pilot tests and main trials. We then explain the basic statistics required for the analysis of individual test items and describe the most usual ways of reporting overall test results.

4.1 Reasons for pretesting

However well designed an examination may be, and however carefully it has been edited, it is not possible to know how it will work until it has been tried out on students. Although item writers may think they know what an item is testing and what the correct answer is, they cannot anticipate the responses of learners at different levels of language ability. Even experienced language teachers and testers are often unable to agree about what an item is testing (see Alderson 1993 and Buck 1991) or how difficult the item is for a given group of students. In a study carried out by researchers at Lancaster University, 21 judges were asked to estimate the difficulty for potential examinees of 30 reading comprehension questions. The judges ranged from highly experienced testers who were familiar with both the test and the ability level of the candidates, to teachers who were familiar with neither. The judges' estimates varied wildly. For example, two judges guessed that 90% of the students would answer Item 2 correctly, whereas one judge thought that only 10% would. The other estimates for the item ranged fairly evenly from 80% to 15%. This was by no means an extreme example. Seven of the other items had as wide a discrepancy between the estimates, and in the case of one item, one judge estimated that 95% of the students would get it right, whereas another estimated that 5% would. The two items that showed the least disagreement among judges had estimates ranging from 100% to 50%. Interestingly, the more experienced judges were no more accurate than those who knew nothing about either the test or the students.

Examiners do not, of course, only need to know how difficult the test items are. They also need to know whether they 'work'. 'Work' has many meanings. It may mean, for example, that an item which is intended to test a particular structure actually does so, or it may mean that the item succeeds in distinguishing between students at different levels so that the more proficient students can answer it better than the weaker ones. It is surprising how often items, however thoughtfully designed, fail to distinguish between students in this way. It is impossible to predict whether items will work without trying them out. The performance of multiple-choice items may be the most difficult to predict, since the presence of a variety of correct and incorrect answers provides plenty of scope for ambiguity and disagreement, but open-ended items and subjectively marked tests can also produce surprises. For example, an open-ended question may turn out to confuse the best rather than the worst students, or an essay task may unintentionally elicit only a small range of language from the candidates. Although the combination of experienced item writers and strict editing procedures ensures that many potentially poor items are discarded, some problems will not be identified at the editing stage and can only be discovered during pretesting. It is essential, therefore, that all tests should be pretested whether they are objectively marked discrete items or subjectively marked open-ended ones.

4.2   Pilot testing

The term *pretesting* in this book refers to all trials of an examination that take place before it is launched, or becomes operational or 'live' as some of the boards put it. Most of the pretesting takes place during the 'main trials' but these should be preceded by less formal pretesting which we will call *pilot testing*. Pilot testing may vary in scope from trying out a test on a small group of colleagues to running a trial on say a hundred students, but in all cases the aim is to iron out the main problems before the major trials. A pilot testing programme could consist of the following:

1. Try the test items out on a few friends or colleagues, of whom at least two are native speakers of the language being tested, to see whether the instructions are clear, the language of the items acceptable and the answer key accurate. These colleagues should take all parts of the exam, not just the objectively marked sections. It is surprising how many faults in a test emerge at this stage, especially if the test constructors do not have the language being tested as their first language.

2. Give the revised test to a group of students who are similar in

background and level to those who will take the final examination. Large numbers are not necessary, but if there are at least 20, so much the better. Such pilots can be run relatively quickly and cheaply, and will provide invaluable information about the ease of administering the test, the time students need for completing it, the clarity of instructions, the kind of language being elicited in the open-ended questions, the accuracy and comprehensiveness of any answer keys, the usability of the marking scales, and so on. The results will reveal many unanticipated flaws in the test, and will save time and effort when the main trials are run.

4.3 The main trials

The scope of the main trialling and the kinds of analysis required depend on factors such as the importance and purpose of the exam and the degree of objectivity of the marking. The most objectively marked tests are those, such as multiple-choice, where the answer does not have to be created by the candidate, but is selected from a range of possible alternatives, and can be marked as accurately by a clerk or a computer as by a trained teacher or tester. The most subjectively marked are those such as oral interviews and written compositions where the marker has only a marking scheme for guidance. Between these two extremes lies a range of item types which demand a greater or lesser degree of subjectivity in the marking (see Chapter 3).

One of the main questions facing any test constructor is the number of students on whom a test should be trialled. It is impossible to give a rule for this as the number depends on the importance and type of exam, and also the availability of suitable students. Since the construction of traditional multiple-choice items is very difficult, and since it is so easy for the item constructor to miss ambiguities in the distractors, it might be argued that such test items need more pretesting than any other type, and indeed when we come to report on the exam boards' pretesting practice it will be seen that multiple-choice items receive the most trialling. However, since other types of objective items, for example gap-filling and open-ended questions, can also behave in unexpected ways, all kinds of objectively marked tests should be thoroughly pretested. Henning 1987 recommends 1000 students for trial multiple-choice tests, but it is so difficult to find samples for trialling that test constructors may have to be content with a sample of 200 or 300, or even 30 or 40. The only guiding rule is 'the more the better', since the more students there are, the less effect chance will have on the results. If, for example, 300 students take a trial test, and one student, who happens to be ill that day, produces an uncharacteristically poor paper, that result will have little effect on the overall test statistics. However, if there are only 10 students in the trial, then that one student's performance will noticeably affect the overall results.

Regardless of how many trial students there are, it is important that the sample should, as far as possible, be representative of the final candidature, with a similar range of abilities and backgrounds. If the pretest students are not similar to the expected test population, then the results of the trials may be useless: tests behave very differently with different populations (for a discussion of this see Crocker and Algina 1986).

It is also important that the trial test students should take the test seriously and do it as well as possible. If they do not appreciate its importance, and treat it as a game, the ensuing results may invalidate the whole trialling procedure. We shall be describing one way of coping with this at the end of this chapter.

The trial test should be administered in exactly the same way as the final exam will be, so that not only will the administration guidelines themselves be tested, but also the test items will be presented under the same circumstances as in the live exam. The only aspect which might need to be different relates to the timing of the exam. If the examiners wish to estimate the test's reliability (see below), the students should be allowed to take as long as they wish to complete the exam. This may be contrary to the procedure of the exam itself, where, for either theoretical or practical reasons, students may be given less time than they would like. If it is necessary to limit the students' time during the trials, it is still possible to assess the test's reliability, but any results will have to be treated with caution as they are likely to overestimate the test's reliability (see Crocker and Algina 1986).

In the statistical discussion about the analysis of objective tests that follows, it will be assumed that the trial exams are *norm-referenced*, that is that they aim to place candidates on some sort of ordered scale, so that they can be compared with one another. If the exam is *criterion-referenced*, and students are compared not with one another, but with a level of achievement or a set of criteria set out in marking descriptors, then such norm-referenced measures may be inapplicable. In many examination systems it is the case that objectively marked tests are treated as norm-referenced, and subjectively marked ones as criterion-referenced. This is probably not from any underlying testing philosophy, but because of practical considerations. Since the correct items in an objective test can be added up to provide a total score, students can be ranked according to these totals, and performance on individual items can be compared to these rankings (see Classical Item Analysis below). For criterion-referenced tests it may not be appropriate to base any item analysis on a ranking of students' papers, and therefore less generally accepted methods of analysis may be required. (See Crocker and Algina 1986 and Hudson and Lynch 1984 for discussions of some of these.) Subjectively marked tests such as essays and oral interviews do not lend themselves to norm-referenced item analysis, and where testers use forms of global marking for stretches of written or spoken performance, where the candidates' performance is compared with a series of descriptions of the language required at each level, these papers may be considered to be criterion-referenced.

4.4 Test analysis

4.4.1 Correlation

Before we discuss ways in which the performance of individual items can be assessed, there is one concept which underpins so much of testing analysis that we need to introduce it before we go any further. That concept is *correlation*, by which we mean the extent to which two sets of results agree with each other. To give some idea of what a correlation is, here are some hypothetical results on a very small number of students.

Figure 4.1 gives the ranks of 8 students (students A – H) on two tests. You will see that in each case the students were ranked identically on the two tests, so that A came first each time, B came second and so on. This is shown graphically in the scattergram. The students' ranks on Test 1 are shown up the side of the graph, and those on Test 2 along

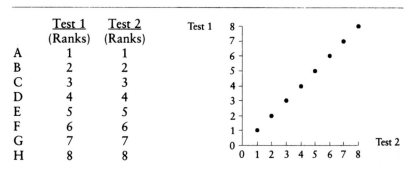

	Test 1 (Ranks)	Test 2 (Ranks)
A	1	1
B	2	2
C	3	3
D	4	4
E	5	5
F	6	6
G	7	7
H	8	8

FIG. 4.1   CORRELATION = +1.0

the bottom. Each dot on the graph stands for a student's rank on both Test 1 and Test 2. In this case, as all the ranks were the same for both tests, you will see that the dots progress diagonally up the graph from bottom left to top right. You will also see that if these dots were joined together they would make a straight line. This line shows that there is a perfect correlation between the two sets of scores. This result is described as a perfect positive correlation, or a correlation of +1.0.

If we now look at Figure 4.2 we shall see what happens when the two sets of ranks, instead of being identical, are as different from each other as it is possible to be. In this case the student who came first in Test 1 came last in Test 3, the student who came second in Test 1 came

	Test 1 (Ranks)	Test 3 (Ranks)
A	1	8
B	2	7
C	3	6
D	4	5
E	5	4
F	6	3
G	7	2
H	8	1

FIG. 4.2   CORRELATION = – 1.0

last but one in Test 3, and so on. The scattergram again shows a diagonal line, but this time the slope is in the other direction; it falls from top left to bottom right. This result is described as a perfect negative correlation, or a correlation of –1.0. It can be seen that there is just as strong a relationship between these two sets of test results as there was between Tests 1 and 2, but that this time the relationship is a negative one. Strong negative correlations are unlikely to occur between the results of two language tests, but might be found, for example, between scores on a language test and some personality measures.

Finally, Figure 4.3 shows the results of Tests 1 and 4. In this case there is no obvious relationship between the two sets of results. They could have been due to chance, and there is no discernible pattern in the scattergram. The dots appear all over the graph. The correlation index for this set of results is +.05, which is so near to .00 that we can say that there is no correlation between the two sets of results.

It is not very common for there to be no correlation between the results of two language tests. Since both are intended to test aspects of the same trait – language ability – they might be expected to show at least some degree of agreement. A more likely correlation between two

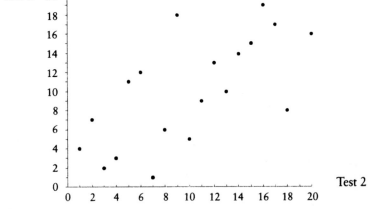

	Test 1 (Ranks)	Test 4 (Ranks)
A	1	6
B	2	3
C	3	5
D	4	1
E	5	7
F	6	8
G	7	2
H	8	4

FIG. 4.3   CORRELATION = +.05

language tests is shown in Figure 4.4. Here you will see from the ranks of the students participating that there was some similarity between the two sets of results. For example, Student B came second in one test, and third in the other, and Student C came third in one test and fourth in the other. However, there is not total agreement. The scattergram shows that there is some similarity between the scores, since the dots tend to progress up the graph from the bottom left to top right, and since there are no outlying dots at the top left and bottom right hand corners. However, it is not possible to join all the dots with one straight line. The correlation this time is +.70 which means that there is quite a strong agreement between the two sets of scores.

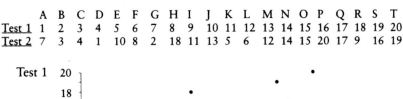

	A	B	C	D	E	F	G	H	I	J	K	L	M	N	O	P	Q	R	S	T
Test 1	1	2	3	4	5	6	7	8	9	10	11	12	13	14	15	16	17	18	19	20
Test 2	7	3	4	1	10	8	2	18	11	13	5	6	12	14	15	20	17	9	16	19

FIG. 4.4   CORRELATION = +.70

There are many ways of calculating correlation coefficients. The method used here was the *rank order correlation* (see Appendix 5 for the formula and a worked example). This correlation index is easy to work out by hand, and is used when there are only a small number of results to be correlated, or when the results are in ranks, as they were in our examples.

Another correlation method, which can be used for correlating test scores, rather than just ranks, is the *Pearson product moment correlation*. This is the most common correlation coefficient and is calculated routinely by statistical programs. However, it is not always appropriate to use it. Firstly it assumes that the two sets of scores are on an equal interval scale, that is that there is the same difference between each mark on the scale, so that, for example, there is roughly the same difference between the scores of say 18/20 and 19/20 as there is between say 5/20 and 6/20. It would often, therefore, not be appropriate to use the product moment correlation coefficient to correlate two sets of marks based on rating scales such as Very Good, Good, and Poor, since even if these are transformed into scores of say 3, 2 and 1, there is no guarantee that there is the same difference between 3 and 2 as between 2 and 1. Secondly, the product moment coefficient is only appropriate if the relationship between the two sets of results is consistent throughout the range of scores. For example, if two tests were taken by a wide range of students and the scores of the top students agreed across the two tests while those of the beginners did not, then the points in the correlation scattergram would tend to cluster round a curve rather than a straight line, and the product moment correlation coefficient would not be suitable. Anyone planning to use this coefficient should read about it first in a standard statistics book such as Guilford and Fruchter 1978.

4.4.2   Classical Item Analysis

OBJECTIVE TESTS

Traditionally there are two measures which are calculated for each objective test item – the *facility value* and the *discrimination index*. The facility value (F.V.) measures the level of difficulty of an item, and the discrimination index (D.I.) measures the extent to which the results of an individual item correlate with results from the whole test.

Facility Value

An item's facility value is the percentage of students to answer it correctly. If there are 300 students and 150 of them get the item right, the F.V. of the item is 150/300, which is 50% (often shown as a proportion: .5). This simple measure immediately gives item writers some idea of how easy the item is for the trial sample of students. If only 6/300 people get an item right, the F.V. is 2%, and it is clear that the item is very difficult indeed. Similarly if the F.V. is 95% (285/300) the item is very easy. Such very easy or difficult items are not very informative since they tell us little about the varying levels of ability of the trial group. To take an extreme case, an item with an F.V. of 0% will give no information except for the fact that the item is too difficult. If the examiners want a wide spread of scores from an exam, that is if they want the students' scores to range from very high to very low, then they will select items which are as near to an F.V. of 50% as possible because such items provide the widest scope for variation among the individual students. (This will be explained more fully under Discrimination Index below.) However, if test constructors are more interested in ensuring that a test is at a particular level of difficulty, they can manipulate the test contents by selecting items with the appropriate F.V. so that the test population achieves the required mean score. (The 'mean' is what is commonly known as the average, that is the sum of all the students' scores divided by the number of students.) For example, if students get a mean score of 70% on a trial test, the mean F.V. of all the items is 70%, and the test must therefore have many items with F.V.s of over 70%. If the test constructors want to make the test more difficult, they can remove or replace easy items, perhaps those with F.V.s of over 80%, so that the mean F.V., and therefore the students' mean score, is lowered. This will be discussed further under Descriptive Statistics (Section 4.5).

Discrimination Index

As well as knowing how difficult an item is, it is important to know how it discriminates, that is how well it distinguishes between students at different levels of ability. If the item is working well, we should expect more of the top-scoring students to know the answer than the low-scoring ones. If the strongest students get an item wrong, while the weakest students get it right, there is clearly a problem with the item, and it needs investigating.

There are many ways of calculating a discrimination index, but one of the easiest involves ranking students according to their total scores on the test, and comparing the proportion of correct answers in the top third of the sample with those in the bottom third. For example, if the top group consists of 10 students, and 7 of them get an item right (.7), whereas only 2 out of 10 in the bottom group (.2) do, then the D.I. is

.7 − .2 = +.5. An item with a D.I. of +.5 is usually considered to be discriminating well since the high scoring students have answered it better than low scoring ones. (See Appendix 3 for worked examples.)

The highest discrimination possible is +1.00, which is achieved if all the students in the top group get an answer right and none of the students in the bottom group does. Such items are very unusual. Often item writers are content with D.I.s of +.4 or above, but there are no rules as to what D.I.s are acceptable, since the possibility of getting high D.I.s varies according to the test type and range of ability of the examinees. Sometimes, however, an item has a negative D.I., which means that more students in the bottom group were correct than in the top group. There is obviously something very wrong with such an item and it should be revised or discarded. For example, when the following item was tried out on 207 French elementary and lower intermediate students, the D.I. was −.31. Only .07 of the top group chose the correct alternative, whereas .38 of the bottom group did. All but 7% of the top group chose alternative A.

This shirt is too dirty _____ .

A	to wear it
B	that I wear it
C	than I wear
D	for me to wear

It is not clear what is wrong with this item, but for some reason it is not working, and should either be altered or dropped from the test.

With multiple-choice items, a low discrimination index can often be explained by the performance of one or more of the distractors. The responses to these can be set out in a table, as in the following example, which shows the results of a pilot testing of a listening comprehension item. The stimulus was played on a tape, and students had to select the appropriate response.

'We're going to a film tonight. Do you want to come along?'

A	Where are you going tonight?
B	Do you want to see a film tonight?
C	Thanks. What time is it?
D	Are you going along now?

The students' marked test papers were grouped into the top scoring third, middle third and the bottom third. For each item a table was constructed showing how many students in each of the thirds chose each alternative. The results for the above item are shown in Table 4.1.

TABLE 4.1 ITEM ANALYSIS TABLE

	A	B	C*	D	Blank	Total	
T	-	-	14	7	-	21	* The correct answer is C.
M	-	-	17	3	-	20	
							F.V. = 71%
B	6	-	13	-	2	21	
							D.I. = +.05
Total	6	-	44	10	2	62	

(T = Top, M = Middle, B = Bottom)

This table shows how the item worked with these students. 44 out of 62 chose the correct alternative, C, but this alternative attracted students almost equally from the three groups. It did not therefore distinguish between students at different levels, and indeed the D.I. is only +.05. If we look at how the distractors behaved, we can see what went wrong. Firstly, alternative B was wasted as no one chose it. Secondly, distractor D attracted the wrong people: 7 of the top scoring students chose it, as did 3 of the middle group and none of the bottom group. Since more of the best students chose the supposedly wrong answer than did the weak ones, there must be something wrong with this distractor. Indeed, it could be argued that 'Are you going along now?', makes perfect sense in the context. This alternative should therefore be dropped. The only distractor which seems to be working well is alternative A, where all those who chose it were in the bottom group. This therefore provided most of what little positive discrimination there was. The distribution of students who left the item unanswered also contributed to this positive discrimination since the only two blanks were in the bottom group.

We mentioned above that if test items are intended to have high D.I.s, they should have F.V.s close to 50%. This is because items of medium difficulty provide more scope for discrimination. Table 4.2, overleaf, demonstrates this by showing what the maximum D.I.s are for items with differing F.V.s. In this imaginary example, 30 students took the test, and the table shows how many students in each of the top, middle and bottom groups answered each item correctly. There were 10 people in each of the three groups.

TABLE 4.2 RELATIONSHIP BETWEEN FACILITY VALUE AND DISCRIMINATION
INDEX

	Top Group	Middle Group	Bottom Group	F.V.	D.I.
Item 1	10 (1.0)	10 (1.0)	10 (1.0)	100%	0.0
Item 2	10 (1.0)	10 (1.0)	8 (0.8)	93%	+0.2
Item 3	10 (1.0)	10 (1.0)	4 (0.4)	80%	+0.6
Item 4	10 (1.0)	10 (1.0)	1 (0.1)	70%	+0.9
Item 5	10 (1.0)	10 (1.0)	0 (0.0)	66%	+1.0
Item 6	10 (1.0)	5 (0.5)	0 (0.0)	50%	+1.0
Item 7	10 (1.0)	0 (0.0)	0 (0.0)	33%	+1.0
Item 8	9 (0.9)	0 (0.0)	0 (0.0)	30%	+0.9
Item 9	6 (0.6)	0 (0.0)	0 (0.0)	20%	+0.6
Item 10	2 (0.2)	0 (0.0)	0 (0.0)	6%	+0.2
Item 11	0 (0.0)	0 (0.0)	0 (0.0)	0%	0.0

Note: The numbers in brackets are the proportions of people in a group
to get the item right.

Obviously if everyone gets an item right (Item 1), there cannot be any
discrimination, and similarly if everyone gets the item wrong (Item 11).
On the other hand, if half the students get it right, so that the F.V. is
50% (Item 6), it is possible to have the maximum D.I. of 1.00, with all
the top group getting the item right, and all the bottom group getting
it wrong. The table shows that with F.V.s from 66% to 33% it is
possible to get maximum D.I.s, but that once the items go beyond those
F.V.s it is no longer possible. For example, if the F.V. is 80% (Item 3),
it is not possible for all the ones who got it right to be confined to the
top group, so the discrimination cannot be higher than +.6. This should
be remembered when D.I.s are being considered. If an item has an F.V.
of 6%, and still has a D.I. of +.2, it is discriminating very well for such
a difficult item.

If the number of subjects is small, as for example in a pilot test, the
D.I. can be calculated using the method described here, or by using the
E_{1-3} *formula* which produces the same result (see Appendix 3).

Nowadays testers usually use computer programs for their test
analysis. These do not generally calculate the E_{1-3} D.I. (see Appendix
3), but calculate the *biserial* and the *point biserial correlations*. Like the
E_{1-3}, both of these correlations compare the item's performance with
that of the whole test, but they use mathematically more complex
correlation procedures. The E_{1-3} and these two correlations all produce
similar results, but the two biserial correlations have the advantage of
making use of all the students' answers, rather than just those from the
top and bottom groups. The biserial correlation, which tends to be

consistently higher than the point biserial, should be used if the pretest sample is likely to be of a different level of language proficiency from the final test population. Otherwise the point biserial correlation should generally be used. The formulae for these correlations are given in any standard book of statistics, and Crocker and Algina 1986 give a clear explanation of their uses. The Microcat computer program ITEMAN automatically calculates the facility value and both biserial correlations of all items, and it also reports on the performance of distractors. Statistical packages such as SPSS and SAS carry out the same processes but are more complicated to use. (For the full names and addresses of these and other computer programs, see Appendix 8.)

One point perhaps ought to be mentioned before we go any further. In order to work out the D.I.s we said that the students' test papers were ranked in order of test score. In the listening test example above, the test score was the score on the listening test. However, if this listening test had been part of a test battery, the students could have been ranked according to their scores on the whole battery. The purpose of ranking these test papers is to order the students according to some measure of language proficiency, and it is often the case that the best measure available is the scores on a complete test battery. However, if the listening test was intended to test very different skills from those of the other test components in the battery, it would not correlate highly with the other tests, and the listening items would not correlate highly with the overall test results. The item discrimination indices would then tend to be low. What test constructors often do therefore is compare items' performance with students' total scores on those parts of the test battery which seem to be testing similar skills to those of the items under consideration. For example, if the test battery contains multiple-choice tests of grammar and vocabulary, and performance tests of speaking and writing, testers might rank the students according to their combined grammar and vocabulary scores, and compare the grammar and vocabulary item results with those ranks.

Since comparing test items with the results of a test of which they are a part, and which has not yet been pretested, is logically suspect, some testers rank the students according to some other measure of language ability, such as teachers' subjective rankings of the students, and compare each item's performance with this external measure. The difficulty here is to find an external measure which is trustworthy, and which measures the relevant language skills. Anastasi 1988 discusses this in some detail.

Items requiring single word answers, phrases or sentences can be analysed in the same way as multiple-choice items, but in this case, of course, there are no distractors to analyse. Apart from calculating the F.V. and D.I., and studying the often informative behaviour of the blanks, the most important aspect of this kind of item analysis is to study the students' wrong answers. These answers will give insights into how the students understood the task and whether the item is testing what is intended. They will also reveal any inaccuracies and omissions in the key, and will highlight ambiguities in the marking scheme. For example, the marking instructions might say 'ignore misspellings', but it may be unclear what this actually means. If the correct answer is 'right', what about 'rigt', 'righ', 'write', 'rite'? Pretesting the key and marking scheme at this stage should remove many problems with the marking of the final exam, since the definitive answer key can take account of these marginally incorrect responses.

Frequently, it turns out that supposedly objective tests are very difficult to mark consistently. For example, it is difficult to design open-ended tests of reading or listening comprehension which have only a closed set of possible answers. In addition to difficulties such as the treatment of spelling mistakes as described above, open-ended answers may include grammatical ambiguities which interfere with the clarity of the answer. In addition, the longer the expected answer, the greater is the likelihood of unexpected acceptable answers. If markers are in a hurry to get through a large number of scripts, they will be tempted to make their own decisions about the acceptability of such answers, and these decisions may be different from those of other markers. It may, therefore, be necessary to check marker consistency by correlating the scores given by two or more examiners (see the Reliability section below). As long as it is possible to make the marking consistent, item analysis can be carried out in the usual way.

SUBJECTIVE TESTS

Although item analysis is inappropriate for subjectively marked tests such as summaries, essays and oral interviews, these tests still need to be pretested to see whether the items elicit the intended sample of language; whether the marking system, which should have been drafted during the item writing stage (see Chapter 3), is usable; and whether the examiners are able to mark consistently. It is usually impossible to try out such tests on large numbers because of the time needed to mark the scripts or run the interviews, but students with a wide range of backgrounds and language levels should be tested in order to ensure that the sample of language produced contains most of the features which will be found in the examinations themselves.

Once the papers or interviews have been administered, there should be trial marking sessions to see whether the test item prompts have produced the intended kinds of responses, and whether the marking guidelines and criteria are working satisfactorily. These trial marking sessions should follow the general pattern described in Chapter 6, and should lead to amendments to the item prompts, the marking guidelines and criteria.

4.4.3 Reliability

If we gave the same test to the same students several times, we should probably find that the students did not always get exactly the same scores. Some of these variations in score might be caused by 'true' or systematic differences such as the students' improvement in the skill being tested, and others might be due to 'error', that is unsystematic changes caused by, for example, students' lapses in concentration, or distracting noises in the examination hall. The aim in testing is to produce tests which measure systematic rather than unsystematic changes, and the higher the proportion of systematic variation in the test score, the more reliable the test is. A perfectly reliable test would measure only systematic changes.

Although it is usually impossible to achieve a perfectly reliable test, test constructors must make their tests as reliable as possible. They can do this by reducing the causes of unsystematic variation to a minimum. They should ensure, for example, that the test is administered and marked consistently, that the test instructions are clear, and that there are no ambiguous items. As we have seen from the section on discrimination indices, ambiguous or faulty items have low discrimination indices, and a test which contains many such items will tend to be unreliable.

Reliability can be estimated in various ways. The classic way is to give a test to a group of students, and then give the same test again to the same people immediately afterwards. The assumption is that the students will have learnt nothing in the meantime, and that if the test is perfectly reliable, they will get the same scores on the first and the second administrations. This is known as *test-retest reliability*. Fairly obviously, it is impractical, and in any case students may do better or worse the second time when they are accustomed to the test method, or are suffering from exhaustion or irritation. We can assess test-retest reliability allowing a longer time interval between administrations, but this also has its problems since during the intervening period students may have changed. For example, they may have learnt more of the language. Another way of assessing test reliability is to assess *parallel-form reliability*, which involves correlating the scores from two very similar (parallel) tests. However, this too is problematic since it is almost impossible to construct two genuinely parallel tests. (The construction of parallel tests is discussed in Section 4.5 below.)

Since all the above are so time consuming and unsatisfactory, it is more common to give the test only once, and to measure what is called *inter-item consistency*. One way of doing this is to simulate the parallel forms method by calculating the *split half reliability index*. This involves dividing a test into two, treating these two halves as being parallel versions, and correlating these two halves (see Appendix 6 for an example). The more strongly the two halves correlate, the higher the reliability will be. A perfectly reliable test would have a reliability index of +1.0. The reliability index is interpreted in much the same way as a correlation coefficient. If the results of a test were only due to unsystematic factors, or chance, the reliability index would be close to .00. This split half method is itself not totally satisfactory since the strength of the correlation will depend on which items are chosen to go into each of the two halves. A more complex reliability index, therefore, is usually calculated, which estimates what the reliability index would be if all possible divisions of the original test were correlated. The two most common formulae are Kuder Richardson (KR) 20 and Kuder Richardson (KR) 21. KR20 is based on item level data, and can be used if the tester has the results for each test item. (As long as the test items are not unequally weighted and are marked as either right or wrong, this reliability index is identical to Cronbach's alpha, which is the reliability index reported in some computer programs.) KR21, which assumes that all items are of an equal level of difficulty, is based on total test scores. Since KR21 uses less information than KR20, it is less accurate, and always produces a lower reliability index. Both formulae assume perfect reliability of scoring. (A worked example of KR21 is given in Appendix 7.) KR20 is difficult to calculate, and is not recommended for those without a computer. The split half reliability index is the easiest of the three to calculate, and generally produces similar results to KR20 and KR21.

The reliability of a test depends on many factors such as the type and length of the test, and the range of ability of the students on whom the test was trialled. A well-constructed and objective test of 100 multiple-choice grammar items, which has been pretested on students with a wide range of language ability, might have a reliability index of +.95. However, an equally well constructed listening test with 20 open-ended items which has been tried out on very advanced students might only have a reliability of +.75. The reliability also depends on the homogeneity of the items. If all the items are intended to test the same skill in the same way, then the test items will intercorrelate highly, and the test will have a high reliability index. If the test contains sections testing different skills in different ways, these sections will not correlate highly with one another, and the reliability will be lower. (This is discussed further in Chapter 8.) When interpreting a reliability index it is important to bear all these points in mind.

As we mentioned above, the Kuder Richardson formulae should preferably only be used if the students have been given as much time as they wish to finish the test. Otherwise some items, particularly those at the end of the test, will not be reached by the less able students, and the reliability index will tend to be too high. (For more about reliability see Guilford and Fruchter 1978; Anastasi 1988 and Crocker and Algina 1986.)

In a subjective test, of course, the marking itself may be unreliable. This may be caused by factors such as variation in the way an oral interview is conducted, ambiguity of marking criteria, the application of different standards by different markers, and inconsistency on the part of individual markers. The reliability of such tests can be assessed by correlating the marks given by two or more raters to the same students, and by correlating marks given by the same rater on different occasions. Since the correlations will compare the order in which the markers place the students, but not the level of the scores, it is possible for two examiners to rank a group of students in exactly the same way, thus achieving a perfect correlation with each other, while one has given consistently higher marks than the other, or has used a narrower range of marks. It is therefore also necessary to compare the mean scores given by each marker. There is a reliability index based on analysis of variance which takes both ranks and levels into account, and this will be discussed in Chapter 6.

4.4.4 Item Response Theory

The results of analyses carried out using the above classical test analysis procedures have one major drawback. The examinees' characteristics and the test characteristics cannot be separated, so that the results of the analyses are only true for the actual sample on which the trials were carried out. The results will not apply to samples of students at different levels of proficiency. It is not, therefore, possible to provide any fixed measure of a test's difficulty. If the items in a test have low facility values, the test may be difficult, or it may have been tried out on low-level students. If the facility values are high, the test may be easy, or it may have been given to highly proficient students. Because of this it is difficult to compare students who have taken different tests, or to compare items that have been tried out on different groups of students.

Measurement using *Item Response Theory* (IRT) is designed to cope with this problem. We can use it to develop an item difficulty scale that is independent of the sample on which the items were tested, so that we can compare the performance of examinees who have taken different tests, or can apply one set of item analysis results to groups of students with different levels of language ability. This means that in order to equate two tests it is, theoretically, not necessary to trial both complete tests on the same group of students. As long as a few identical 'anchor' items are included in the two versions of the test, each version can be tried out on a different group, and the two can be equated using these anchor items.

IRT is based on probability theory, and shows the probability of a given person getting a particular item right. Students' scores and item totals are transformed on to one scale so that they can be related to each other. If a person's ability is the same as the difficulty level of the item, the person has a 50/50 chance of getting that item right. The relationship between examinees' item performance and the abilities underlying item performance is described in an item characteristic curve (ICC). This shows how, as the level of students' ability increases, so does the probability of a correct response. Figure 4.5 shows a simple example of an ICC. The probability of an examinee answering the item correctly is shown on the left side of the graph, and students' levels of ability are shown across the bottom. The ability levels here range from −3 to +3. This scale, which is called a *logit scale*, is quite arbitrary. If the user does not like the negative figures, the levels could be transformed to range from, say, 100 to 0, with a mean of 50. In this example it can be seen that students with an ability level of 0 have a 0.3 (or 30%) probability of answering the item correctly.

There are three main IRT models, and views vary about which

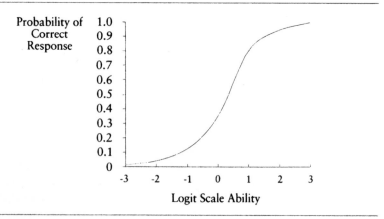

FIG. 4.5

models are most appropriate for different circumstances. Anyone planning to use IRT for test analysis should get advice before embarking on it. All we can do here is briefly outline the main advantages and disadvantages of each model.

ONE-PARAMETER (RASCH) MODEL

This is the simplest of the three models. It is comparatively easy to understand and requires fewer subjects in a sample than the other two models. A minimum of a hundred students is usually considered sufficient. Of course, in many testing situations this is an impossibly large number, but if a smaller sample is used, the results will have an unacceptably high margin of error.

This model is handy for simple, practical analyses, but is limited in scope because it is only concerned with two aspects of a test – person ability and item difficulty. It does not take item discrimination into account.

Two useful computer programs for running Rasch analyses are BIGSTEPS and QUEST (see Appendix 8).

TWO-PARAMETER MODEL

This model does everything that the one-parameter model does, but also takes account of item discrimination. It is, therefore, more complex and requires a sample of at least 200 students.

THREE-PARAMETER MODEL

The three-parameter model not only does everything that the one- and two-parameter models do, but it also takes guessing into account. It is much more sophisticated than the other two models, and its supporters say that it can be modelled to fit the real world. However, it is very complicated to understand and use, and it requires a data set of at least a thousand students.

The mathematics behind IRT is too complex to be explained here, but Henning 1987 and Crocker and Algina 1986 contain brief introductions to it, and Wright and Stone 1979, Wright and Masters 1982, Lord 1980 and Hambleton, Swaminathan and Rogers 1991 explain it more fully.

A computer program which can be used for running one-, two-, or three-parameter analyses is BILOG (see Appendix 8).

IRT is a useful additional tool for the test constructor. It can be used for identifying items which do not fit into a test or for identifying students who do not fit in with their testing group. It is useful for detecting test bias, and can be used for the analysis of the results of subjective as well as objective tests. It is also invaluable for computer-adaptive testing. However, it is not necessary for the basic item analysis of a new test.

ITEM BANKING

IRT is ideal for those wishing to store items in *item banks*. Pretested items or sets of items can be 'calibrated' according to characteristics such as person ability, item difficulty and powers of discrimination, and stored in a bank to be called upon when needed. Then, when test constructors are devising a new version of a test, they can select from the bank items which will not only be of a suitable level for the test population, but will also, when assembled together, combine to form a test which is equivalent in difficulty and discrimination to previous tests in the series.

Such item banking depends on the availability of at least two hundred people for each trial, and the existence of a set of anchor items which have already been calibrated so that their level of difficulty is known. The new items will be placed on the same scale of difficulty as the existing ones.

4.4.5 Descriptive statistics

In addition to analysing the performance of individual items, it is useful at the trialling stage to report on the overall performance of a test paper, or on the performance of sections within the test. Here again different exams will have different requirements, but in all cases graphs of the distribution of scores should be presented, showing where the scores cluster, and how wide the spread of scores is. The most important statistics to be reported are the *mean*, the *mode* and the *median*, which show how the scores cluster together, and the *range* and *standard deviation*, which show how widely the scores are spread out (see Appendix 4 for worked examples). The histograms in Figure 4.6 show three different distributions of scores which can be described using these five statistics.

In all three cases, 12 students have taken a test of 10 items. We can see from the histograms that although the mean is 6 each time, the overall test results are very different. In (a) and (b), for example, more students got the mean score than any other score – 4 students scored 6 in (a), and 6 students scored 6 in (c). However, in (b) more students got a 7 than a 6. The score gained by the largest number of students is called the mode, so in (b) the mode is 7. It is useful to report the mode as well as the mean, particularly when the test is very easy or very

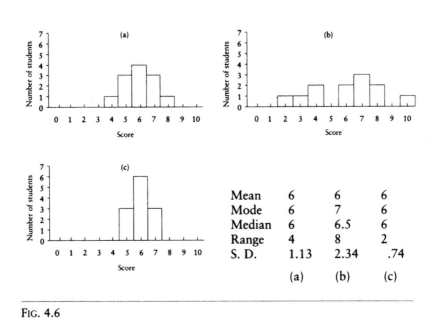

	(a)	(b)	(c)
Mean	6	6	6
Mode	6	7	6
Median	6	6.5	6
Range	4	8	2
S. D.	1.13	2.34	.74

FIG. 4.6

difficult, or when it appears that students of two levels of ability have taken the test. Figure 4.7 gives an example of the results of a test that was very easy for the students. The mode is 20, whereas the mean is 15.55. Such a distribution of scores, where scores cluster at the top end of the histogram, is described as being 'negatively skewed', because the scores tail off towards the left end of the graph. If a test is very difficult, and the scores tail off towards the right end of the graph, then the results are 'positively skewed'.

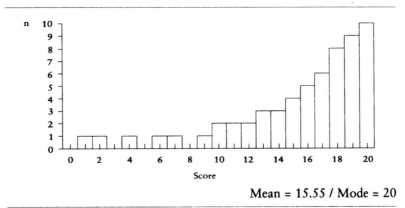

Mean = 15.55 / Mode = 20

FIG. 4.7

93

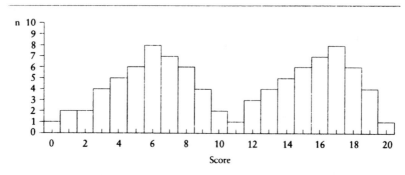

Mean = 11 / Modes = 6 and 17

FIG. 4.8

Figure 4.8 shows the results of a test that might have been taken by students at two different levels of ability. For example, the tester might have given the test to two different classes, one intermediate and one advanced. In this case the distribution is described as 'bimodal', as it has two modes. If we only reported the mean score, we should not have a clear picture of the results since only one student got a score of 11. If the mean and the modes are both reported, the distribution is described more informatively.

The third measure of 'central tendency' (measures that show where the scores cluster) is the median, which is the score obtained by the student who is in the middle of the student rankings. If for example, five students took a test and had scores of 9, 7, 6, 2 and 1, the median score would be 6. The median is particularly informative when the tester feels that the mean is in some way not representative of the whole group's level of ability. For example, if all but one of a group of 10 students get scores between 8 and 10, but one student gets a 1, the mean score will be sharply reduced by that one maverick score. To compensate for any such misrepresentation of the scores, it is best to report the median as well as the mean. In Figure 4.6 it will be seen that in the symmetrical distributions of (a) and (c) the median is the same as the mean, but that in (b) the median, 6.5, is different.

Once these measures of central tendency are reported, we get a clearer idea of the differences in the distributions of scores in the examples in Figure 4.6. However, none of these measures accounts for the differences in the spread of scores. For example, (a) and (c) have identical means, modes and medians, but it can be seen at a glance that (a) has a much wider spread of scores than (c). The most simple way to report this difference is to report the range of each distribution. The range is the difference between the top and the bottom scores. So the range in (a) is 8–4 which is 4, and in (c) it is 2. Once we know the ranges, some of the differences in the widths of the three distributions are shown. It is now clear that (c), with its range of 2, has a very narrow spread of scores, whereas (b), with a range of 8, has a wide one.

The range is a very useful measure of 'dispersion', but it has one weakness: it does not take account of any gaps in the distribution, that is scores which were achieved by no one. So in (b), where no students got a score of 5 or 9, the range is perhaps an overestimate of the spread of scores. The measure of dispersion which takes account of every single score is the *standard deviation*. This is a very important statistic and should be reported whenever possible. Any introductory book of statistics will explain the standard deviation, and as it is more complicated than the other measures we have described, we shall only describe it very briefly here. The standard deviation (S.D.) is, approximately, the average amount that each student's score deviates (differs) from the mean. If a student has a score of 4, and the mean score is 6, then that student deviates –2 from the mean. Similarly a student with a score of 10 will deviate +4 from the mean. The S.D. reports the average amount by which all the scores differ from the mean. If we look at Figure 4.6 again we shall see that (a) has an S.D. of 1.13, (b) has one of 2.34 and (c) has .74. By comparing these figures we can instantly see that (c) has a smaller spread than either (a) or (b).

There are other statistics and graphs which are used to describe the distribution of scores (see any introductory statistics book), but a histogram and the five measures mentioned above are adequate for most purposes. With these measures it is possible to compare the difficulty level and the spread of scores of different sections of a test, or of different tests with each other.

These measures of central tendency and dispersion will show how appropriate the draft test is for the purposes for which it is intended. For example, it will be possible to see whether the test is of a suitable level of difficulty. It will also be possible to see whether the test is capable of discriminating between different students. If a test has to distinguish between many levels of students, then a very easy or difficult test with a skewed distribution will not be suitable, as too many people will be clustered at either the top or the bottom end of the distribution. What is required in this case is a wide spread of scores with only a few students getting any one score (see Figure 4.9 overleaf). For such a test, items should have high D.I.s since these will cause the students to be spread out widely. However, if the test is a pass/fail one, with one cut-off score, the test may require a bimodal distribution with bunching either side of the cut-off and only a few students scoring at the point of cut-off itself (see Figure 4.8). If a test is designed to select only students at the top or the bottom of the ability range, then the

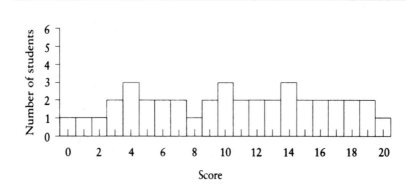

F<small>IG</small>. 4.9

items' facility values should reflect that. So, for example, if a test is designed to select the weakest 20% for further tuition, then the items should have high facility values. This will lead to more discrimination among the weakest students, as can be seen from Figure 4.7, where the high-level students are clustered together, and the weakest 20% are spread out at the lower end of the distribution. For more about this see Crocker and Algina 1986 and Anastasi 1988.

4.5 Parallel and equivalent versions

It is frequently necessary to produce parallel or equivalent versions of a test. Parallel forms are used, as we have seen, to assess test reliability, and equivalent forms are needed whenever a single test version cannot for some reason or another remain secure.

Although the terms 'parallel' and 'equivalent' are sometimes used interchangeably, we shall keep them distinct. *Parallel tests* are designed to be as similar to each other as possible. They should, therefore, include the same instructions, response types and number of items, and should be based on the same content. They should also, if tried out on the same students, produce the same means and standard deviations. Each student should get almost identical scores on each test – any differences being due to test unreliability – and if there are more than two parallel versions of the test, all the versions should correlate equally with each other (see Magnusson 1966 and Crocker and Algina 1986). Such parallel tests are very difficult to construct, and apart from their uses in reliability studies are possibly most often used in studies where experimental subjects are given similar but not identical tests.

Many examination boards produce one or two new versions of their exams each year. For these they do not produce parallel forms but seek to produce equivalent ones, which are based on the same specifications, but which may vary as to the number of items, the response types and the content. Boards often have a range of test types which may be used in an exam, and they often do not expect or indeed want all of these to be used each time. What is important with *equivalent tests* is that they each measure the same language skills and that they correlate highly with one another. It is to be hoped, of course, that equivalent versions will be of a similar level of difficulty and have a similar spread of scores, but if the means and standard deviations are not identical, the scores reported to the students can be adjusted to take account of this (see Chapter 7). In order to calibrate two versions of a test, the two tests should ideally be given to the same group of students. However, if the equivalent forms of a test are produced from an item bank, or if it is possible to have some anchor items and to use IRT analysis (see Section 4.4.1), then this may not be necessary. However, some check on the equivalence of the tests must be carried out at some stage. It is not enough to rely on item writers' and examiners' judgements.

4.6 Native speakers

One area of pretesting which has not so far been discussed is the question of trials using native speakers. Whether foreign language tests should be tried out on native speakers is controversial (see Alderson 1980; Angoff and Sharon 1971 and Hamilton, Lopes, McNamara and Sheridan 1993). Attempts to define 'native speaker' have proved problematic (see Davies 1991). Nevertheless, although we are aware of the complexities of the matter, our view is that the performance of suitably defined and selected native speakers is an important aspect of a test on which data ought to be gathered.

Some testers say that since examinees are not being compared to native speakers, such pretesting is unnecessary. This may be reasonable if the tests are at elementary and intermediate levels, although even then we would argue that such tests should at least be *piloted* on native speakers, since there is always the danger that test writers may write items which follow the rules of the language, but do not reflect native-speaker usage. Certainly it is not clear how much use should be made of native speakers during trials of speaking and writing tests since native speakers themselves vary so widely. However, for objective tests, native-speaker trials are invaluable. Since most candidates cannot be expected to produce as high a level of language as well-educated native speakers, any items which turn out to be too difficult for such native speakers should be omitted.

4.7 Survey of EFL Examination Boards: Questionnaire

Before compiling the exam boards' answers to the questionnaire, the boards' information booklets were studied to see whether there were any discrepancies between them and the responses. The only mismatch we found concerned a board which said it did not carry out any pretesting, although its published materials showed that it did. We have adjusted our report to take account of this. It may be that other boards have misrepresented themselves, but we can only rely on the information we have been given. Our only other departure from the questionnaire responses was to follow the recommendation of one board which asked us to refer to a Ph.D. thesis for information about the statistics used during the pretesting stage.

Since UCLES not only completed separate questionnaires for most of its examinations, but also completed questionnaires for many of the different papers within the exams, it is difficult to compare its responses with those of the other exam boards. In some cases, therefore, the UCLES responses have had to be treated separately.

QUESTION 21: *Are items/questions pretested? If Yes, how are students selected, and how many take each item/question?*

Of the twelve boards, six said their items were pretested, and six said they were not.

Of the six who said they did pretesting, two appeared to be referring to piloting – one said it pretested items on a few students 'as security of material is essential' and the other said test-types and difficult items were pretested informally 'by setters/examiners in their own schools using secure candidates. Exam security is paramount'. Of the other four boards, one said it only pretested items during the developmental stage of an exam, and one only pretested multiple-choice items.

The remaining two boards who said they carried out pretesting were UCLES and the AEB. UCLES' pretesting varied according to exam and test paper. All components of IELTS, CCSE (Certificates in Communicative Skills in English) and CEIBT were pretested. Of the other five exams, Reading, Listening and parts of the Use of English papers were pretested, but only two of the Writing papers were, and none of the oral tests. Not all the UCLES respondents said how many students were tested in these trial runs, but the scale of pretesting seemed to vary from paper to paper. In one case (CEIBT) there were too few students for statistical analyses to be carried out, but in the cases of the CAE and CPE reading tests, items were pretested on 200–400 students. The CCSE was pretested on about 100 students, but curiously no statistical analysis was carried out of the results.

The AEB TEEP test, as was pointed out earlier, is an exceptional exam in that not only is there only one version of it, but it is now no longer administered by the AEB. However, since it was in the AEB's remit at the time the questionnaire was answered, it will be considered here. After some pilot testing, it was pretested on approximately 100 native and 300–400 non-native speakers. The non-native sample was designed to be as representative of the overseas student population in Britain as possible, with students being classified according to their first language, academic level and academic discipline. (See Weir 1983.)

Of the six boards who said they did no pretesting, one said that initial pilots were run 'to establish levels' and one said 'questions and whole exam papers are pretested during the developmental stage, but not once a series is fully launched'. One board said that its student numbers had so far been too small for pretesting to 'provide reliable statistics', but that 'with the rapid expansion of take-up this is a procedure we shall be implementing from now on'. The LCCI said that 'banking of a selection of proven items for future use is projected'. Three boards, referring to their testing of spoken English, said that pretesting was inapplicable.

It seems from the boards' answers that some are planning to carry out more pretesting in the future. However, the fact that at the time the questionnaire was completed no boards appeared routinely to pretest all new items, and that only three carried out large-scale pretests on any of their items, is cause for grave concern. There must inevitably be suspicions that students are not receiving the fair testing that is their due.

There seem to be two reasons why so many exams are not pretested. Firstly, some boards feel that trialling is not necessary because of the thorough way in which items are prepared and edited and because of the experience of the item assessors. Secondly, it may be difficult to trial a secure test without revealing information to future candidates.

From our comments at the start of this chapter, it must be clear that we do not subscribe to the first of the reasons given above. Since there is evidence that even experienced examiners can misjudge the level and effect of test items, we feel that it is essential that all items should be pretested. The second reason is a more powerful one: anyone who has attempted to pretest an exam will know how difficult it is to find appropriate trial candidates even when security is not an issue. However, the problem is clearly not intractable, since some exam boards do manage to run trials. We shall be discussing one way of tackling this problem at the end of the chapter.

It was surprising that so many of the subjective tests were not pretested. It seems that very few boards pretest writing papers, and almost none pretest oral tests. Three boards said that pretesting oral tests was 'not applicable'. A possible explanation for this is that the boards may have misunderstood the expression 'pretesting'. One of the UCLES respondents demonstrated this by saying that whereas the CAE English in Use paper was pretested on between 100 and 300 people, the Writing paper was trialled (their underlining) on a much smaller scale. It may be that at least some of the boards thought that 'pretesting' referred to the large scale trialling of objective-type questions, and therefore said that pretesting oral papers was inapplicable. If they do not run trials of any kind, then this is worrying as there are many things that can go wrong with the setting, administering and marking of subjective tests. If boards do not try out their subjective tests in advance, they presumably try to compensate for flaws once the marking stage is in progress, but this is clearly too late.

QUESTION 22: *If items/questions are pretested, what statistics are calculated on the results?*

One of the boards which did not do large-scale pretesting said, 'No statistics are needed. If any moderator has any serious doubts about the suitability of an item, it is not used.'

Another board said, 'No official statistics are calculated' but, 'Information gained from informal pretesting is used to improve/reject questions.'

Only three boards appeared to carry out statistical analyses of the pretesting results. One of these, City and Guilds, presents the following information for each multiple-choice item: the facility value, the point biserial discrimination index, the percentage of candidates to choose each of the test options, the mean score on the test of candidates choosing each option, and the percentage of students in the top and bottom 27% of the sample to choose each alternative (City and Guilds 1984).

Once again, procedures varied at UCLES. The board did not carry out statistical analyses on any of the CCSE components nor on most of the subjectively marked tests. In addition, it did not calculate any statistics for CEIBT because too few students were involved in the pretesting. However, on all the other multiple-choice tests it calculated facility values and point biserial correlations, and for the other kinds of objective tests it reported 'overall statistics', by which they may have meant means, standard deviations and other measures of distribution. For IELTS, item and test statistics were reported using the Microcat ITEMAN program referred to earlier in this chapter. Items were also calibrated 'across versions using anchor items'. Presumably Item

Response Theory test analysis was used for this. For CEELT (Cambridge Examination in English for Language Teachers), facility values and point biserial correlations were reported on each item, and means, standard deviations, skew and kurtosis (the steepness of the distribution curve) were reported on each section or complete test.

The AEB calculated facility values and point biserial correlations for each item, and means and standard deviations for all sections of the exam (see Weir 1983 for more details). All the statistics were reported for native and non-native speakers.

It is surprising that three of the boards which do pretest items do not then analyse the results. Presumably the pretesting is only used to study students' answers, check the administration of the exam, and so on. If this is the case then useful information is being wasted.

Weir's Ph.D. thesis (Weir 1983) showed that the AEB had calculated reliability indices of its objective tests, but no other board mentioned assessing the reliability of their objective tests during the pretesting stage. For some of the UCLES responses, however, reliability may have been included under 'overall statistics', as the Microcat ITEMAN program automatically prints out Cronbach's alpha.

No board made any reference to checking on the reliability of the subjective tests during pretesting. In some testing situations it is not possible to calculate the reliability of subjective items until after the live test has been given, but in large-scale examinations it should be possible to do so at the trialling stage so that adjustments to tasks and to the marking criteria can be made before the final exam is given. The reliability of subjective tests will be discussed more fully in Chapter 6.

QUESTION 23: What happens if trial items/questions are unsatisfactory?

The six boards which pretested their items said that if items proved to be unsatisfactory, they were either rewritten or discarded. Three of the UCLES respondents said that any revised items went through another pretesting cycle.

Every time an item is rewritten it should be tried out again, since there is no guarantee that an edited item will be any more successful than its predecessor. However, for many testing centres such retrialling of items seems to be impossible. In these cases, item analysis should be carried out after the live test has been administered, and faulty items should be omitted from the final scores.

QUESTION 24: What steps, if any, in addition to the above, are taken to monitor the quality of individual items/test writers?

Within UCLES the respondent for the PET, FCE, CAE and CPE oral papers said that feedback was collected from examiners, candidates and centres. The designers of the objectively marked papers were involved in editing sessions and were monitored by the overseeing chair and the subject officer. One respondent mentioned a training course for item writers, but it was not clear if this took place before or after items had been pretested.

Of the other exam boards, five either did not answer this question or said it was not applicable to them. Three said that draft tests were monitored and feedback was given to writers before the exam, and the remaining three said that markers provided feedback after the administration of an exam, and that the item writers' work was then monitored. One said that 'moderation revealed quality', and that unsatisfactory writers were 'discontinued'.

4.8 Survey of EFL Examination Boards: Documentation

The documents which the boards sent us contained almost nothing about pretesting, so we cannot expand on the above responses. However, UCLES sent us a covering note in which they pointed out that a pretesting unit within the EFL Division had recently been set up and that pretesting and electronic item banking were in the process of being extended. No further details were given.

4.9 Discussion

The main concern from the above results must be that so many boards do not pretest their items. It is unfortunate, to say the least, that the thorough moderation and editing of the tests which is undertaken by most boards is not followed up by any empirical checks.

The difficulty in finding suitable trial students is indeed great, and those boards who do not carry out pretesting would profit by finding out how the other boards manage to run trials.

One way to get round the problem of finding representative samples, and at the same time ensuring that the test material is secure, is to give trial items to candidates while they are sitting live examinations. If these extra items are inserted into the exam without the candidates' knowledge, the candidates will not only be of the appropriate level and background, but will also take the items with the seriousness which is often lacking in trials. The scores on these trial sections of the exam will not, of course, be reported to the candidates, but once the items have been checked, satisfactory ones can be stored in an item bank for future test administrations. One disadvantage with this method of pretesting is that the addition of testing material may make the testing session too long and demanding. However, it is thought to be the easiest way of administering such a trial and of gaining the most valid results. If examiners are worried about giving candidates untried items which might be unclear and therefore cause anxiety, they can always tell the candidate that some of the items are for trial and will not be marked. However, this might cause problems. Candidates might pay less attention to items they think are being pretested – which would result in unrepresentative performances. Moreover, there might be a security problem, since if candidates feel they have successfully identified items being pretested, they may memorise such items for the benefit of future candidates.

4.10 Checklist

PRETESTING PROCEDURES

Pilot testing (on a small number of people including native speakers of the language being tested)
Check test administration, timing, instructions, content, answer key etc.

Main trials (on as many students as possible, including native speakers for advanced tests)
Check test administration, instructions, content, answer key, etc.

Objective tests
Item analysis: discrimination index and facility value
Whole test: reliability, e.g. KR20 or KR21

Subjective tests
Mark a sample of scripts or interviews to check tasks, marking criteria, etc.
Reliability:
Check inter-marker and intra-marker consistency
(See Chapter 6)

For all tests calculate distribution statistics
Histogram
Mean, mode, median, range, standard deviation

After pretesting, change administration procedures, timing, etc., edit items and, if possible, try out altered items again.

Bibliography

Alderson, J. C. 1980. Native and Non-native Speaker Performance on Cloze Tests. *Language Learning* 13(1): 59–76.

Alderson, J. C. 1993. Judgements in Language Testing. In Douglas, D. and C. Chapelle, *A New Decade of Language Testing*. Alexandria VA: TESOL.

Anastasi, A. 1988. *Psychological Testing*. Macmillan: London.

Angoff, W. and A.J. Sharon. 1971. A comparison of scores earned on the Test of English as a Foreign Language by native American college students and foreign applicants. *TESOL Quarterly* 5: 129.

Bachman, L. F. 1990. *Fundamental Considerations in Language Testing*. Oxford: Oxford University Press.

Buck, G. 1991. *Expert estimates of test item characteristics*. Paper presented at the Language Testing Research Colloquium, Princeton.

Crocker, L. and and J. Algina. 1986. *Introduction to Classical and Modern Test Theory*. Chicago, Ill.: Holt Rinehart Winston.

Davies, A. 1991. *The Native Speaker in Applied Linguistics*. Edinburgh: Edinburgh University Press.

Guilford, J.P. and B. Fruchter. 1978. *Fundamental Statistics in Psychology and Education*. Tokyo: McGraw Hill.

Hambleton, R.K., H. Swaminathan and H.J. Rogers. 1991. *Fundamentals of Item Response Theory*. Newbury Park, Calif.: Sage Publications.

Hamilton, J., Lopes, M., McNamara, T. and Sheridan, E. 1993. Rating Scales and Native Speaker Performance on a Communicatively Oriented EAP Test. *Melbourne Papers in Language Testing* 2: 1–24.

Henning, G. 1987. *A Guide to Language Testing*. Cambridge, Mass.: Newbury House.

Hudson, T. and Lynch, B. 1984. A Criterion-Referenced Measurement Approach to ESL Achievement Testing. *Language Testing* 1: 171–202.

Lord, F.M. 1980. *Applications of Item Response Theory to Practical Testing Problems*. Hillsdale, N.J.: Lawrence Erlbaum.

Magnusson, D. 1966. *Test Theory*. Reading, Mass: Addison Wesley.

Weir, C.J. 1983. *Identifying the Language Problems of Overseas Students in Tertiary Education*. Ph. D. thesis, University of London.

Wright, B. D. and Stone, M.H. 1979. *Best Test Design: Rasch Measurement*. Chicago, Ill.: Mesa Press.

Wright, B. D. and Masters, G.N. 1982. *Rating Scale Analysis: Rasch Measurement*. Chicago, Ill.: Mesa Press.

5 The training of examiners and administrators

In this chapter we address the nature of the training that is necessary for examiners and administrators of tests. Examiners need to become familiar with the marking systems (schemes or scales) that they are expected to use and they must learn how to apply them consistently. They also need to know what to do in unanticipated circumstances or with answers which they have not been trained to expect. Even experienced examiners need constant updating and retraining, and so we describe in some detail the nature of the training that is necessary, especially for those who assess students' written and spoken performances. This chapter should be read in conjunction with Chapter 6 for a complete picture of how to ensure reliability in marking.

5.1 Who is an examiner?

The term *examiner* indicates the person who is responsible for judging a candidate's performance in a test or examination. We will use this term to cover all those who have this responsibility, regardless of whether they mark objective or subjective sections of the test, and regardless of whether they have been involved in the design or administration of the examination. We distinguish between examiner and *interlocutor* in the testing of speaking: the former refers to the person who assesses the candidates, while the latter refers to a separate person who interacts with the candidate while the examiner assesses the candidate's performance.

5.2 The importance of training examiners

The training of examiners is a crucial component of any testing programme, since if the marking of a test is not valid and reliable then all of the other work undertaken earlier to construct a 'quality' instrument will have been a waste of time. No matter how well a test's specifications reflect the goals of the institution or how much care has been taken in the design and pretesting of items, all the effort will have been in vain if the test users cannot have faith in the marks that the examiners give the candidates.

Measurement, according to Mathews 1985: 90, 'implies a standardised instrument of assessment and an operative who can consistently apply it'. He goes on to state that there are at least three sources of inexactness which may threaten the soundness of any test:

1. uncertainty about the nature of the attributes of students which are to be examined and the units of measurement which can be attached to them;

2. uncertainty about the degree to which the questions and answers actually relate to those attributes even if their nature is identified;

3. inexactness in mark schemes, and variety of interpretation and application of the mark schemes by the markers.

The first two of these sources have been discussed in Chapters 2 (Test specifications) and 3 (Item writing and moderation). The third source becomes apparent only when examiners are being trained. In the pages that follow we shall discuss the steps that can be taken to lessen both the inexactness of the mark scheme and the variation that can occur between examiners when they begin to interpret and apply their mark schemes.

5.3   What is involved in training examiners?

5.3.1 Types of marking

There are basically two types of marking: *objective* and *subjective*, as presented in Chapters 3 and 4. Each of these will be described more fully below, to contextualise the discussion of examiner training.

OBJECTIVE MARKING

Objective marking is used for multiple-choice, true/false, error-recognition, and other item types where the candidate is required to produce a response which can be marked as either 'correct' or 'incorrect'. In objective marking the examiner compares the candidate's response to the response or range of responses that the item writer has determined is correct. The full set of acceptable answers may be called a 'key' or a 'mark scheme', depending on how much need there is for examiners to exercise their discretion in marking (Mathews 1985: 90 and 101). The term *key* is generally used when there is one and only one correct answer for each item (as is supposed to be the case with the item types mentioned above). The marking of tests which have keys is mechanical and may be carried out by clerical staff or by machine. The term *mark scheme* is used when there is more than one possible response for an item (as might be the case with grammatical transformation, for example, or cloze tests) or when candidates are allowed to use their own wording to express the required idea (as in some short-answer reading tests).

As mentioned in Chapter 4, the main problem that arises in some forms of objective marking (although not multiple-choice testing) is that item writers cannot foresee all of the responses that candidates might come up with to answer their items correctly. It is useful during pretesting to make a record of which unpredicted answers are acceptable and which are not; however, it is possible that when the whole population takes the test, even more responses will appear that no one has anticipated. The training programme for examiners of objective sections should give these examiners time to analyse all items carefully, to write down their own responses as if they were candidates, and to go through a large number of sample scripts to see if any new acceptable responses occur that should be added to the mark scheme. The goal of the training is to expand the mark scheme so that the examiners, who often do their marking alone and from their homes, will not have doubts about whether responses should be considered correct or not. In addition, examiners need to know what to do when they are faced with the unexpected, in order to ensure that they do not act independently of each other and reach different decisions.

SUBJECTIVE MARKING

Subjective marking is usually used for marking tests of writing or speaking. Examiners are required to make judgements which are more complicated than the 'right-wrong' decisions referred to earlier: their job is to assess how well a candidate completes a given task, and for this they need a *rating scale*. This scale may consist of numbers, letters or other labels (e.g. 'Excellent' or 'Very good'), which may be accompanied by statements of the kind of behaviour that each point on the scale refers to. These statements are called 'descriptors'.

There are basically two types of scales. Examiners may be asked to give a judgement on a candidate's performance as a whole, in which case they will use a *holistic scale*. An example of a holistic scale is given in Figure 5.1.

FIG. 5.1   A SAMPLE HOLISTIC SCALE

18–20	Excellent	Natural English with minimal errors and complete realisation of the task set.
16–17	Very good	More than a collection of simple sentences, with good vocabulary and structures. Some non-basic errors.
12–15	Good	Simple but accurate realisation of the task set with sufficient naturalness of English and not many errors.
8–11	Pass	Reasonably correct but awkward and non-communicating OR fair and natural treatment of subject, with some serious errors.
5–7	Weak	Original vocabulary and grammar both inadequate to the subject.
0–4	Very poor	Incoherent. Errors show lack of basic knowledge of English.

From: *UCLES International Examinations in English as a Foreign Language General Handbook*, 1987

When examiners use this type of scale, they are asked not to pay too much attention to any particular aspect of the candidate's production, but rather to make a judgement of its overall effectiveness. This type of scale is sometimes also called an *impression scale*, especially when examiners are asked to make their judgements quickly.

Other examiners may be asked to judge several components of a performance separately (e.g. handwriting, paragraphing, grammar, choice of vocabulary). This type of marking requires an *analytic scale*, where descriptors are given for each component (see Figure 5.2). In analytic marking the candidate may receive a higher rating on one component of the performance than on another; it is up to the institution to decide whether or how to combine these different ratings to provide an overall mark. (See the discussion on 'weighting' in Chapter 7.)

These scales (Figures 5.1 and 5.2) are only two of many that are available in EFL testing. The number of points on the scale and the number of components that are to be analysed will vary, given the distinct demands that different writing or speaking tasks can place on candidates. The challenge to examiners is to understand the principles behind the particular rating scales they must work with, and to be able to interpret their descriptors consistently. This is the main purpose of training programmes for examiners of writing and one of

---

Fig. 5.2   A Sample Analytic Scale

Relevance and Adequacy of Content

0. The answer bears almost no relation to the task set. Totally inadequate answer.
1. Answer of limited relevance to the task set. Possibly major gaps in treatment of topic and/or pointless repetition.
2. For the most part answers the task set, though there may be some gaps or redundant information.
3. Relevant and adequate answer to the task set.

Compositional Organisation

0. No apparent organisation of content.
1. Very little organisation of content. Underlying structures not sufficiently apparent.
2. Some organisational skills in evidence but not adequately controlled.
3. Overall shape and internal pattern clear. Organisational skills adequately controlled.

Cohesion

0. Cohesion almost totally absent. Writing is so fragmentary that comprehension of the intended communication is virtually impossible.
1. Unsatisfactory cohesion may cause difficulty in comprehension of most of the intended communication.
2. For the most part satisfactory cohesion though occasional deficiencies may mean that certain parts of the communication are not always effective.
3. Satisfactory use of cohesion resulting in effective communication.

Adequacy of Vocabulary for Purpose

0. Vocabulary inadequate even for the most basic parts of the intended communication.
1. Frequent inadequacies in vocabulary for the task. Perhaps frequent lexical inappropriacies and/or repetitions.
2. Some inadequacies in vocabulary for the task. Perhaps some lexical inappropriacies and/or circumlocution.
3. Almost no inadequacies in vocabulary for the task. Only rare inappropriacies and/or circumlocution.

Grammar

0. Almost all grammatical patterns inaccurate.
1. Frequent grammatical inaccuracies.
2. Some grammatical inaccuracies.
3. Almost no grammatical inaccuracies.

Mechanical Accuracy I (Punctuation)

0. Ignorance of conventions of punctuation.
1. Low standard of accuracy of punctuation.
2. Some inaccuracies of punctuation.
3. Almost no inaccuracies of punctuation.

Mechanical Accuracy II (Spelling)

0. Almost all spelling inaccurate.
1. Low standard of accuracy in spelling.
2. Some inaccuracies in spelling.
3. Almost no inaccuracies in spelling.

From: *Test of English for Educational Purposes,* Associated Examining Board, UK, 1984

---

the two main purposes for examiners of speaking. In the next sections we shall first discuss a general set of procedures for training examiners of writing, and then explain how the same procedures can be modified for examiners of speaking. We will then discuss a second dimension in the training of examiners of speaking: the need for special skills if they are to interact with candidates while assessing them.

5.3.2 Training examiners of writing

The procedure described below is one which would be suitable for a test with a large number of examiners, where for practical reasons it is impossible for all the examiners to have an equal say in determining marking policy. This description assumes that there is a 'Chief Examiner', who either alone or with a small group of colleagues sets the standards for the marking and passes these on to examiners who may mark centrally or individually in their own homes. If an institution counts on only a few people to mark all of the scripts produced by its population and if these people mark in the same place at the same time, then certain steps in the following procedure can be modified to allow for input from all examiners. However, the procedures described should ideally be followed by all testing programmes, no matter how small.

DESIGNING THE RATING SCALE

The designer of a writing task should also be responsible for designing the scale which will be used to mark the writing (see Chapter 3). We would recommend never using a scale which contains numbers only or one where the descriptors are simply one-word statements like 'Excellent', 'Very good', etc., as these statements can be interpreted in different ways by different examiners. We would recommend scales with no more than about seven points, as it is difficult to make much finer distinctions, and we would also recommend that explicit descriptors accompany most of the points on the scale. It may be important to develop different scales for different tasks or types of tasks: one rating scale is rarely appropriate for the assessment of all written or spoken performances. Both the tasks and the rating scales should be tried out during the pretesting phase of the examining process (see Chapter 4).

SETTING THE STANDARD

Soon after the test has been administered, the Chief Examiner (or 'CE') should read quickly through as many scripts as possible, to become familiar with the types of writing that the candidates have produced and the problems they have had in trying to complete the writing task. Keeping the rating scale in mind (though not adhering to it rigidly at this stage), the CE should extract scripts which represent 'adequate' and 'inadequate' performances, as well as scripts which present problems that examiners are often faced with but which are rarely described in rating scales: bad handwriting, excessively short or long responses, responses which indicate that the candidate misunderstood the task etc. These scripts we will call 'consensus' scripts and 'problem' scripts respectively. The number of scripts that a CE selects will depend on several factors (time, duplicating facilities, etc.), but it would be useful to extract at least 20: perhaps 15 consensus scripts representing various levels of performance (mostly in the middle range, however) and 5 presenting the types of problem mentioned above.

   The next step is to try out the rating scale on these scripts and to set and record standards. Although some institutions expect the CE to do this alone, we recommend that the CE work with a small number of interested colleagues, forming a standardising committee. All of the members should be given copies of the scripts selected by the CE, in random order, and each member should mark all of these scripts before the committee meets to set standards. During the meeting the members should compare their marks and discuss any differences of opinion they might have. They should aim to reach a 'consensus mark' for each of the scripts, and, in doing so, to refine the rating scale so that it is easier to understand and to use. Once they have reached agreement, they should record the reasons for each of their decisions. The CE should then divide the scripts – both consensus and problem scripts – into two batches: the first batch should be used during the initial stage of examiner training and the other batch during the second stage.

THE STANDARDISATION MEETING

The CE should be the coordinator of the standardisation meeting, which will either be directly with examiners or, in the case of large tests, with Team Leaders who will later go on to train their own examiners. It goes without saying that the coordinator of such a meeting, whether CE or Team Leader, should be thoroughly familiar with the rating scale, all of the scripts that will be used during training, and the reasons given by the committee for awarding their marks.

A complete day should be set aside for the standardisation meeting. Although this is likely to be expensive, it is the safest way of ensuring that enough discussion will take place for all examiners to understand thoroughly the rating scale and the procedures for marking. (It may be that in small testing programmes one whole day is not needed, but only experience will tell.)

The standardisation meeting should be held shortly before the official marking period begins. Both novice and experienced examiners should attend such a meeting, though not necessarily the same meeting. Our observations have shown that unreliability can be introduced into a marking programme by experienced examiners who have become complacent in their job.

Before attending the meeting examiners will have been sent the same batch of sample consensus scripts (half of the scripts worked on by the committee) and a rating scale. They should have tried out the scale on the sample scripts before the meeting and should be prepared to explain their marks to their colleagues. The first stage in the standardisation meeting is devoted to discussing these consensus scripts to find out if all examiners agree on the marks they have given and to work out why they have had problems if they do not agree. If disagreements stem from unclear concepts or wording in the rating scale, this should be edited further. The goal of this stage is to help all examiners to match the marks of the original committee, but they should not be shown the record of the original committee's reasons until they have gone through the process of marking on their own and have discussed their marks with their colleagues. This is to prevent examiners from being in-fluenced by the original committee's reasoning before they have had a chance to try out the scale and think for themselves. After the consensus scripts have been dealt with, the problem scripts should be presented, together with guidelines on what examiners should do in these cases.

The second stage of the training process provides for further practice in marking. The scripts that the examiners practise on will be the second batch of scripts marked by the committee. These will include both consensus and problem scripts and will have been duplicated so that each examiner has one copy of each. Here again the goal is to reach agreement about what each script is worth and this agreement should match the judgements of the committee. This stage should take less time than the initial stage because many typical problems should already have been resolved.

It is important for the CE (or Team Leader) to pay attention to how each of the examiners is marking during both stages of training. If any examiner finds it difficult to understand the rating scale or to provide judgements which are similar to those provided by the committee, then the CE should consider asking that examiner not to mark this section of the test. (This, of course, applies to both large and small testing programmes.)

Part of this meeting will also need to be devoted to explaining the procedures for marking and recording marks. These will differ according to whether the marking is to be done centrally or elsewhere. It is especially important that the examiners learn about the procedures which will be used to check the reliability of their marking. These are explained in Chapter 6.

Immediately after this meeting the CE should edit the rating scale to incorporate agreed changes, and should send copies of the new scale to all the examiners who will proceed into the marking phase. It is important to note that no further changes should be made to this scale. It is especially important for Team Leaders to understand this: any alterations after this point could perhaps lead to an unacceptable amount of variability in marking.

By the time the marking period begins then each examiner will have gone through a full training programme, will have a set of the sample scripts for future reference and will have a copy of the final rating scale.

Note that examiners should go through this training process at regular intervals, not just when tests are being administered for the first time. It is also crucial that 'experienced' or 'trained' examiners undergo this type of training regularly, not just new examiners. It is all too easy for individual examiners to develop their own idiosyncratic ways of examining, which the training is intended to remove.

5.3.3 Training examiners of speaking

The training of examiners of speaking follows the same pattern as the training of examiners of writing, with three main differences. The first difference is that in most institutions, where the examiners give their marks during the test rather than afterwards, the training needs to take place before the test administration.

The second difference is that the institutions need to use recordings of student performances instead of written scripts, both when the committee is setting standards and during the standardisation meeting. Audio recordings are sometimes used for this purpose, but it is increasingly common to use video tape recordings unless the test is designed to be taken in a language laboratory. Arranging for either type of recording to be made and edited is a complicated and time-consuming affair. It is desirable to tape as many performances as possible, so that the Chief Examiner has plenty of scope for choosing sample performances at each level. After the sample performances have been chosen, it is best to edit them together onto a single tape so that coordinators of standardisation meetings can find the performances they need immediately. The committee's notes about the agreed mark for each performance should be accompanied by appropriate counter numbers. All of the recordings should be of a very high quality so that examiners-in-training have no problems with visibility or audibility of candidates. This may mean recording in a studio rather than in a mock classroom.

It will probably not be possible for examiners to listen to the tapes before the standardisation meeting, so time must be allowed during the meeting for listening to each performance and re-listening to parts of most performances. Coordinators need to be realistic about how many sample performances they can fit into a single standardisation meeting: this is likely to be less than half the number of sample scripts that examiners of writing can hope to deal with in the same amount of time. The procedures followed in the meeting should be basically the same as those followed in meetings for examiners of writing: listening/viewing, independent marking, discussion of marks, refinement of marking scale if need be and arrival at consensus marks.

Some institutions also invite volunteer students to be 'tested' during the standardisation meeting. The examiners thereby get the chance to try out their skills (which may include interacting with the candidates – see below) in a realistic situation. The problem with using live performances is that it is not possible for the examiners to view the performance again, which is sometimes desirable when they have given different marks – unless, of course, the performances are also recorded.

The third difference between training examiners of writing and examiners of speaking is that in many tests examiners of speaking are present in the testing room and must interact with the candidate while the test is going on. In some tests a separate person (often a teacher) may take on the role of 'interlocutor', eliciting language from the candidate while the examiner is freed to assess, but it is much more common to find the examiner single-handedly giving instructions, asking questions, reacting to the candidate's contributions – and trying to assess the performance at the same time!

In this case, a separate training session should be held to allow the examiners to 'walk through' the testing situation, with their colleagues playing the role of candidates, or, if possible, with volunteer candidates. The examiners should be given instructions about where to sit in relation to the candidates, what kinds of questions to ask in order to bring out the best in the candidate, how to manage the many papers that they will be holding (not only their own instructions, rating scale and scoring sheet but also all of the material that the candidate will need to refer to), how to enter their marks discreetly, how to welcome the candidate and bring the test to a close, and so on. For some tests this training may take as much as half a day, which needs to be added to the day already set aside for standardisation. This is essential to ensure reliable administration and marking.

Examiners and interlocutors need to be thoroughly familiar with the tasks they will be administering, the roles they are expected to play, the cue cards they must manage and the questions they must ask (see also Section 5.4.1 below). For those who must examine as well as elicit, this is an extremely difficult task, and suitable training must be developed to ensure adequate familiarity on the part of examiners.

5.4 The importance of training administrators

Discussing the need for some oral examiners to administer the test as well as to assess the candidates leads us to an aspect of training which must not be ignored: the training of all administrators. The administrators of a test are those people who 'deliver' the test to the candidates, and they are responsible for seeing that the conditions in which the test is given provide all candidates with the best chance possible to display the abilities which are being tested. Though the training of administrators need not be as complex as that provided for examiners, it is still important that the administrators understand the nature of the test they will be conducting, the importance of their own role and the possible consequences for candidates if the administration is not carried out correctly.

5.4.1 Tests of speaking

The administrator's role is particularly important in tests of speaking, because it is always necessary for at least one person to elicit language from the candidate and to react in an encouraging way to keep the language flowing. As explained above, some tests are designed so that an 'interlocutor' takes this role while the examiner observes the interaction and assesses the candidate. In other tests the examiner must talk to the candidate and try to assess at the same time. Whether interlocutor or examiner, the person who interacts with the candidate must be in control of techniques which will help each individual to feel at ease, while at the same time paying attention to details such as timing and wording of prompts, to ensure that all candidates have an equal opportunity to display their abilities. The task of the administrator becomes more complicated if two or more candidates are tested together: making sure everyone understands the task, keeping track of the number and types of contributions offered by each person, and thinking of ways to bring into the discussion candidates who have not been able to speak earlier.

For some speaking tests it may be necessary to employ a further administrator to give instructions to the candidates and to provide them with the materials they need to study before they enter the testing room. This person is sometimes referred to as the 'usher'. The usher may also be responsible for getting candidates into and out of the testing room on time, and for making sure that candidates who have already been assessed do not communicate with those who are waiting their turn.

The success of a speaking test will depend on each of these people carrying out their duties well. We have already suggested that an extra half day of training would be in order for examiners who are also expected to interact with the candidates, and we would also recommend at least a half day of training for teachers who will be acting as interlocutors while someone else serves as examiner. Ushers may not need to spend so much time learning their job, but it would be useful for them to discuss what needs to be done and to practise the routine several times before the day of the test.

All of the administrators should have clear written instructions telling them what to do and when to do it. It would also be useful for all parties if all the material that they need to use with candidates (task sheets, photos, reading passages, etc.) could be bound together, so that they do not waste time either before or during the speaking test trying to locate or put in order recalcitrant papers.

An important task for the administrators of speaking tests is to create an environment which will help candidates to feel at ease.

Comfortable waiting rooms should be provided, and the examination room should be large enough so that all participants can sit comfortably, but not so large that it overwhelms the candidates. The interlocutor (or the examiner who serves both as interlocutor and assessor) should be near enough to the candidates for them not to have to strain to make themselves heard – unless, of course, the task they are to perform calls for voice projection, as in tests of public speaking or dramatic arts.

5.4.2 Tests of listening

In the case of listening tests the choice of room is particularly important, as is the decision about how many candidates can take the test at the same time. Some institutions try to fit as many people as possible in one room, believing that it is administratively easier; however, rooms which are large enough to handle large numbers often have poor acoustics which make it difficult for candidates to understand the listening input (the voice of a live speaker, or a cassette or video recording). It is crucial for administrators to do a trial run of listening tests to check whether the person who is speaking is visible and audible from all parts of the room and to check whether recordings can be heard equally well no matter where a candidate is seated.

It is also important to learn how equipment is to be set up, when and how it is to be used, and what to do if there is a malfunction. Checks must be made of all the microphones, cassette and video recorders, loudspeakers and tapes that will be used. If the test is to be held in a language laboratory, it is important to check all of the control equipment and the equipment in each individual booth.

As in the administration of speaking tests, those responsible for conducting listening tests need clear written instructions about what to say and what to do throughout the test. If the candidates are to listen to a live speaker, this person must have time to prepare thoroughly. The institution should not underestimate the time that a speaker needs to complete this preparation. In the case of a person who is to conduct a dictation, for example, it is first of all necessary to understand the passage that is to be read out in order to decide on the intonation and phrasing, to be able to pronounce all the words without stumbling, to control the pace of the dictation and the length of the pauses, and to read the passage loudly enough for all the candidates to hear. If the candidates are to listen to recordings, the person responsible for running the machines needs to know when to start the recording, when or whether to pause, and when or whether to play the recording again.

5.4.3   Tests for all skills and aspects of language

We have indicated that many of the people involved in the administration of speaking and listening tests may require training. There are other administrators, however, whose work is not so specialised: those who are responsible for distributing and collecting test papers, keeping track of timing, and making sure that the candidates cannot help one another during the test. These administrators are often referred to as 'invigilators' or 'proctors'. It is usually not necessary for invigilators to undergo special training; however, it is important that they understand all of their duties and what to do should unexpected problems arise. The institution should provide the invigilators with clear written instructions and should discuss these instructions and any questions the invigilators might have before the administration of the test.

5.5   Survey of EFL Examination Boards: Questionnaire

We asked the examination boards about the criteria they used for choosing markers and how long they appointed markers for. We also asked about the types of marking carried out by the boards and the procedures they followed for standardising examiners. (Note that the questions in the questionnaire asked about 'markers' rather than 'examiners', but for the sake of consistency with earlier parts of this chapter we will continue to use the term 'examiners'.)

QUESTION 31: *What criteria are used in the appointment of markers?*

The criteria for appointing examiners seemed much the same as those for item writers (see Chapter 3): the most commonly mentioned were relevant teaching experience (including teaching for this particular examination), examining experience and appropriate professional qualifications. Those who mentioned professional qualifications did not elaborate on what these were, but we presume they mean a certificate or degree in language teaching or applied linguistics.

Several boards mentioned that examiners-to-be must perform well at standardising meetings (see Question 34 below), and one mentioned that they must successfully complete a self-access training manual. No details were given about what counted as successful completion.

Age was mentioned by several boards: one stated that examiners should be younger than 55 on first appointment, and three mentioned retirement ages of between 65 and 70.

Other factors that were only mentioned by one or two boards were: good references, competence in the language, expertise in the candidate's area, reliability, punctuality, commitment to a communicative approach to teaching and testing, and having the right sort of personality for oral examining. No details were given.

QUESTION 32: *For how long are markers appointed?*

Length of appointment varied considerably from board to board: some boards appoint examiners by the examining session, but most seemed to give yearly renewable contracts. Several boards reported that they take examiners on for an indefinite period, as long as they continue to render satisfactory service. It is not clear how 'satisfactory service' is measured, but the overall picture seems to be that those known and acceptable to a board will continue as examiners, possibly rising to the status of Chief Examiner if appropriate.

QUESTION 33: *Are any parts of the examination a) objectively marked, e.g. by machine or clerically; b) marked centrally, i.e. by teams working together; c) marked locally, by individuals, e.g. the test administrator or equivalent?*

Only two boards said they did objective marking. One of the boards pointed out that 'clerical markers are ordinary temporary staff who are trained to implement mark schemes under strict supervision'.

Four boards did central marking; eight did not. One of the boards referred to a 'writing weekend', but did not give details of how this was organised. The other boards did not describe how their central marking operated.

Only four boards said that they did local marking; however, this question may have been interpreted in different ways by different boards since several boards, whose examiners are known to work at home, responded negatively. In our experience most boards do in fact operate a sort of 'cottage industry', where examination papers are sent to examiners' homes for marking within a specified time. Though this is more convenient for the examiners and no doubt less expensive than central marking, this procedure has implications for the monitoring of marking and the operation of reliability checks. Perhaps the most important point is that there is a time lag between an examiner marking a script and a Chief Examiner being able to check whether the marking is appropriate. This is discussed further in Chapter 6.

QUESTION 34: *Does your board hold a meeting to standardise markers? If so, what is this meeting called? How long does it typically last?*

Eleven of the twelve responding boards held standardising meetings for markers; only one did not. The board which did not hold such a meeting said that the standardising of examiners was 'done informally by the Chief Examiner'.

The name for this type of meeting varied, according to the particular exam. The most commonly reported name was 'standardisation meeting', but also used were 'standardising meeting', 'coordinating meeting', 'assessors' meeting', 'examiners' meeting' and 'briefing meeting'.

The time allotted for the meeting varied, from half a day to a day. One board reported that the training of its examiners to mark 10 different levels took one day only, which seems hardly likely to ensure adequate familiarity with rating scales and procedures.

QUESTION 35: *If your examination board holds a 'standardising meeting', what normally happens during this meeting?*

Most of the boards held standardisation meetings which resembled the description given in Section 5.3.2: markers marking sample scripts or video recordings, discussing assessment criteria with other markers and the Chief Examiner, and reaching agreement on the final mark and problem areas. The details of the standardisation procedure varied (who provided the sample scripts, how many sample scripts the markers had to mark, whether the Chief Examiner 'imparted' the standard by lecturing or allowed it to be 'discovered' through group discussion), but the general pattern was similar.

In some cases, however, it is not clear whether all examiners had access to the same scripts. Nor is it clear whether the examiners work individually before they discuss marks with their colleagues, or whether they work together from the start. If they work together from the start, examiners with stronger personalities or more firmly held views (or prejudices) may tend to dominate the discussion, thereby depriving the other examiners of the opportunity (or need) to make up their own minds. It is important to pay attention to the amount of access that examiners have to the sample scripts (including being able to take them home for future reference) and the amount of time they have for deciding on marks on their own before discussing them.

One board described its procedures for training oral examiners:

Live demonstration of candidates and assessors and officiating assessors. Report sheets individually marked by attending assessors.

Results discussed orally at the time and written comments critically assessed and moderated following the meeting.

There are two important points in this procedure: the first is that the board provides live demonstrations, and the second is that the assessors are allowed to give their marks individually before they discuss them with colleagues. However, there are points that need attention: Do the examiners who are being trained just observe others interacting with the 'candidates' or do they themselves get a chance to practise? Also, what is the nature of the moderation which takes place after the meeting? This process must be the board's way of checking whether individual examiners are competent enough to begin marking. Unfortunately, however, we know very little about how Chief Examiners identify incompetence and how they inform examiners that they should not mark.

One board seems to hold meetings for standardising Team Leaders but there is no such meeting between the Team Leaders and the ordinary examiners ('assistant examiners'). Although the examiners have an opportunity to discuss scripts with their Team Leader on an individual basis, they miss out on potentially valuable discussions with other examiners.

One board sent examiners a self-access manual, and it certified examiners once they demonstrated that they were competent to mark scripts on their own. The board presumably uses such a manual because the examination is given 'on demand' in many countries and must be marked locally within a short amount of time. Unfortunately, though, no details were given about how the manual is constructed or used, nor about how markers who train themselves finally become 'certified'.

QUESTION 36: *What steps are taken at the end of the standardising meeting to establish the degree of agreement among markers?*

Many of the boards mentioned that they aimed for 'agreement' at the end of their standardising meetings, but it was not clear how they decided whether sufficient agreement had been reached. The following description illustrates this well:

The markers will have had the scripts for about one week and will have marked provisionally about 10 at each level. At the meeting the mark schemes will be discussed and revised where necessary and a common approach agreed.

The clearest description we received was this one:

> By the end of the meeting team leaders reach agreement on contentious items. Armed with the minutes of these briefings, the team leaders then conduct their own standardisation process. Markers have to mark the 'criterion' (performances) and compare their results with the briefing meeting results. Marking does not start 'for real' until full agreement is reached across the teams.

Here there are references to two meetings: one in which the team leaders are standardised and one in which the team leaders standardise the examiners. What we do not know, however, is whether this 'full agreement' is the result of negotiation, or whether the examiners are tested in any way on their ability to give satisfactory marks. No board mentioned either giving any sort of test to examiners to determine whether they were ready to mark, or calculating inter-rater reliability to see how much agreement there was between each examiner and the Chief Examiner and colleagues. A question which has not been answered is how much an examiner is allowed to deviate from agreed marks before being considered unfit for marking. (See Chapters 4 and 6 for a discussion of reliability.)

5.6 Survey of EFL Examination Boards: Documentation

5.6.1 Training markers of writing

The documents that the boards sent us contributed very little to our understanding of their training procedures. There were only four documents which mentioned training; most did not include any information about how markers were trained to do their job.

The document from the ESB said only that:

> Assessors meet regularly to compare notes and discuss assessment techniques.

(page 1)

They did not say how this happened.

The fullest description of a training programme came from the AEB, in a booklet that describes the procedure that was followed for their GCE (O level and A level) examinations prior to 1986. We do not know if the same procedure was followed for the TEEP test, and in any case TEEP procedures will have changed as the examination has been passed on to another institution; however, it is worthwhile reproducing the description of the AEB procedure as it is the type of description that would be most likely to give users confidence in the care taken by a board to train examiners:

> Copies of the question papers, marking schemes and mark sheets are despatched from the Board to the examiners so as to arrive immediately after the examination has been taken. The Examiners' first task is to study the questions and the marking schemes and to carry out trial marking of a number of scripts. At this stage they will also be looking for unexpected answers which the scheme does not readily fit.
>
> Within two or three days of the examination all Examiners attend a standardisation meeting. At this meeting the Chief Examiner discusses each question and its marking scheme. What is required for each mark is noted; acceptable alternative answers are agreed and noted as well as those which are only partly correct and those which are not acceptable. A variety of points are raised concerning answers which have already been seen and decisions are taken on all of them. In addition the method of marking is discussed to ensure that all Examiners mark in the same way. The purpose of this meeting is to ensure correct application of the marking scheme by all examiners to all scripts so that, no matter who marks it or when it is marked, a particular answer will always receive the appropriate mark. In many subjects the Board arranges for all Examiners to mark photocopies of the same scripts in order to check that all are marking to the same standard in the same way before they leave the meeting.

(page 11)

MATERIALS FOR TRAINING

One of the most useful findings in the survey of documents was that both Oxford and UCLES publish booklets for teachers who want to prepare students for the examination. These booklets contain past examination questions, sample scripts written in response to the questions, and the boards' marks and comments for each sample script.

The goal of these publications is to familiarise teachers not only with the tasks that candidates will have to perform on the examination but also with the way that they will be judged. We presume that the sample scripts and comments were (or are) used for training purposes as well; however, we do not know how they have been used.

5.6.2 *Training of markers of speaking*

There was very little in the documentation about the training of markers of speaking.

Oxford-ARELS says this about the standardisation of Team Leaders:

> About a week after each scheduled examination, co-ordination meetings of Examining Team-Leaders are held to establish standards in relation to the very detailed marking guides already issued ...
>
> Marking Guides for all examinations are extremely detailed. They are printed in booklets known as Keys, and one booklet is used for each marking. As an example, the Key for a Higher level examination contains about 90 separate assessments ...
>
> The standards required vary with each individual task; in some, only an error-free response is awarded marks; in others 2, 3 or 4 grades of correctness are recognised. The Marking Key gives full details. In a few cases, markers are required to make a subjective assessment, since there is no alternative. In these cases as much guidance as possible is given in the Key.

No details are given about the procedures for the standardisation meeting, and nothing is said about the way that ordinary markers are trained. However, Oxford-ARELS does give some information about the quality control procedures, which is reported in Chapter 6.

MATERIALS FOR TRAINING EXAMINERS

Both the LCCI and UCLES publications refer to videos that they have produced for their exams. LCCI offers two types of video to interested parties: one which is produced for teachers and students and illustrates the various levels of oral performance, and another which is produced for training. This type of video is 'not intended to illustrate the principles of oral examining in general but to provide matter for criticism and discussion among LCCI examiners in training.' This gives us some insight into the LCCI training procedures – namely that examiners do mark sample performances in their training sessions – but we do not have details about how they train their examiners. We presume, but do not know, that there are notes to accompany each type of video, to help teachers and examiners to understand what they are seeing.

UCLES mention videos in their description of FCE and CPE, but we know only that the videos show performance levels for the exams. We do not know if there are accompanying notes or how the videos are used in training.

5.7   Discussion

It was reassuring to learn that so many boards do hold standardisation meetings, but disturbing to find that two do not. It was useful to read the descriptions that the boards offered of their training procedures; however, the descriptions were sometimes very brief. We still have questions about various stages in the training and we are especially unclear about how the boards decide whether examiners are ready to mark 'for real'. Several boards mentioned that examiners have to reach agreement on criterial scripts or taped performances, but whether this agreement is the result of discussion (in which case examiners may be persuaded rather than convinced) or whether there is a test that examiners have to pass, we do not know. If this is the case, it would be unreasonable to expect every examiner to agree entirely with every mark given by the Chief Examiner and Team Leaders, but if variation ('deviation') is allowed, how much is acceptable?

It was surprising to learn that at least one of the boards trains its examiners by post or telephone, rather than face-to-face. The board takes the trouble to train the Team Leaders together, but the Team Leaders do not train their examiners in person. It is not known whether the board feels that it would be a waste of time to bring all the examiners together for discussions, but this is certainly a false economy. If, nevertheless, the board were able to give convincing reasons for training by post or by phone, the examiners would still begin sending sample scripts to the team leaders after they had started marking for real. It would seem more sensible to ask examiners to send in sample marked scripts before they begin marking for real, and to ask the examiners to wait for feedback before continuing to mark further.

We discovered two interesting developments: the 'writing weekend' which one board holds to train examiners of writing and to monitor them while they are marking, and the self-access training manual which one board uses to train examiners who cannot attend training sessions. The writing weekend would appear to provide a good environment for discussing criteria for marking and for discussing and re-discussing scripts which do not fit easily into any of the points on the rating scales: if the markers do not have to travel to and from the meeting and are not distracted by pressures at home, they can concentrate totally on marking. The self-access training manual might be a good idea for countries where travel is very difficult and where the examination board has no option but to provide distance training. However, it would be important to know more about how the training manual works and how the board decides that an examiner can be certified before we could recommend such a practice.

One final point: the materials provided by some boards to help teachers to understand how writing and speaking are evaluated were very interesting. It would be useful for all boards to offer video tapes (or audio cassettes) which illustrate the criteria that they use in evaluation and which provide examples of different levels of performance. It is especially helpful when such recordings are accompanied by the marks that the Chief Examiner would give to the performances, together with notes explaining the reasons.

There is always a danger that chapters such as this one, which set out procedures to achieve a desirable goal, will be seen as too prescriptive by some or as impractical by others. It is clear that every institution has its constraints and that it is sometimes necessary to make compromises. We would not argue that every step in the procedure that we have described needs to be followed exactly, but we would argue that there are certain things which do need to be done to make sure that examiners are well prepared. Amongst these are the following:

The institution must have a training programme of some sort. Institutions should never assume that mark schemes and rating scales are flawless or that examiners can apply them without practice.

Institutions must set aside a reasonable amount of time for training, especially if examiners are being trained for the first time. It is not possible to do thorough training of examiners of writing or speaking in a couple of hours.

Institutions should provide photocopies of scripts which are to be discussed so that examiners can make notes and keep these for future reference.

Examiners must be given the opportunity to make their own decisions and discuss these with other examiners and the Chief Examiner or Team Leader, rather than having the CE or Team Leader just explain what is to be done.

Institutions should have a policy about the amount of agreement they expect from their examiners, and there should be some kind of defined standard that examiners have to meet before they are allowed to examine for real.

5.8 Checklist

A mark scheme or rating scale needs to be designed which is appropriate to the tasks candidates are being asked to perform.

In advance of the training, the Chief Examiner needs to set the standards by applying the scheme or scale to sample scripts/performances. Where necessary, the scheme/scale should be modified in the light of this trial.

The CE should select suitable scripts/performances for the training programme.

Suitably qualified and experienced examiners need to be selected.

At the standardisation meeting, both consensus and problem scripts/performances need to be considered, and agreement reached on how schemes/scales are to be applied.

Examiners who perform unsatisfactorily during the training need to be retrained or rejected.

If necessary, schemes/scales and written guidelines for their application should be revised in the light of the standardisation meeting before they are used 'for real'.

For speaking tests, performances for training purposes will need to be recorded in some fashion and then edited onto one tape.

At the training meeting for speaking, arrangements will need to be made for the viewing/hearing of the tapes. Alternatively, live performances may need to be arranged.

Examiners of speaking will need practical advice such as where to sit and what to do with their papers, and clear written instructions should be prepared before the actual examining.

Separate training should be arranged for interlocutors, and for examiners if they also have to elicit as well as to assess. This training should enable interlocutors/examiners to elicit spoken performances appropriately.

Those who administer the tests also need training in what to do when.

For listening tests, the room(s) will need to be checked for size/seating and acoustics, the availability and condition of any special equipment should be checked, and a trial run in advance of the actual examination should be arranged. If the test is to be delivered live rather than by recording, the speaker(s) need training, and clear written instructions should be prepared on what to do when.

Bibliography

Mathews, J.C. 1985. *Examinations: A Commentary*. London: George Allen and Unwin.

6 Monitoring examiner reliability

In this chapter we discuss the nature of examiner reliability and its importance, and how the reliability of marking can be established. It is important that a candidate's score on a test does not depend upon who marked the test, nor upon the consistency of an individual marker: an unreliable examiner is somebody who changes his or her standards during marking, who applies criteria inconsistently, or who does not agree with other examiners' marks. We describe in some detail the sorts of procedure that should be followed in an effective monitoring programme.

6.1 The importance of monitoring examiner reliability

In Chapter 5 we stressed the importance of thorough training for all examiners, especially those who assess writing and speaking. Training will help examiners to understand the rating scales that they must employ and should prepare them to deal with many problems, including ones which could not be foreseen when the writing or speaking tasks were first designed. Training should give the examiners competence and confidence; however, it cannot on its own guarantee that examiners will mark as they are supposed to. There are many factors which can interfere with an examiner's ability to give sound and consistent judgements: problems with the rating scales, time pressures, domestic and professional worries, and so on. Even very experienced examiners can be affected by these problems. It is the institution's responsibility to design quality control procedures to assure the users of the ... the marks are as reliable as possible.

... le can be applied to several aspects of examining (see ... on objective testing), but in this chapter we shall ... marking of writing and speaking. There is also a ... marking of objective tests, but this simply means ... ners have applied the marking key or mark scheme ... heir arithmetic is accurate. Though mistakes will ... ese areas, the procedures for monitoring are straightforward. Those for subjective marking are more complicated, hence our concentration on it in this chapter.

Two terms will appear often in our discussion: 'intra-rater reliability' and 'inter-rater reliability'. An examiner is judged to have *intra-rater reliability* if he or she gives the same set of scripts or oral performances the same marks on two different occasions. The examiner may still be considered reliable even if some of the marks are different; however, not much variation can be allowed before the reliability becomes questionable. Intra-rater reliability is usually measured by means of a correlation coefficient or through some form of analysis of variance. The notion of correlation was discussed in detail in Chapter 4. An analysis of variance essentially compares the distributions (means and standard deviations – see Chapter 4) of two or more populations. For example, the marks that four different examiners have given to the same set of written scripts can be contrasted. If the different examiners have given the same marks each time, the means and standard deviations will be identical. Analysis of variance is a way of assessing how significant any differences might be (see any introductory statistics textbook for more details).

Inter-rater reliability refers to the degree of similarity between different examiners: can two or more examiners, without influencing one another, give the same marks to the same set of scripts or oral performances? It would not be realistic to expect all examiners to match one another all the time; however, it is essential that each examiner try to match the 'standard' all the time. This standard is set either by the Chief Examiner or the standardising committee, as discussed in Chapter 5. Though there is bound to be some variation between examiners and the standard some of the time, there must be a high degree of consistency overall if the test is to be considered reliable by its users. This reliability is also measured by a correlation coefficient or by some form of analysis of variance.

There are several ways in which an institution can monitor the marking of its examiners. The precise methods chosen will depend on several factors – amongst them, whether the marking is done centrally or elsewhere, and whether the marking is of written scripts or of oral performances. In the following sections we will describe methods which are suitable for each situation.

6.2   Central marking

The easiest situation to imagine is one in which the marking is done centrally, with written scripts. In this case there are at least three ways of monitoring.

6.2.1 Sampling by the Chief Examiner or Team Leader

When marking takes place centrally, examiners are usually divided into teams: each team has a coordinator and a maximum of 10 or 12 examiners. If the test is a small one (say only a hundred or so candidates), there may only be one team, coordinated by the Chief Examiner. If there are more candidates, there may be several teams, each one coordinated by a Team Leader. All of the team leaders will have been standardised by the Chief Examiner, and they in turn will standardise the members of their teams (see Chapter 5). Each team will mark in its own area of the marking hall or in a separate room: this will allow the Team Leader to monitor all the marking efficiently and will make it easy for the team members to discuss marking problems as they arise.

The examiners should be instructed to mark as they were trained to mark, and should be especially careful not to write on any candidate's script. They should not underline, make any corrections or write any comments anywhere on the script, and they should record their marks on separate record sheets designed for the purpose. Some examining bodies ask examiners to record their marks on the front or back cover of the testing booklet, but we advise strongly against this practice, as it becomes very tempting for other examiners – either Team Leaders or 'second markers' (see Section 2.3 below) – to look at the mark before they give their own mark.

The sampling procedure should begin soon after the marking begins. The following paragraphs will explain the steps of the procedure. (Note that in this illustration and the other illustrations in this chapter we will assume that the marking coordinator is a Team Leader.)

Each examiner is expected to mark a certain number of scripts on the first day of marking. The Team Leader collects a percentage of marked scripts from the examiner (often 1 or 2 scripts out of every 10), and reads through them again in order to give an independent mark. (This is called *blind marking*, because the Team Leader should not be aware of the examiner's marks while making his or her own assessments.) If the Team Leader's marks agree with those of the examiner, then the examiner will be allowed to continue marking. If, however, the Team Leader's marks do not agree with the examiner's and the differences are serious (e.g. a difference of more than one point on a scale from 1 to 5), then the Team Leader needs to discuss this with the examiner. The aim of the discussion is to narrow the differences in opinion between the two parties, so there must be a thorough reading of the problematic scripts and the rating scale. Occasionally the examiner will be able to convince the Team Leader to reconsider, but in institutions where sampling takes place it is generally assumed that the Team Leader will know best and in the end the examiner will have to reconsider.

The process of sampling should continue throughout the marking period, even when The Team Leader feels confident that the examiners are marking well. One of the most common causes of unreliability in marking is complacency – but fortunately it is also one of the most preventable!

6.2.2 Using 'reliability scripts'

The second method of monitoring marking is to ask each examiner independently to mark the same packet of 'reliability scripts'. These scripts will have been chosen by the Chief Examiner to represent different points on the rating scale and different problems that examiners are faced with (similar to the sample scripts used for training – see Chapter 5), and they will have been marked by the Chief Examiner and the standardising committee. This reliability exercise should take place after the examiners have begun marking 'for real', but early enough in the marking period for changes to be made to scripts which may already have been marked incorrectly by unreliable examiners. The afternoon of the first day of marking or the second morning would be suitable times.

It is not necessary to make photocopies of the sample scripts for each member of the team: these can be circulated amongst the team members. It is important, however, that the team members do not write on the scripts that they read since any such marking would undoubtedly influence later examiners. The examiners should record their marks on a separate marking sheet and hand these to the Team Leader at the end. The Team Leader then compares the marks that each examiner gave with the marks that were agreed by the standardising committee. If the Team Leader finds that any examiner's marks differ greatly from the committee's marks, there should be a discussion to determine why. If the Team Leader finds that the whole team is giving marks which are different, there should be a meeting to discuss what is happening and to gather suggestions about how to solve the problem. The goal of this exercise is to reinforce the standardisation which took place during the training period (see Chapter 5), and if it turns out that the examiners are applying the rating scale in ways which are different from the committee, then marking must stop and a re-standardisation take place.

There are two ways in which the Team Leader can determine whether the examiners are marking in the way they are supposed to be marking. The quickest way, known as 'eyeballing', is to place each examiner's scores side by side with the committee's scores. Obvious differences of opinion will stand out immediately, and the Team Leader can begin appropriate action, such as more intense sampling of certain examiners, straightaway.

'Eyeballing', however, will reveal only the most conspicuous of problems. A more informative method is to correlate each examiner's marks with the standardising committee's marks, and to compare means and standard deviations. The correlation will indicate whether the examiner has ranked the reliability scripts in the same order as the committee (a reasonable correlation to aim for would be .8) and the comparison of means and standard deviations will indicate whether the examiner is stricter or more lenient than the committee. If the examiner's mean score is significantly lower than the committee's, this will mean that the examiner is stricter; if it is significantly higher, it will mean that the examiner is more lenient. (A significant difference is one which is large enough not to be due solely to chance. The usual test of whether the difference between two means is significant is the t-test, and analysis of variance is used for comparing more than two means. See Guilford and Fruchter 1978 or any introduction to statistics.) The best outcome is for an examiner to have a correlation of .8 or above with the standardising committee's marks, and a mean score which is not significantly different from that of the committee. If either of these conditions is lacking, then the Team Leader should discuss the problem with the examiner and try to find a remedy.

The Team Leader will need to check all of the team members in the same way. This requires a fair amount of calculation, which can be done by hand or by calculator. Some institutions may prefer to do the calculations by computer, using a statistical program such as SPSS or SAS (see Appendix 8). Readers interested in more sophisticated analyses (such as generalisability theory, which is based on analysis of variance and which can estimate the reliability of a whole group of markers at once) should refer to Crocker and Algina 1986.

6.2.3 Routine double-marking

The third way of monitoring examiners and ensuring that their marks are reliable is to require routine double-marking for every part of the exam which requires a subjective judgement. This means that every piece of writing is marked by two different examiners, each working independently. The mark that the candidate receives for a piece of writing is the mean of the marks given by the two examiners.

Administratively, the easiest way is to arrange for two examiners from the same team to mark each script, but it is not necessary for the same two people to work together all the time. As in the previous two methods, the examiners should refrain from writing anything on the script itself, so as not to influence each other. Each enters the mark on a separate marking sheet. It is then the responsibility of the Team Leader to note whether the two marks are similar or not. If they are similar (that is, if they are in the same general area of the rating scale), then the candidate's final mark will be the mean of the two marks; if, however, the marks are very different (say, two points or more apart on a five-point scale), then the examiners need to read the script again and carefully study the rating scale. If the examiners cannot come any closer in their assessments, then the writing should be referred to another examiner, who may be another member of the team or perhaps the Team Leader. It will be up to the institution to decide whose view should prevail in the case of a disagreement, or whether the two closest marks or all the marks should be averaged.

6.3 Alternatives when marking is carried out elsewhere

All the methods given above apply to central marking, when the members of a marking team work together in the same place at the same time. If, however, the marking takes place elsewhere, either in examiners' homes or in an examining centre, then some modifications may have to be made to the above procedures. We will look first at the case where marking takes place in examiners' homes.

6.3.1 *Marking in examiners' homes*

The procedure where the Team Leader analyses a sample of the examiners' scripts must be modified. If examiners are marking at home they may not be in a position to guarantee to mark a certain number of scripts a day; it is therefore not practical to expect them to be able to send in a sample of each day's marking. It would be practical, however, to ask them to send in a sample from each batch of marking they are asked to do, or, preferably, to send the finished batch to the Team Leader for random sampling. This allows the Team Leader access to scripts that the examiners have marked at all times of the day and under varying conditions: if the examiners choose their own sample, they may send scripts which they have marked when their judgement is fresher, or scripts which they have spent more time on and considered more carefully. If the Team Leader chooses the sample, it will be more representative of the examiners' normal marking.

The biggest problem with this system is timing: it may delay the marking process if the examiners have to wait to hear from the Chief

Examiner before they begin a new batch of marking. However, this is better for all parties than if the examiner rushes through all of the marking and then perhaps has to go back to re-mark (or if the Chief Examiner has to arrange for another examiner to mark because the original examiner was not able to mark well). It is the responsibility of the Team Leader to communicate with the examiners as soon as possible, to inform them that it is all right to go ahead or to advise them of any problems that they are having. In the latter case the Team Leader should send the problematic scripts back to the examiner, so that the examiner can study the changes the Team Leader has made and try to internalise them. Subsequent marking by this person would need careful monitoring.

The second monitoring procedure, which involves all the examiners in marking the same packet of reliability scripts, can also be carried out with examiners marking from home. The principal modification is that photocopies of all scripts need to be sent to each examiner, but this should not be too time-consuming or expensive, especially when compared to the costs of re-marking all an examiner's scripts if the marking does not conform to the institution's standards. There is always the possibility that markers will mark the 'reliability scripts' more carefully than other scripts, and that the Team Leader will not be getting a true picture of the marker's ability to adhere to the marking scale under normal conditions; however, the exercise will prove useful in uncovering those examiners, if any, who are having problems even when they know they need to mark carefully.

The third method of marking, routine double-marking, is also possible for examiners marking from home. The main difficulty is that it will probably not be easy for separate examiners to discuss their differences of opinion in the cases where they are important enough to require attention. However, the Team Leader could be asked to read all scripts where these types of difference have occurred and to make the final decision.

6.3.2 Marking in testing centres

The second type of non-central marking takes place in the individual testing centres, most notably during oral tests. This type of marking is notoriously difficult: examiners have only a short time in which to make their decisions and they usually have no way of reviewing a candidate's performance after the test to confirm or change their decision about the level of performance. Ironically, however, there are few well-used monitoring procedures for oral tests. The most common procedure is sampling. This is usually done by the Team Leader, who visits the testing centre and sits in on oral tests conducted by the examiner. The Team Leader observes the test administration and independently marks the candidate. When the test is finished, the Team Leader and the examiner compare their marks and discuss the instances where they have serious differences of opinion. Although this procedure is doubtless useful for the examiners who are observed, the likelihood of any one examiner being observed in any one year is limited, especially when institutions examine in many centres.

It is rare to find anything equivalent to the 'reliability scripts' for oral tests, or routine double-marking. Institutions plead that it is not practical to introduce these procedures: when there are many examiners it would be expensive to copy 'reliability tapes', and it would be administratively difficult as well as expensive to have two examiners in every testing centre. However, institutions which run tests for their own purposes (internal promotion, final achievement) might very well consider these options: if the examiners are also members of staff, they could view or listen to a single copy of the reliability tape at the same time and do routine double-marking without requiring more travel than normal from the examiners. An interesting possibility for institutions which test many candidates on different sites would be the taping of candidate performances, so that they can be sampled by a Team Leader or even double-marked. This is a procedure which is used in the testing of foreign languages in the UK and is also used by Oxford-ARELS for their EFL exams. The suggestion may not be suitable for all institutions, but it could certainly be developed by many.

6.4 Intra-rater reliability

All the procedures detailed above are attempts to improve inter-rater reliability: the agreement among markers. However, it is sometimes the case, especially in language testing, that differences of opinion between examiners about the quality of a candidate's performance may be quite legitimate. That is why we recommend routine double-marking in the majority of circumstances: this system allows examiners to differ (by a certain amount), and simply averages the marks to arrive at a final score.

In all cases it is crucial that any one marker should be internally consistent: that is, each examiner should agree with him or herself marking the same performance on a different occasion. This intra-rater reliability can normally be assumed to have been monitored when inter-rater reliability is being checked. This is because any agreement between examiners will be limited by the internal consistency of any and all examiners. However, it may be important to establish intra-rater reliability, either at the end of examiner training, or routinely during marking.

The only way in which intra-rater reliability can be established is by getting examiners to re-mark scripts they have already marked. This will only make sense if the first marks are not on the scripts (which is why we strongly advocate that examiners never write on their scripts). Examiners should not be told that they are re-marking scripts, and the Team Leader should be responsible for selecting a sample of scripts previously marked by each examiner and devising a means of including those in later batches of scripts to be marked by that examiner. The correlation between first and second marks, and their respective means and standard deviations can then be checked, and suitable action taken if intra-rater reliability proves to be low.

Similar procedures can be devised for oral examining provided that performances have been taped. In this case, audio tapes may be preferable to video tapes, to avoid the chances of the examiner recognising the candidate, although we acknowledge that ratings based on audio-taped performances may be somewhat different from ratings based on live performances.

6.5 Survey of EFL Examination Boards: Questionnaire

In the questionnaire we asked EFL examining boards whether they practised routine double-marking, how they resolved conflicts between examiners, and what kinds of statistics they calculated to investigate the reliability of marking in their exams.

QUESTION 37: *Once marking is under way are any scripts double-marked? If so, what proportion of scripts?*

Our assumption when writing this question was that examining boards would attempt to improve the reliability of their subjective marking by asking two examiners to mark every piece of writing and perhaps every oral performance by a candidate. We discovered, however, that only three boards used this system: one board said that it double-marked all of the writing in its only EFL exam, one reported that it double-marked writing in several of its exams, and one reported that it routinely double-marked all oral performances at its highest level.

Six other boards seemed to interpret 'double-marking' in the way that we use 'sample marking' above: they reported that at some point during the marking process the Chief Examiner, or Team Leader, would analyse a percentage of the scripts marked by any one examiner. Some boards did not report how many papers were analysed in this way; others reported that they analysed 10 or 15% of each examiner's output. One board reported that it double-marked scripts only 'on appeal': presumably if a candidate or a centre was not satisfied with a final grade and asked for a re-scrutiny of the script.

It is not always clear when the sampling takes place. One board reported that:

> An initial sample of 10–15 scripts for each section (approximately 10%) is moderated by the Chief and Assistant Chief Examiners. If there is cause for concern further scripts are considered. If necessary, a complete re-mark would take place.

This indicates that scripts are normally checked by a senior examiner only at the beginning of the marking period, when examiners are presumably at their freshest and on their best behaviour. Only those examiners who do not perform satisfactorily at this stage are subject to further sampling. It seems risky to allow examiners to mark for such a long time (the rest of the marking period) without some appraisal of their work, since there are so many pressures which may lower their attention level and make them mark less well than they should. However, at least one board continues to sample throughout the marking period:

> Scripts from *all* examiners are sampled by the Chief Examiners at the beginning, middle and end of the marking process. At the end examiners are statistically and empirically correlated. This may lead to re-marking of scripts marked by poor examiners (who will not be re-hired) or to the scaling of 'dovish' or 'hawkish' examiners.

(For a brief explanation of 'scaling' see Question 41 below.)

It is important to note at this point that most of the boards who replied to the question about double-marking referred to their written examinations, perhaps because our question referred to 'scripts'. Only four mentioned oral assessments. One board mentioned that recordings made of all performances at its higher level were marked by two examiners, and by more in cases of disagreement. A respondent from another board mentioned that they sometimes use interlocutors as well as assessors in some of their exams, and that the interlocutors may contribute to the assessment (though if there is a difference of opinion between the interlocutor and the examiner, the examiner's view prevails). Two other boards which give oral tests wrote that double-marking was 'not applicable', although both referred to 'sampling' or 'moderating' in their answers to Question 41. We therefore know very little about the procedures which are used by most boards to make sure that their examiners of speaking are upholding their standards consistently.

QUESTION 38: *What happens in the event of disagreements between first and second markers? Please circle those that apply:*

1   *A third marker is brought in, and the two closest marks used*
2   *The two marks are averaged*
3   *The second marker's opinion holds*
4   *The two markers discuss and reach agreement*
5   *Other*

The boards which reported using 'double-marking' in the sense that we meant it – i.e. using two independent examiners to mark each script or performance – had different ways of arriving at a final mark when the two examiners disagreed. The practice of asking the two examiners to discuss and reach agreement was favoured by one board, but two reported that for some of its exams the decision was referred to the Team Leader or Chief Examiner. The fourth board reported that the process did not necessarily end there. If the Chief Examiner's decision was not satisfactory, examiners from other teams might be called in to give an opinion: 'and some candidates have been privileged to have up to nine markings before a final decision has been made'.

The boards who used sample marking reported that the second marker's opinion held. This marker was a senior examiner (Chief Examiner or Team Leader) in all cases.

QUESTION 39: *Are inter-marker correlations routinely calculated?*

Five boards claimed that inter-marker correlations were routinely calculated, and three claimed that they calculated correlations on occasion.

One replied that it did not calculate correlations routinely, but did not state whether it calculated them at all. Three boards felt that the question was 'not applicable': two because they did not do double-marking, and one 'because the Chief Examiner marks all the scripts'.

It was intriguing that at least eight boards reported calculating correlations at least some of the time, since only four reported doing routine double-marking. We do not know who the boards correlate with whom. It would be interesting to know this, and to see the results of the calculations. As far as we know these are not made public.

QUESTION 40: *Are markers' means and standard deviations routinely calculated?*

Eight boards said that they routinely calculated markers' means and standard deviations; two said they did on occasion. Another two said this was not applicable to their exam, either because 'the Chief Examiner marks all scripts' or because the exam was 'oral assessment'.

We are again intrigued by the number of boards who report doing these calculations because we do not know whose means are compared to whose, and we have no evidence of the results of these calculations.

QUESTION 41: *Are any other procedures routinely followed to calculate or to check upon marker reliability?*

Several boards referred back to their training and sampling procedures, which have already been reviewed in Chapter 5; several others mentioned new procedures. Two boards referred to the procedure called 'scaling': an exam board will 'scale up' (i.e. adjust the mark given to) scripts that have been marked by someone who is found to be too strict in marking, and 'scale down' in the case of examiners who are found to be too lenient. The boards presumably decide on the direction and degree of scaling by looking at the means and standard deviations of their examiners, but it is not clear who they compare each examiner with, nor exactly how the 'scaling' is done.

The problem with scaling is that there may be a tendency to believe that reliability of marking has been achieved because examiners' scores have been adjusted to 'account for disagreement'. However, scaling may actually exacerbate problems: unless examiners who have been shown to lack inter-rater reliability are known to have intra-rater reliability – and this is unlikely – then the adjustment of marks for individual candidates may result in less, not more, justice. In short, the correctness and accuracy of scaling is in some doubt, and test developers ought at least to check that the scaling actually achieves what they wish it to. It is better, we argue, to ensure examiner reliability in the ways we outline above.

Other procedures reported included reports on each examiner which are compiled by the Chief Examiner (confidential to the board), and 're-standardisation'. The board that mentioned re-standardisation did not give details of who needed to be re-standardised and when this would be done. A further board wrote that for oral examiners there was a process of 'observation and group examining and retraining', but it is not clear what the term 'group examining' refers to nor who would need to be retrained. (We are assuming that 're-standardisation' and 'retraining' are both procedures which take place in addition to the normal standardisation meetings held regularly during the year.) The final procedure mentioned was described as 'computer screen record only', but no details were given. It is a pity that the board did not elaborate more, as others could surely profit from learning about new procedures using micro-computers.

6.6 Survey of EFL Examination Boards: Documentation

We received documents from four boards which contained some information about the monitoring of examiners. We shall first review the procedures used for monitoring the marking of writing, and then review the procedures for monitoring the marking of speaking.

6.6.1 Monitoring the marking of writing

We received information about the monitoring of the marking of writing from three boards: the LCCI, the AEB and UCLES.

The LCCI, in their *Handbook of Duties of Examiners and Moderators for Business Studies Examinations*, devote a page to what they call 'Standard Re-scrutiny Procedures'. These procedures are described briefly below:

1. Assistant Examiner (LCCI's term for 'examiner') sends 12 scripts from initial packet (preferably in the 40–60% range) to the Chief Examiner.

2. Chief Examiner analyses scripts. 'If desired, the Chief Examiner may telephone the Assistant Examiner, to give a report (favourable or unfavourable) on the re-scrutiny. In any case, the Assistant Examiner's scripts ... will be returned to him ... with instructions, e.g.

   a. The standard of marking is quite acceptable: 'OK. Carry on'.

   b. The standard of marking requires minor adjustment.

   c. The standard of marking requires major adjustment. In this case, the Chief Examiner may require the Assistant Examiner to make appropriate adjustments, but to refrain from returning scripts to [Headquarters] until a sample of adjusted marked scripts has been re-scrutinised.

3. Subsequent sampling

The Chief Examiner may require subsequent sampling of Assistant

Examiners' marked scripts, 'to check that they are keeping to the established standard'.

At the end of the marking period, the Chief Examiner should make a report on the performance of Assistant Examiners whose work has been re-scrutinised, e.g.

    a.   Marking satisfactory. Re-use for subsequent papers.

    b.   Initial marking slightly askew but appropriate adjustment was made, so Assistant Examiner may be re-used for subsequent papers.

    c.   This Assistant Examiner could not adapt his marking to the required standard. Do not re-use.

There are several positive features in this description – namely, that the Chief Examiner re-scrutinises the examiner's adjusted marks, and that the board keeps a record of which examiners should be allowed to mark again in future. However, there are several points which need clarification:

1. Why does the examiner select the scripts which are to be re-scrutinised, rather than sending the whole batch to the Chief Examiner and letting the Chief Examiner decide which scripts to mark? As stated earlier, asking the examiner to choose the scripts might result in a sample of scripts which have been marked more carefully than others.

2. Why does sampling not continue throughout the entire marking period for all examiners? If the examiners are not 'kept on their toes', then complacency may set in.

3. How does the Chief Examiner decide that the examiner is not marking well enough? There is no mention made in this document of the procedures that the board uses or the results they will accept as evidence for reliability or unreliability.

4. What happens to the scripts that have been marked by an examiner who could not 'adjust to the required standard'? Some boards state that they will re-mark all of the scripts of an examiner who proves to be unreliable; we presume this to be the case here but do not know for sure.

The AEB's booklet *How to set and mark GCE examinations* presents a procedure which is very similar to the LCCI procedure, but it suggests that all examiners' scripts are sampled throughout the marking period and states explicitly that total re-marks will be carried out if necessary (page 12).

The AEB also gives details about what happens at the end of the marking period as a further check on the reliability of marking. Although this procedure does not apply to EFL exams (the AEB no longer produces such exams), we assume it is used for foreign language examinations. It is useful to reproduce this description in full as it contains several good ideas that could be adopted by institutions which deal with large numbers of candidates:

> In subjects where more than fifteen Examiners are required to mark a paper, Assistants are divided into teams. One team is supervised by the Chief Examiner while the others are supervised by Senior Assistant Examiners. All queries which arise after the standardisation meeting are dealt with by the Chief Examiner either directly or through a Senior Assistant Examiner.
>
> As soon as possible after the standardisation meeting each Assistant Examiner sends to the Team Leader (Chief or Senior Assistant Examiner) a sample batch of marked scripts. By re-marking these the Team Leader checks that each Assistant is marking correctly. If necessary the Assistant is instructed to make minor or major changes in order to get the marking right. If not entirely satisfied, the Team Leader asks for additional sample scripts after the inaccuracies have been pointed out and Assistants have modified their marking. [Further sampling of marked scripts, some randomly selected, ensures that the marking is continued satisfactorily and that all Assistants are marking to the correct standard. Should there still be difficulties with any Assistant – there are some good teachers with good subject knowledge who find work of this kind very difficult – arrangements are made to have all of that Assistant's scripts re-marked. In some cases the difficulties may be limited to the marking of only one question in the paper and only that question has to be re-marked.]
>
> When the marking is completed the Chief Examiners and their Senior Assistants come to the Board to review the work of all Assistants. They re-mark more of the scripts marked by all of the members of their teams and these 'Office Review' scripts are selected so as to ensure that each Assistant's work is sampled across the full range of marks, the range of centres from which they come and the period during which they were marked. The sample scripts already re-marked may have indicated some problems; the statistical information which the Subject Officer has may also indicate possible problems but the work of every Assistant receives the same thorough scrutiny. For each of them scripts are re-marked until a decision about the quality of the work can be made with confidence. In most cases the marking is found to be correct and the marks are accepted. In a few cases the re-marking evidence indicates that a small numerical adjustment would correct the marking and this adjustment is made. Where neither of these decisions can be taken all of the scripts are re-marked. Thus, by the end of the Office Review meeting the Board has confirmed the marking of most of its

examiners and has taken appropriate action about the rest so ensuring that the marks awarded do not depend on who marked the work or when it was marked.

The marking of objective test papers presents none of these problems. The answer sheets containing coded responses are scanned by a special machine and it is only necessary to ensure that the machine has been set up with the correct response codes. There is a special procedure to ensure that candidates who fail to follow instructions for using the answer sheets are credited with marks for their correct answers.

How to set and mark GCE examinations, AEB (page 12).

The points that are worth highlighting in this description are that sampling continues to take place for every examiner even after marking finishes, and that some statistical information is used to help in the decision-making process. Unfortunately, we do not know what kind of information is used.

UCLES also describes its monitoring procedure for FCE and CPE in the *General Handbook*. What is worth noting about the UCLES procedure is that there does not seem to be a clear division between training and monitoring: the examiner receives sample scripts for training purposes at the same time as the first batch of 'live scripts' (scripts to be marked for real), and returns both the sample scripts and a selection of live scripts at the same time. Although this system is doubtless quick to operate if the examiner marks the training scripts well, it must be difficult to decide what to do if there are problems with these scripts. No detail is given about what happens in such instances.

It is important to note that none of the three reports mentions the statistical procedures used to make decisions about the reliability of the marking.

6.6.2 Monitoring the marking of speaking

Oxford-ARELS publishes a short description of how it monitors the marking of speaking, in a booklet entitled *Oxford-ARELS Examinations in English as a Foreign Language: Rationale, Regulations and Syllabuses*. The description is as follows:

The candidates' tapes are all marked in the UK by qualified examiners. At the two higher levels, independent marking by two examiners is mandatory; and if they disagree by more than a small amount the senior examiner is brought in to give a third – and definitive judgement. At the Preliminary level all tapes which, at first marking, are close to a grade boundary (e.g. Pass/Fail) are double-marked; again, if there is more than a minor disagreement, a third marking is called for. At each

143

examination at least 10% of the whole entry is reviewed by the senior examiners.

(page 7)

It is reassuring to know that this board does so much double-marking and that third judgements are also asked for in the case of disagreements. It is curious though that the lower-level exam is marked by only one examiner, except when the first examiner's mark is near a borderline.

We found only one further reference to monitoring procedures in the documents we received from the boards. The LCCI, in its booklet *Languages for Industry and Commerce: Oral Examinations. Syllabus Booklet, Regulations and Teacher's Guide, 1990–1992*, had this to say about oral examining:

> The Co-ordinators act as chief examiners for the panel and are
> responsible for supervising all the examiners on their panel and will
> periodically sit in with them on examinations to maintain training and
> standards.
>
> (page 41)

Unfortunately this description is too general to be of use to institutions wishing to design new examination systems or reform old ones.

6.7   Discussion

It is clearly important to monitor the marking of a test in order that the reliability of the mark may be raised. The most common way of doing this in examination boards is by sampling the examiners' marks and asking for adjustments to be made if the marking is not satisfactory. In tests with large populations the sampling is done by Team Leaders, whose own judgements are often not questioned; in some exams, though, the Team Leader's marking is sampled by the Chief Examiner, whose judgement is final.

Only a few of the exam boards gave the details of their sampling procedures. The descriptions they gave were useful, but we have several questions that need clarification:

1. Why do so many boards use sampling rather than routine double-marking?
2. Why do some boards sample only at the beginning of marking, and not all the way through?
3. Why do some boards ask the examiner to choose the scripts which are to be sampled, instead of conducting random sampling?

Has a system for monitoring markers been decided on? Will it be by sampling, by reliability scripts or by routine double-marking?

If monitoring is to be done by sampling, are the details of the system known to all?

What percentage of each examiner's marked scripts will the Team Leader sample?

Whose view will prevail if the Team Leader's assessment of a script differs from the examiner's?

Will sampling take place only at the beginning of the marking period or continue throughout the marking process?

If an examiner has been asked to re-mark certain scripts, will the Team Leader sample them again?

If monitoring is to be done by 'reliability scripts', are the details of the system known to all?

Have the scripts which are to be used for the reliability study received a 'consensus mark' from the Chief Examiner and the Standardising Committee?

Have enough sets of scripts been photocopied for all the teams to carry out the reliability exercise at approximately the same time?

Has a decision been made about what level of correlation indicates acceptable inter-rater reliability?

Do the Team Leaders know how to calculate correlations so that they will be able to give feedback to their examiners soon after the reliability study takes place?

If monitoring is to be done by routine double-marking, are the details of the system known to all?

Has a decision been taken about how wide a discrepancy must be between two examiners before they have to confer about the marks they have given?

Has a decision been taken about what should be done in a case where neither examiner is prepared to change his or her marks?

Has a system been created for monitoring oral exams? Will there be a recording of each performance, or at least of a sample of performances?

If it is discovered late in the process that an examiner has not been consistent in marking, or has been too generous or strict, is there a

4. Do all boards ask examiners who have been 'out of lin adjusted scripts back for further sampling?

Clarification of these points would be valuable for institutio setting up new tests and wish to adopt practical means of r without sacrificing too much reliability.

Although we noted that some boards practise routin marking, we feel that some attention ought to be given to the issues:

Double-marking is clearly possible with large test popu well as small ones and ought therefore to be more prevale It is equally important to do double-marking when exami in their homes rather than mark centrally.

Marking ought to be conducted in such a way that the first does not influence the second examiner's judgement.

We also believe that more needs to be known about the proce the boards use when monitoring the marking of speakin aware that Chief Examiners and Team Leaders sometimes examiners as they are marking, but we doubt that this syst for more than a few examiners to be monitored every possibility we have suggested is to operate a system of mon tape recordings, so that Team Leaders or Chief Examiners ca hear the candidate's performance but can also hear how the conducts the test and can check that the mark given reasonable. We believe that all boards that run oral tests ou this routinely.

6.8   Checklist

We present below a series of questions that institutions sl themselves when setting up procedures for monitoring reliability:

Have the examiners been divided into teams, and is it clea Team Leader is in each team?

Have the examiners been given the latest edition of the marl or the rating scales, which incorporates clarifications a improvements decided upon at the time of training?

Have the examiners been told not to make any mark candidates' scripts?

system in place to correct the wrong marking? If 'scaling' is to be used, is there a system for deciding when and how to scale?

Will complete records be kept so that examiners who have not marked well will not be asked to mark again in future?

Will any of the information gained during the monitoring process be published? If not, how will users of the exam know that the marking has been reliable?

Bibliography

Crocker, L. and J. Algina. 1986. *Introduction to Classical and Modern Test Theory*. Chicago, Ill.: Holt Rinehart Winston.
Guilford, J.P. and B. Fruchter. 1978. *Fundamental Statistics in Psychology and Education*. Tokyo: McGraw Hill.

7 Reporting scores and setting pass marks

This chapter addresses the questions that need to be considered once the test has been marked. Decisions need to be taken on whether simply to add marks up to arrive at a total score for the test, or whether to give some items more importance than others. Testers need to decide in what form to report scores, and they also often have to decide which candidates can be considered to have performed adequately, and thus to have passed the test, and which have failed.

7.1 Scores

Once tests have been marked, it will be possible to calculate, for each candidate, some form of score. If the test consists of a number of objective subtests (for example, multiple-choice or error-recognition tests), then each item may have been assigned a mark of 1 if correct and 0 if wrong. These item marks can then be added together to arrive at a total for each subtest, or a total for the whole test, or both. If the test is subjectively marked, then holistic or analytic ratings (see Chapters 5 and 6) may be given for performance on the whole test or on individual tasks. If the latter, these ratings can also be aggregated to arrive at a score for the test as a whole.

Scores on objective tests are sometimes corrected for guessing. In such cases, a student's total correct score is adjusted by subtracting an amount derived from the chances of getting the item correct by guessing alone. On a true/false test, where the likelihood of guessing correctly is 50%, students can expect to answer one question correctly for every question they answer incorrectly, and thus the correction is to subtract the number of wrong answers from the number of correct ones. The general formula is:

$$\text{Corrected score} = \text{Right answers} - \frac{\text{Wrong answers}}{\text{Number of alternatives} - 1}$$

However, the use of such corrections is controversial and only recommended where blind guessing is known to occur, and if a large number of items are omitted by some or all of the students. Otherwise correction has little effect and is not recommended (Ebel and Frisbie 1991: 213).

7.2 Weighting

7.2.1 Item weighting

Test designers often believe that some items are more important than others and that such items should therefore carry more weight. Giving extra value to some items is known as *weighting*. However, differential weighting of items very rarely leads to improved reliability or validity.

Items are usually weighted because they are thought to require more advanced proficiency or knowledge to complete, or to take more time to answer, or because they are believed to be more central to the curriculum or to the concept of proficiency. Ebel, however, unambiguously condemns item weighting:

> If an achievement test covers two areas, one of which is judged to be twice as important as the other, then twice as many items should be written in relation to the more important area. This will result in more reliable and valid measures than if an equal number of items is written for each area and those for the more important area are double-weighted.
>
> Complex or time-consuming items should be made, if possible, to yield more than one response that can be independently scored as right or wrong.
>
> (Ebel 1979: 199)

The simplest method of weighting is *equal weighting*: to give the same mark to each item. It is important to note, though, that if subtests are unequal in length, and if each item receives the same mark, then the subtests will be unequally weighted unless the scores are transformed in some way.

7.2.2 Weighting of test components

Test designers may also consider that different test components (not items) should have different values. They may believe that some

149

aspects of language proficiency are more important than others in a given context – that is, relative to the test's purpose. If the test is screening applicants for academic study, then accuracy in writing may be more important than correct pronunciation. If the test is for selecting international air traffic controllers, the ability to identify numbers and directions in spoken discourse may be much more important than the ability to write grammatically accurate and coherent essays.

A further reason for weighting might be pedagogic: to emphasise to students the importance of particular parts of the curriculum. For example, it may be difficult to produce many items or tasks for the oral component of a test, but teachers may regard oral abilities as crucial and therefore assign weighting to that component in disproportion to the number of items.

Another reason for indicating the weighting of different components might be to ensure that candidates allocate their time appropriately when taking the test.

The relationship between subtests as established by correlations may be an important consideration in deciding how to weight them. If different test components are highly correlated with each other, then the issue of whether to weight or not is not a problem: the natural 'unweighted' weighting will give marks almost as valid as those resulting from more sophisticated statistical procedures (Ebel 1979: 252).

If test components are not to have equal weight, normally the most reliable test should have the higher weighting. If components are of equal reliability, then judgements about relative importance may be legitimately used: it should be stressed, however, that these are subjective.

A low correlation of one subtest with other subtests is often taken to mean that it is measuring something different from the others. Such a subtest might receive weighting in order to increase its contribution to the total score.

If test components of varying length are to be equally weighted, then scores should technically be weighted to make their standard deviations equal (for a detailed explanation and discussion, see Ebel 1979: 252–5). In general, however, the best advice is not to weight components by some formulaic adjustment of scores, but rather to weight components at the test design stage by including more or fewer items in the individual components.

7.3   Transformation

If, despite the differences in length, each subtest is considered to be equally important, then it will be necessary to transform the subtest scores before adding or comparing them. The commonest form of transformation is to convert the subtest scores into percentage scores: divide each subtest score by the number of items and multiply by 100. More complex forms of score transformation are possible (standardised scores, z scores and so on): these are dealt with in most textbooks on educational measurement and will not be described here. Suffice it to say that the net effect of such score transformations is to make subtest scores comparable and usually, if they are added up, equally weighted.

Judgements about transformation may involve a comparison of a given candidate's performance on one subtest with performance on another subtest. It may be decided to adjust scores on one subtest in the light of scores on the other. For example, a candidate's score on a subjectively-marked speaking test might be adjusted to agree with the same person's score on an objectively-marked listening test: this might be justified if one test is thought or known to be more valid or reliable than another. The justification for transforming scores is often subjective and influenced by applied linguistic, pedagogic and psychometric considerations.

It may be important to know whether and how the components of a test have been transformed since this directly affects how the final score is arrived at, and therefore what that score means. If, for example, scores from a writing subtest worth 20 marks are added to scores from a reading subtest worth 50 marks to arrive at a total score out of 70, that total score will clearly normally be 'composed more' of reading than of writing: in other words, a person's reading ability will have a greater influence on the final total score than that person's writing ability, provided that the two subtests are of roughly equivalent difficulty, variability and reliability.

7.4   Score aggregation

In the case where the score to be reported is a single letter or number grade, this grade will obviously be made up of component parts: the aggregation of subtest scores. This aggregation is often done in a somewhat complicated manner. To illustrate, we take the case of UCLES' First Certificate in English – not because the test is exemplary, but because it is well known to many readers.

The FCE examination consists of 5 'papers' or subtests. Each paper has a varying number of possible marks:

Paper 1 (Reading) is worth 55 marks (made up of 25 items worth 1 mark each and 15 items worth 2 marks). The candidate's score on this paper is then transformed to a score out of 40.

Paper 2 (Written Composition) has five subjectively marked questions, marked on a scale of 0–20. The candidate's initial marks are converted to scores out of 40.

Paper 3 (Use of English) is 'marked out of a working total arrived at in the course of the examiners' meeting' (*UCLES General Handbook* 1987: 48), usually in the range of 70–80 marks. The candidate's 'working total' is then transformed to a score out of 40.

Paper 4 (Listening) has a total score of 20. 'This final total of 20 may involve adjustment of initial scores on a number of individual items; this is to give control over the desirable weighting of answers for discrimination purposes, and to offset, for instance, the guessing factor in true/false selection items' (*UCLES General Handbook* 1987: 57).

Paper 5 (Speaking) has a maximum total of 30 marks and the candidate's score is transformed to a score out of 40. However, this mark out of 40 is then adjusted if it is 'not in line with expectation as shown by the candidate's performance in the other papers' (*UCLES General Handbook* 1987: 4).

The result of this process is five scores adding up to a possible combined maximum of 180. In other words, candidates have scores for each paper (Reading, Written Composition, Use of English, Listening and Speaking) and these are, roughly, equally weighted. It must be said that this process is somewhat complex, and in principle it is usually better to avoid the need for such complexity by adjusting the balance of items in the test and ensuring marker reliability by adequate training.

7.5 Reported scores

What is often of greatest importance in understanding test scores is the *reported score*: the score that is reported to candidates or employers or schools. In principle, having weighted and transformed the subtest scores as desired, it is now possible to report each of the subtest scores separately, or to combine them in some way for decision and reporting purposes. The simplest approach is to combine the scores by addition, and to decide on a single 'pass' mark for the examination as a whole. This, indeed, is a very common procedure for school tests, and is often used in national exams as well. In this approach, a candidate's performance in one subtest can indeed compensate for poor performance in another section. However, this compensation will not be explicit and it will obviously be affected by the nature of the weighting of subtests. A slight refinement to this pass/fail approach is to have several different cut-off points: one score is the border between Pass and Fail, a second and higher score is the border between Pass and Credit, and a third score is the border between Credit and Distinction. This is, for example, the custom in GCE O level examinations in many countries. In the case of UCLES' FCE and CPE, candidates pass with a grade A, B or C, and fail with D or E. A further refinement is to set cut-off points for each test component, and candidates are only allowed to 'pass' the test as a whole if they reach a minimum level on each component (see Section 7.7, below).

For many UK examinations, the reported score is a simple letter or number grade. However, a simple total grade need not be reported: it is possible separately to report scores on important components of the test, typically the subtests. For example, an exam board may report a profile score, on a scale of A–D, for five different subtests: Writing, Editing, Reading, Listening and Speaking (the JMB's UETESOL test). Some tests do both – the IELTS, for example, reports scores on a scale of 0–9 for the four test components of Speaking, Listening, Reading and Writing, but then also reports an Overall Band Score, which is a straightforward addition and averaging of the four component scores.

7.6 To combine or not to combine?

It is often argued that the simple approach of reporting a single letter grade, whilst easy to administer, may be unfair to some candidates since it does not give due recognition to their abilities in component parts of the examination or test. The alternative mentioned above is to treat each component completely separately, and to report scores or grades on a profile, such that a candidate might 'pass' two components and 'fail' three: no overall 'pass' or 'fail' would be computed or reported. The problem with this approach is that it ignores the requirements of the real world: decision-makers often need a single piece of information, not several pieces which demand more complex consideration. When deciding on employment or admission to higher education, personnel officers and admissions tutors need to know whether the candidate is or is not adequate in broad terms, and may not accept that such a decision is actually a complex matter.

A somewhat different approach is taken if it is decided simply to report scores, but not to stipulate a 'pass' mark. In such cases, the responsibility for deciding whether a score is adequate or inadequate rests with the test score user. This is the approach taken by ETS, which does not set any 'pass' mark for TOEFL scores, although individual institutions will set their own admission cut-offs. The same approach is taken by the IELTS test, although verbal descriptors, which provide guidance to score users in how to interpret the meaning of the score, are provided for each band score.

It is informative to examine actual practice in the use of IELTS profile scores. The intention in reporting four profile scores without indications of pass or fail is to allow individual institutions to decide what the appropriate profile for candidates is. For example, it may be that students of Electrical Engineering do not need a high score in speaking, but do need a good score in reading, whereas students of Law need to perform well in speaking as well as in reading. Thus the decision to admit or not to admit would vary according to the discipline of the institution and the candidate. However, in practice, most admissions tutors probably ignore the profile scores and only consider the overall band score – the average of the four skill scores. Even here, it is possible to argue that a potential student in Linguistics needs a higher overall score than a potential student in Agriculture, for example, since the linguistic demands of one discipline may be higher, overall, than those of another. Yet many admissions tutors simply consider an overall score of 6.5 to be 'adequate' and any score below to be 'inadequate', regardless of intended discipline. In other words, the value of the profile scores for fine-tuned placement decisions may be ignored – some would say, misused – by decision-makers.

7.7 Using subtest scores to reach decisions

Let us assume, then, that it is important, for practical as well as theoretical reasons, to produce an overall decision about a candidate on the basis of subtest scores. One could decide that a candidate would have to 'pass' each subtest in order to pass the exam as a whole. Alternatively, one might allow a failure on one paper out of the five, i.e. a candidate could still pass the exam as a whole despite having unsatisfactory performance in one component. Or one might decide that if a candidate fails one paper, he or she will have to achieve a compensatingly high mark in one of the other papers to pass the exam (known as 'compensation'). Or one might stipulate that a candidate can only pass the exam as a whole if he or she has gained a stipulated minimum score in one particular component (known as a 'hurdle').

It should be clear that the notion of 'passing' the examination as a whole presents potential conceptual problems, and may result in a great deal of arbitrariness. Individuals may reach the same overall score in a variety of different ways, and thus be awarded a pass, although their profiles are different. This is one of the main reasons why profiling of test results is considered by many to be superior to reporting one overall result, whether it is a pass/fail result or a score to be interpreted by test users.

Another problem we have seen with the notion of labelling a test performance as 'pass' or 'fail' is that one performance, or score, may have different values depending upon the purposes for which it is being used: what is considered adequate for one purpose or for one population of candidates may be quite inadequate, or more than adequate, for another purpose or population. This is the reason why many exam results are reported on a scale, and not as a simple pass/fail decision, thus the Pass/Credit/Distinction scale mentioned above. Even when a number of grades are reported, it is often common to find that more than one grade is labelled as a failing grade, as for example in A level results in the UK.

7.8 Setting pass marks

Despite the considerations in previous sections, it remains the case that, for many purposes, testers are obliged to determine whether a candidate's performance is adequate (a pass) or inadequate (a fail). In the UK, for example, it is common practice for examination boards to set cut-off scores. As we have seen, this decision may be taken at the level of each subtest, or at the level of the test as a whole. In subjectively marked tests, especially criterion-referenced tests, this decision may be made at the level of each task, where the examiner decides whether the candidate has performed the task adequately or not. However, for many tests, the final score will be a combination of subjectively and objectively marked items. How can pass/fail boundaries be determined for a test as a whole?

It is worth pointing out at this juncture that in many contexts the setting of a pass mark is not thought to be a problem, and a fixed percentage is considered to be appropriate. This may be 50%, or 75%, or some other magic number. This is usually simply a matter of historical tradition, yet there is absolutely no reason why any particular figure 'must' be the pass/fail boundary.

One aspect of the issue of how to determine pass marks is the distinction between norm-referencing and criterion-referencing, much discussed in the testing literature (see, for example, Ingram 1977). We have already touched upon this topic in Chapter 4, but a brief reminder of the distinction is appropriate here.

In norm-referencing, essentially what happens is that each candidate is compared with other candidates, either those who have taken the test before in some operation to establish norms for the test, or those who have taken the test at the same time. The simplest case is where candidates are rank-ordered in terms of their scores, and an arbitrary number or percentage of students are considered to have 'passed'. This arbitrary number may be determined by the availability of places in an institution or by class size. For example, an institution may be able to offer remedial classes in reading and writing to 40 students only. A placement test might be used to identify the lowest 40 candidates in those skills. Students scoring higher than the 40th candidate from the bottom will be considered to have 'passed': they will not be admitted to the classes, because of lack of space, or whatever.

Most decisions are more complex than that, and are not dictated by availability of resources so much as they are influenced by the judgements of teachers, administrators or even politicians on the basis of their experience of teaching or their notions of the educational standards appropriate for given populations. An educational system may believe that standards of achievement in the secondary schools are such that roughly 40% of the population has not reached the standard. This then is translated into setting a pass-mark at the score which is reached by 60% of the population, past or present.

An alternative, only slightly more sophisticated approach, is to 'grade on the curve'. This refers to the normal distribution or bell curve (see any introductory statistics book), and assumes that normal distributions occur and are appropriate distributions for language proficiency and learning. (We will not discuss here whether that assumption is justified.) Basically, the idea is to categorise candidates taking the test according to their score expressed in terms of standard deviations. Those who are more than, say, two standard deviations above the mean may be considered to be 'excellent', or 'exceptional', and receive the highest grade; those scoring between one and two standard deviations above the mean are considered to be 'good' and classified accordingly; and so on down to 'exceptionally weak' for those whose score falls more than three standard deviations below the mean. Unfortunately a given score is not necessarily 'exceptionally good' or 'bad' simply because it is more than three standard deviations above or below the mean: it is just an extreme score, and its quality needs to be interpreted with respect to test content and test purpose, as well as with respect to the population of candidates taking the test.

A similar approach is taken when the distribution curve is inspected for breaks in the distribution: bi-modal curves (see Figure 7.1) are obviously useful for this, since the dip in the frequency curve provides a natural potential cut-off point (although it would need to be interpreted in terms of the meaning of the score and the difficulty of the test as well as its purpose).

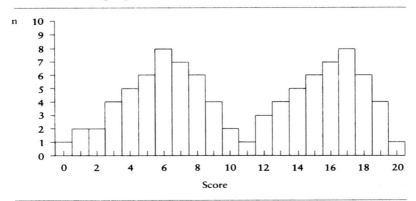

FIG. 7.1   BI-MODAL DISTRIBUTION

Criterion-referenced testing is different, at least in principle. A standard or criterion is defined *a priori* – before the test is administered – and any candidate reaching that standard is considered to have passed. Needless to say, reality is never so simple: the problem comes in deciding what the standard is to be for any given test. In tests of speaking and writing, it is possible to argue that the rating process itself can be criterion-referenced, since most descriptors for rating criteria contain, essentially, definitions of adequacy, and raters have to judge whether or not the candidate meets the standard for that criterion. Although this is itself not straightforward, it is much more complicated to apply such a principle to discrete-point tests of grammar or vocabulary, or even to integrative cloze tests intended to measure reading ability. What is an adequate score on this grammar test? What can be considered to be a pass on this cloze test?

One way to answer this question non-arbitrarily is to identify 'masters' – people who are known to possess the ability being measured – and see how well they perform on the test. For example, one might select people who are known to be good readers, and see how well they perform on a reading test. This performance is then compared with 'non-masters' and some decision is reached about where, between the two performances, a cut-off point should come. For proficiency tests, one obvious source of such 'masters' is educated native speakers who can competently use the language on which the candidates are being tested. However, for most achievement tests (see Chapter 2 for a discussion of the differences between proficiency and achievement tests), it is much more problematic to identify suitable masters, and it may be that the only way to do this is to select as 'masters' students who have already succeeded in the curriculum being tested.

An alternative approach, known as 'standard setting', is to ask expert judges – trained professionals with relevant expertise – to inspect the content of the test and decide what the likely performance of *barely-adequate* candidates on this test would be. One way to do this is for judges to estimate the probabilities, for each item, of a barely-adequate candidate getting the item correct. These probabilities can then be aggregated for the test as a whole, much as real scores are aggregated, to arrive at a probable percentage pass mark for a barely-adequate candidate. For example, judges might agree that the probability of a barely-adequate candidate getting Item 1 correct is 75%, whereas for Item 2 it is 50% and for Item 3 25%. The aggregation would be 75 + 50 + 25 divided by 3 = 50%. The pass mark for this three-item test would thus be 1.5.

It has to be said that this procedure is time-consuming and tedious: a short cut that may be more practical is to ask judges to look at subtests and estimate what score they consider a barely-adequate candidate ought to achieve on the subtest.

An alternative procedure, detailed in Ebel and Frisbie 1991, uses the scale which will be used to report scores. First, the grade to be assigned to a minimally-adequate performance is established (say, for instance, a D). A description is developed of the knowledge and ability of a student who just passes, and then similarly for each of the other grades (in this case, C, B and A). Then an 'expert' reads the first test item and decides if a minimally-adequate student can answer this item correctly. If so, the item is labelled D. If not, the expert decides whether a C-level student can answer it correctly, and so on. This procedure is repeated for each item in the test. The number of items labelled D is counted, and that number represents the approximate cut-off score for a D student. The number of items labelled C is then counted and that number is added to the cut-off score for D, to arrive at the cut-score for C. Similar procedures are followed to arrive at the other cut-off scores, which will then need to be adjusted downwards somewhat to allow for measurement error. Other standard-setting procedures are described in the criterion-referenced testing literature (see, for example Popham 1990).

It goes without saying that for these procedures to have any semblance of validity there must be reasons for believing that the judges are indeed experts, and the reasons for believing this need to be made explicit. In practice, whilst these procedures could be followed by large exam boards, the decision on pass marks is usually much more arbitrary and often – inappropriately – simply refers to some global percentage which has been used historically.

In summary, the process of weighting and combining item-level marks to arrive at reportable scores can be complex. The procedures one uses will depend to a large extent upon what the purpose of the test is, and should reflect what one believes or, better, knows, about the nature of language proficiency and language learning. Arriving at pass/fail decisions is an equally complex and difficult matter, and for that reason is often avoided by test constructors, who believe that the decision is best left up to individual institutions and users to suit their own particular purposes. Where pass/fail decisions are expected, however, despite the difficulties, there are ways in which one can arrive at cut-off points empirically and rationally, or at least defensibly, and not simply randomly, or arbitrarily.

We turn now to how UK EFL examination boards reach such decisions.

7.9 Survey of EFL Examination Boards: Questionnaire

We addressed these issues through the questionnaire in Questions 42 and 43. Question 42 enquired about meetings that might take place once the examination marking was complete. We expected that it might be at such a meeting that decisions on score weighting, transforming and combining might be made, and that suitable pass marks might be discussed.

QUESTION 42: *Do any further meetings (grade awarding meetings, examiners' meetings) take place before results are issued? If Yes, what form do such meetings take?*

Half the boards responding said that some further meeting does indeed take place, usually known as the 'awards meeting'. At this meeting, to quote one board: 'Grade boundaries are set; borderline reviews carried out; and scripts with which individual examiners experienced difficulties/uncertainties are considered.'

For the meeting, to quote another board, 'Examiners have available current and previous years' statistics, all current year scripts and borderline scripts from previous years. Using this evidence pass/fail boundaries are established, borderline scripts reviewed and an administrative report made on the grading.' The process of 'borderlining' was referred to by three boards as 'a re-appraisal of the work of all candidates on or just below each grade boundary'. It should be noted, however, that only four boards described anything like this process.

Of the boards that said they did not hold such meetings, one said: 'This used to happen but now a grade is given for each skill' and another replied: 'Examinations are available on demand. Markers are instructed to double-check borderline results and if in doubt submit recommendations to the Board for onward transmission to moderator if necessary.'

The only UCLES examination that did not have such meetings was IELTS, which does not report pass/fail grades (see the discussion in Sections 7.4 and 7.6 above). All other UCLES examinations followed similar procedures to those mentioned above.

Question 43 asked explicitly about procedures to fix pass/fail boundaries, on the grounds that this might not happen in a meeting, but be done routinely by board officials, possibly by computer.

QUESTION 43: *Are any special procedures followed to decide upon pass/fail boundaries?*

Three quarters of the boards reported special procedures that were followed to decide upon pass marks. Usually these were similar to those described above, although one board added the following information: 'The administrative report after the award meeting accounts for any discrepancies between present and former years' pass-rates (e.g. with our present rapid expansion the change in size and nature of candidate population).' Only three boards made any reference to statistics of the current or previous years' performance. The Chief Examiner appeared to be important in this process for at least one board: 'The Chief Examiners' assessments of the difficulty of the paper and standard of candidates, together with statistical analyses provided by the Board, are all used.'

Of the boards that replied No to this question, one board pointed out that 'Grade boundaries are fixed before the examination'. How they are able to compensate for unexpected difficulty in any one year's examination is unknown.

Most UCLES examinations appear to have special procedures to decide upon grade boundaries, but only two officers amplified their responses:

> Examiner reports/ item-level data/ comparison with previous performances (FCE, CAE, CPE, Paper 4)

> In each paper a candidate may only fail one task. In order to pass the exam, candidates must pass each paper. (CEIBT)

This final response was the only case in the questionnaire survey where respondents referred to pass/fail decisions at subtest level. This may occur in other exams also, but the questionnaire did not explicitly request information about test weighting, score transformation, or decisions at the level of components/subtests. However, we were able to gather some information on these matters by inspecting the documents we received (see Section 7.10 below).

Responses to these two questions were quite detailed and varied. It would appear that it is fairly common to hold a meeting at which pass/fail cut-offs are discussed, presumably by examiners and board officials. Since in the context of UK GCSE and A level results quite a lot of publicity is given to changes in pass rates year by year, and since the pass rates of different exam boards are often compared – one of the few areas of examinations that is fairly closely scrutinised by the public – it is perhaps not surprising that care is given to maintaining standards from year to year. Whether the standards are appropriate is, however, another matter, which may or may not be addressed by such meetings. Nevertheless, it is reassuring to know that the same procedures seem to hold for EFL/ESL examinations (which do not form part of the GCSE/A level system). The procedures appear to be a combination of norm and criterion-referencing. What we do not know in detail is exactly how the pass marks are arrived at: we can only assume that those involved make judgements on the basis of all the evidence assembled in front of them as to what would be a minimally adequate performance. Having sample performances at the grade boundaries obviously greatly assists this process and gives one more confidence in its validity. For tests that include oral components this is, of course, more problematic.

The award meeting, when it has available information on the current year's performance, the previous year's statistics, candidates' papers and previous year's borderline papers for review, gives one reasonable confidence that standards are kept as constant over the years as is possible, if we can assume that the exam population is constant in ability and performance. However, this is clearly not the case when the population is expanding – or contracting – or when innovations have occurred in test format, content or marking criteria. Furthermore, it is unclear what confidence one can have in the consistency of results for boards with small populations, or in the results of those boards that do not have such grade-awarding procedures.

7.10 Survey of EFL Examination Boards: Documentation

The documentation we received from the boards contained quite a lot of information about how scores are reported, but it contained less information on how pass marks were determined and what the pass rates were.

7.10.1 Weighting

Most exam boards do not give much information about the weighting of their exams. Exceptions are the Oxford Delegacy/ARELS Examinations Trust and UCLES.

For example, the *Rationale, Regulations and Syllabuses* includes a mention of the weighting of questions for the Oxford tests as follows:

> Except for Question 1, the precise number of marks allocated varies
> from examination to examination, in order to make adjustments for the
> amount of work required in each question. The proportion is generally:
>
> | | |
> |---|---|
> | Question 1 | 33 to 35% |
> | Question 2 | 40 to 54% |
> | Question 3 | 11 to 15% |
> | Question 4 | 5 to 6% |
> | Question 5 | 5 to 6% |
>
> Questions 1 and 2 carry the greater proportion of marks, but
> candidates often fail to do themselves justice by paying insufficient
> attention to the later questions, where there are still many marks to be
> gained.
>
> (*Rationale, Regulations and Syllabuses*, no date: 4)

UCLES' *General Handbook* (1987) makes reference to 'an intensive research programme in which the desirable relative weighting of subjective and objective elements in the testing of the written and spoken language was established' (1987: 3), but no further details of this research are given. Nevertheless, some information is given on how subtest scores are calculated and combined. It is said that the 'strengths and limitations of various accepted testing formats are balanced against each other ... . Scores in the objective Papers 1 and 4 are cross-referenced to the marks gained in more traditional ways, i.e. those awarded on impression for performance in various communicative tasks' (1987: 3).

In effect, as we have seen in Section 7.4 above, what happens is that scores on the subjective papers are adjusted in the light of the objective papers 'taking into account any examiner variation' or, in the case of Paper 5 (Speaking), 'where its contribution to the aggregate is not in line with expectation as shown by the candidate's performance in the other papers' (1987: 4). In other words, if a candidate does unusually well in the speaking test by comparison with performance on the other papers, his/her mark is presumably adjusted downwards.

The *General Handbook* gives the following information about what happens after the marking process:

> ... the initial marks are converted to 'standardised scores', by calculating the mean and standard deviation of all the scores awarded by a given examiner, and adjusting these to be the same as the mean and standard deviation for the scores obtained by those candidates on Paper 1 ... so that the subjectivity of marking is minimised ... . The use of standardised scores has the effect of reducing the 'bunching' of marks commonly found in essay marking and in particular of ensuring that many candidates obtain the maximum of 40 marks.
>
> (1987: 17)

The problem with this approach is, of course, that it does not allow for much difference between a candidate's ability in writing or speaking and in the other skills: if the performance is 'out of line', it is adjusted to make it more like the performance in the other papers. We would like to have seen more justification, especially from the research programme cited, for this dubious practice. The adjustments may be made to compensate for the low reliability of the interview compared with the other papers, but this is likely to be at the expense of validity. It might have been more suitable if the issue of low reliability had been addressed by better training and monitoring of markers.

In *A Brief Guide. EFL Examinations and TEFL Schemes*, PET is described as being marked out of 100 with 25% of the marks being allocated equally to each component (Reading, Writing, Listening and Speaking). No reasons are given for using equal weighting rather than the much more complicated weighting process described above for other UCLES exams. No information is available on whether poor performance in one component can be compensated for by good performance in another.

7.10.2 Score reporting and setting pass marks

Several boards simply report overall grades and appear to have fixed pass marks. For example, CENTRA produces a booklet describing its *Tests in English Language Skills* 1992. In this, it states that:

> Grades will be awarded as follows:

Pass 40%. Credit 55%. Distinction 70%

No justification for these is given.

A further example is Trinity College London, which offers a series of Oral Examinations, whose syllabus includes the following information about scores:

> Certificates will be awarded to candidates who achieve the necessary minimum marks as follows: pass certificate: 65%; pass with merit certificate: 75%; honours certificate: 85%.
>
> (Syllabus of Grade Examinations in Spoken English for Speakers of Other Languages 1990: 7)

No further information is available on how these scores are arrived at or how the boundaries are determined or scrutinised.

No justifications are offered by Pitmans or the ESB for the pass marks reported, nor is there any discussion of how variations in the difficulty of the examination from year to year or the quality of the candidature are taken into account when applying these pass marks.

Some boards, however, do better than this. The LCCI produces a number of documents which are somewhat more helpful in defining scores and describing pass marks. For each exam there are Pass, Credit and Distinction grades, which are roughly described in behavioural terms. A mark of 50% appears to be the pass mark, and 75% the distinction mark. A credit mark is 60%. Unlike the previous boards, the LCCI gives more details:

> Borderline marks for a pass are 48% and 49%, where scripts are reassessed to see if a pass is to be awarded. Similar borderlines for credit and distinction are 58/59% and 73/74%.

In addition (for two exams), 'marks falling into the 45–49 range after this re-scrutiny process will entitle the candidate to a pass one level below that taken' (1987: 9).

The following additional remarks are found in the *Handbook of Duties for Examiners*:

> Examiners are advised not to award a pass, credit or a distinction as a result of the 'chance' aggregation of marks. A paper should be judged, in the last resort, as a whole: the Marking Scheme must aid judgment not distort it. The chief criterion for success in the Board's examinations is the practical one of employability. Our examinations are 'criterion-referenced', in this sense, not 'norm-referenced': we set out to pass those who deserve to pass (and to fail those who deserve to fail), regardless of the statistical outcome.
>
> (1987: 10)

This degree of explicitness is to be welcomed: the problem is, how do examiners know who should pass, and how reliable are their judgements (see Chapter 6 for more discussion of this)? The document contains considerable detail, but no evidence is presented on the validity of the employability criterion, nor is there much discussion of the issue of variation of difficulty of an examination from one year to the next.

7.10.3 Pass rates

Most boards did not provide information on the percentages of students passing and failing their examinations. An exception to this was the JMB. In the Examiners' Reports for the 1990 exams, information is given on the mark ranges of the grades in each test: a table is presented showing the marks taken for each grade together with the cumulative percentage of candidates at each grade for each component. This amount of information is quite unusual in our experience, and is most welcome. In addition, the Report points out:

> It must be appreciated that the marks reflect the nature of a particular question paper and the way it has been marked and do not represent an absolute standard: grades, not marks, report the examiners' decisions on the levels of performance.

> (1990: 1)

The following comment is found in LCCI's *Guide to English for Commerce*:

> The pass and failure rates are not fixed as a proportion of the total entry (candidates taking the examination) but vary with the quality of scripts submitted in any one series. As much the same examiners set, mark, moderate and re-scrutinise the papers from year to year, the standards are kept reasonably constant so fluctuations in the pass rate can be safely attributed to candidates' performance, which in itself can vary from good days to bad days.
> No very revealing conclusions can be drawn from pass rates therefore ... . For what they are worth, however, the worldwide pass rates in the period 1980–1985 varied within the following ranges:
>
> Elementary: 64–72%
>
> Intermediate: 35–48%
>
> Higher: 29–49%

These figures are merely a function of the performance of candidates who happened to take the examination over that period and are in no sense ideal proportions of the test population, which in any case was at least four times larger at Intermediate than at either of the other two levels. This in turn affects the significance that can be attached to the figures and they should be used with great caution.

(1986: ii)

This candour is admirable: however, it does not explain how LCCI can have confidence that its pass marks are indeed appropriate, despite its assertions, without evidence for the reliability and validity of the judgements of the examiners.

7.11 Discussion

Practice obviously varies a great deal across the different boards with respect to explanations of score reporting and grade awarding. Some boards provide considerable detail on how they combine, weight and transform scores, and arrive at grades and pass/fail decisions. Others give information that is quite inadequate.

Since some boards feel able to provide informative reports and descriptions, it surely cannot be for reasons of security that the other boards do not.

The problem of deciding when a candidate has met the standards of the particular test is obviously a complex and difficult one. Much depends upon the purpose of the test, the nature of the candidates, the composition of the test, as well as its reliability, and the consequences that will follow for candidates: the more important the test, the more important it is to ensure that valid and reliable decisions are made. Shrouding the decision-making process in mystery or secrecy is not an adequate response to the problem. Test-makers have a duty to inform candidates and other stakeholders about the procedures they follow to ensure that standards are maintained and reasonable decisions taken, and also to give people faith in the standards themselves and their meaningfulness for the purpose for which they will be applied.

Obviously the nature of the information provided will vary with the nature of the tests referred to, but it ought not to be too difficult, time-consuming or costly for test constructors to make available standard information on procedures they follow and the statistical results of their examinations.

Such information should include timely and easily-understood score reports that describe test performance clearly and accurately. It should also explain the meaning and limitations of reported scores. Information should also be provided about how pass/fail decisions are arrived at.

Suitable information might include the following:
1. What procedures are followed once the test has been marked, before results are issued.
2 What the weighting is or is likely to be for individual test components.
3. What scores will be reported and in what form.
4. How the reported score relates to the marks on the test as a whole, and/or to individual components.
5. Whether and how borderline reviews are conducted and what the range of acceptable marks is for each component.
6. What the reported score means in terms of the test's purpose and real world language use.

When deciding what information ought to be made available, it is instructive to note what standards have been established elsewhere.

Nevo and Shohamy 1986 include the following categories of evaluation standards for assessment instruments that are of relevance to this chapter (for more details, see Chapter 11):

Information scope: Information collected by the test should be of such scope as to address pertinent questions about students' achievements and be responsive to the information needs and interests of specified audiences.

Justified Criteria: Criteria used to determine test scores and marks are clearly described and justified.

Report Clarity: Testing results are presented in forms readily understood by identified audiences.

Balanced Reporting: Test results are complete and fair in their presentation of strengths and weaknesses of the individual tested.

The *Code of Fair Testing Practices in Education* (see Chapter 11) says that test developers should:

Provide timely and easily understood score reports that describe test performance clearly and accurately. Also explain the meaning and limitations of reported scores. (Statement 9, Test Developers)

Provide information that will help users follow reasonable procedures for setting passing scores ... (Statement 12, Test Developers)

Furthermore, test users should:

Explain how any passing scores were set and gather evidence to support the appropriateness of the scores. (Statement 12, Test Users)

7.12 Checklist

After the test has been marked, those responsible need to consider a number of things. Some of these decisions will have been taken at the test specification or test construction stage. They can, however, still be reviewed and revised after marking, before results are issued.

Is each item to be given the same mark as any other item, or are some to be given more marks than others? Are the disadvantages of doing the latter outweighed by empirically established advantages?

How are individual item marks going to be added together? Are results for each candidate needed for each paper, or for each subtest? Will scores for some papers be adjusted in the light of performance elsewhere? Are different components to be weighted differently and if so, how?

How will scores be reported? Will they be converted into a letter grade or into percentage scores? Will a profile of results be issued, whether in letters, bands or numbers? Will an overall grade be reported?

Will candidates pass or fail? Can candidates pass or fail each component (paper/subtest), or will they be passed or failed on the whole test?

If pass marks are needed, are these fixed for all time by tradition or belief, or can they be varied?

How will the pass marks be set – by simply counting down from the top or up from the bottom until a required number is reached; by norm-referencing, using previous years' statistics as well as the current examination; by criterion referencing, using sample performances of 'masters' or of actual candidates; by getting expert judgements on the test itself; by a combination of these methods?

Will there be a borderline review for candidates who come close to the pass mark? How will this be conducted?

Will pass rates be calculated and published?

What information about standards, weighting, pass marks and pass rates will be published, for whom and in what form?

What do the reported scores mean, and what will be reported to whom?

Bibliography

Ebel, R.L. 1979. *Essentials of Educational Measurement.* 3rd edition. Englewood Cliffs, NJ: Prentice-Hall.

Ebel, R.L. and D.A. Frisbie. 1991. *Essentials of Educational Measurement.* 5th edition. Englewood Cliffs, NJ: Prentice-Hall.

Ingram, E. 1977. Basic Concepts in Testing. In J.P.B. Allen and A. Davies (eds.), *Testing and Experimental Methods.* Oxford: Oxford University Press.

Joint Committee on Testing Practices. 1988. *Code of Fair Testing Practices in Education.* Washington, DC: American Psychological Association.

Nevo, D. and E. Shohamy. 1986. Evaluation Standards for the Assessment of Alternative Testing Methods : an Application. *Studies in Educational Evaluation* 12: 149–158.

Popham, W.J. 1990. *Modern Educational Measurement: A Practitioner's Perspective.* 2nd edition. Boston, Mass.: Allyn and Bacon.

8 Validation

This chapter addresses the most important question of all in language testing: does the test test what it is supposed to test? This issue should be of central concern to all testers, since if a test is not valid for the purpose for which it was designed, then the scores do not mean what they are believed to mean. In this chapter we will describe different ways of assessing validity and discuss the relationship between reliability and validity. We will also seek to answer the question: how do I know if my test is valid?

8.1 The importance of validity

Henning 1987 defines *validity* as follows:

> Validity in general refers to the appropriateness of a given test or any of its component parts as a measure of what it is purported to measure. A test is said to be valid to the extent that it measures what it is supposed to measure. It follows that the term *valid* when used to describe a test should usually be accompanied by the preposition *for.* Any test then may be valid for some purposes, but not for others.
>
> (page 89)

The centrality of the purpose for which the test is being devised or used cannot be understated. One of the commonest problems in test use is test misuse: using a test for a purpose for which it was not intended and for which, therefore, its validity is unknown. This is not to say that a test cannot be valid for more than one purpose. However, if it is to be used for any purpose, the validity of use for that purpose needs to be established and demonstrated. It is not enough to assert, 'This test is valid' unless one can answer the follow-up question: 'How do you know?' and 'For what is it valid?'

Note also that Henning's definition allows for degrees of validity: tests are more or less valid for their purposes: validity is not an all-or-nothing matter. This important point means that users will have to use their own, or somebody else's, judgement when deciding, on the basis of evidence, on the relative validity of a test.

8.2 Types of validity

Validity can be established in a number of different ways, which leads most writers on the topic to talk of different types of validity. We shall follow this custom, since it makes explanation easier, but we emphasise that these 'types' are in reality different 'methods' of assessing validity (see Bachman 1990). We should also emphasise that it is best to validate a test in as many ways as possible. In other words, the more different 'types' of validity that can be established, the better, and the more evidence that can be gathered for any one 'type' of validity, the better.

Over recent years the increasing interest in different aspects of validity has led to a confusing array of names and definitions, but most testers, even if they have used different terms, have identified three main types of validity: *rational*, *empirical* and *construct* validity (see Thorndike and Hagen 1986). Rational (or 'content') validation depends on a logical analysis of the test's content to see whether the test contains a representative sample of the relevant language skills. Empirical validation depends on empirical and statistical evidence as to whether students' marks on the test are similar to their marks on other appropriate measures of their ability, such as their scores on other tests, their self assessments or their teachers' ratings of their ability. Construct validation refers to what the test scores actually mean. What do they tell us about the examinees? If the test is supposed to test the students' ability to use reference and cohesion in writing, does it in fact do so? To assess this the tester must formulate theories and predictions about the test and then test them out.

However, as research into test validity has progressed it is no longer useful to make the rational/empirical distinction, since both methods of validation may include empirical data. Content analyses of tests often include systematic studies of the test content, with experts being asked, for example, to rate the test content in various ways, some of which can then be evaluated statistically (this is discussed in more detail in Section 8.3.2 below). We shall therefore use the terms *internal* and *external* validity, with the distinction being that internal validity relates to studies of the perceived content of the test and its perceived effect, and external validity relates to studies comparing students' test scores with measures of their ability gleaned from outside the test. External validity is also called 'criterion validity' (see American Psychological Association 1985) because the students' scores are being compared to other criterion measures of their ability, but we shall avoid using that term in this book since we are already using 'criterion' in a different sense.

Construct validity is the most difficult of the three to understand. It has many of the same attributes as both internal and external validity, and is considered by some to be an umbrella term for both. We shall discuss it in more detail in due course.

8.3 Internal validity

Since internal validity is likely to be conceptually more familiar to the reader, we deal with this topic first. There are many ways of assessing the internal validity of a test, but three of the most common are: 'face validation', where non-testers such as students and administrators comment on the value of the test; 'content validation' where testers, or linguistic or subject experts judge the test; and 'response validation' (Henning 1987: 96), where a growing range of qualitative techniques like self-report or self-observation on the part of test takers are used to understand how they respond to test items and why.

8.3.1 Face validity

Face validity refers to the test's 'surface credibility or public acceptability' (Ingram 1977: 18), and is frequently dismissed by testers as being unscientific and irrelevant (see Stevenson 1985). Essentially face validity involves an intuitive judgement about the test's content by people whose judgement is not necessarily 'expert'. Typically such people include 'lay' people – administrators, non-expert users and students. The judgement is usually holistic, referring to the test as a whole, although attention may also be focused upon particular poor items, unclear instructions or unrealistic time limits, as a way of justifying a global judgement about the test. Face validity is often said to boil down to the comment: 'This test does not *look* valid'.

However, there has been increased emphasis on face validity since the advent of communicative language testing (CLT), and many advocates of CLT (see, for example, Morrow 1979 and 1986 and Carroll 1980 and 1985) argue that it is important that a communicative language test should look like something one might do 'in the real world' with language. Insofar as this is not systematically or rigorously defined (for example, the concept of 'authenticity' is frequently cited to justify the validity of a test, yet the concept itself is rarely explained) then it is probably appropriate to label such appeals to 'real life' as belonging to face validity. However, more systematic attempts to define real life, as in Bachman's frameworks of *Communicative Language Ability* and *Test Method Facets* (see

Chapter 2) probably belong more properly to the domain of content validity.

We would warn the reader to check whether the term 'face validity' is being used derogatively (in which case it may well mean 'no real validity'), or whether it is being used positively, when it may be better glossed as 'acceptable to users'. Our own position on the issue is that face validity is important in testing. For one thing, tests that do not appear to be valid to users may not be taken seriously for their given purpose. For another, if test takers consider a test to be face valid, we believe that they are more likely to perform to the best of their ability on that test and to respond appropriately to items. In other words, we believe that face validity will affect [illegible]onse validity of the test.

Data on face validity may be g[illegible]dents or asking them to complete a ques[illegible]s and reactions to, and their feeling[illegible]ken or looked at. The results can be su[illegible]nd the acceptability of items and test c[illegible]

8.3.2 Content validity

'Content validity is the *representativeness* or *sampling adequacy* of the content – the substance, the matter, the topics – of a measuring instrument' (Kerlinger 1973: 458). Content validation involves gathering the judgement of 'experts': people whose judgement one is prepared to trust, even if it disagrees with one's own. This is for us perhaps the most important distinction between content and face validity: in face validation we do not necessarily accept the judgement of others, although we respect it, and appreciate that for those people it is real and important and may therefore influence behaviour. In content validation we gather judgements from people we are prepared to believe.

Typically, content validation involves 'experts' making judgements in some systematic way. A common way is for them to analyse the content of a test and to compare it with a statement of what the content ought to be. Such a content statement may be the test's specifications (see Chapter 2), it may be a formal teaching syllabus or curriculum, or it may be a domain specification. Indeed, Henning (1987: 94) says: 'It is precisely in the area of content validity of achievement measures that criterion- or domain-referenced tests have certain profound advantages over more traditional norm-referenced tests.'

An editing or moderation committee meeting of the sort described in Chapter 3 may meet the requirements for content validation but only if the committee members can be considered to be experts, and if they are required to compare the draft test with its specifications or some other statement of content in a systematic way. In our experience this rarely happens. Instead, committee members opine on the content of items without much preparation, with no independent systematic attempt to gather their opinions, which means that the group dynamics of the committee meeting are likely to have a considerable influence on the outcome.

Better procedures for content validation would involve the creation of some data collection instrument. Expert judges would then be told how to make and record their judgements. For example, a scale might be developed on which experts rated the test according to the degree to which it met certain criteria. Bachman, Kunnan, Vanniariajan and Lynch 1988 used two rating scales, The Communicative Language Ability (CLA) Scale and the Test Methods Characteristics (TMC) Scale, to find a quantifiable way of comparing the content of two test batteries. The CLA facets were rated on a five-point scale and related to the level of ability required of test takers in the areas of grammatical, textual, illocutionary, sociolinguistic and strategic competence. The TMC facets related to test items and test passages and concerned the testing environment, test rubric, item type and nature of test input. Among the facets of test input were: complexity of language, rhetorical organisation, degree of contextualisation, test topic, cultural bias and pragmatic characteristics. For each facet raters assessed an item or passage according to a scale which generally had three points. For example:

	Very simple		Very complex
RHETORICAL ORGANISATION	0	1	2

Some facets were rated according to the number of occurrences of a feature, for example:

	No occurrences	One occurrence	Two or more occurrences
CULTURAL REFERENCES	0	1	2

Clapham 1992 used an adaptation of Bachman's TMC scale to evaluate the content of three reading comprehension tests. She asked three EAP teachers to rate aspects of the test input, including the propositional content, organisational and sociolinguistic characteristics of the test items and reading passages.

An alternative used in Alderson and Lukmani 1989 is to provide judges with a list of skills supposedly being tested by a set of test items, and to ask them to indicate against each item which skill or skills the item tested. These judgements could then be pooled to gain some idea of the degree of consensus among judges. Items on which there was little consensus would be considered to have low content validity.

A further alternative is that mentioned in Chapter 2.3, where we describe how, during the development of an international ESP test, teachers of a range of academic subjects at university level in the UK were asked to make judgements about the texts used for reading tests and the sorts of task students were going to be required to complete (Alderson 1988b). This survey was carried out during the development of the test specifications and trial test examples, and shows how early in the test construction process content validation should start.

What these different approaches have in common is firstly that they use as informants experts in the content being judged, and secondly that the judges are given a list or some precise indications of the aspects of the test which are to be considered. The resulting judgements are then pooled in order to arrive at an estimate of the content validity of the test or its components.

Finally, a word of caution is necessary about the use of experts. It has long been assumed in language testing that experts are experts: all one has to do is to select the right people to make the judgements, and valid judgements will result. Unfortunately, this is not necessarily the case. Recent research in language testing has begun to examine the nature of the judgements that experts make (see Alderson 1993). With hindsight, it is not surprising that it has been found that quite often experts do not agree with each other. Sometimes only one or two individuals have widely divergent opinions, but sometimes it is very difficult to perceive any consensus among them. It is interesting for testing researchers when such a variety of judgements appears: it suggests that the aspects being judged are less clear cut, more controversial, perhaps more complex, than was originally thought. From further inspection of such complexity can spring all sorts of interesting new insights. However, the test developer faces a dilemma in such circumstances. If 'experts' do not agree on what an item or a test is testing, what is the test or item testing? Unlike the researcher, who can afford to investigate the issue over a period of time, test developers need evidence of the validity of their instruments as quickly as possible. If agreement has not been reached, should the test be abandoned?

The answer to this dilemma, we believe, lies in the fact that test validity is relative rather than absolute. If content validation procedures reveal problems for aspects of the content validity of the test, then test developers need to gather other sorts of evidence for validity: external validity, face, response, and ~~so~~ ___ ___er term, they could call for research into the problem that h: ___ ___ revealed, but in the short term, they should not despair. Rather they should accept that in language testing as elsewhere there is much we do not know, and continue the search for validity, or amend their test design or test specifications in the light of the disagreements.

One way out of the dilemma that should probably be resisted is to gather experts together who are known to agree with each other, or to arrange things, by training or other means, so that disagreement is minimised. Throughout this book we have emphasised the value of training – of examiners, of item writers, of administrators. However, the training of judges in order to encourage or ensure agreement is fraught with risk, the risk of cloning. When experts are being used, it is important to use as judges people whose opinion you will respect. To seek to change that opinion, through training, because it does not agree with others, is a mere expedient, and puts reliability ahead of validity.

8.3.3 *Response validity*

As indicated above, an increasingly common aspect of test validation is to gather information on how individuals respond to test items. The processes they go through, the reasoning they engage in when responding, are important indications of what the test is testing, at least for those individuals. Hence there is considerable current interest in gathering accounts from learners/test takers on their test-taking behaviour and thoughts.

Gathering introspective data during test-taking is not a simple matter, since the data-gathering can interfere with the process being investigated. Nevertheless, research has revealed interesting insights into test performance through such learner-centred accounts (see Cohen 1984; Faerch and Kasper 1987 and Grotjahn 1986). For example, introspection on a cloze task will show whether the student has to answer an item by using the range of reading skills intended by the test designer, or whether all that is needed is some knowledge of the grammatical structure of the phrase in which the item appears. Similarly, introspection during a reading comprehension task may identify weaknesses in test items and may produce cases where students get an item wrong although they understand the passage, or right although they do not understand the passage (see Alderson 1990).

How should introspective data be gathered? The simplest way is retrospectively. After candidates have taken a test, or a component, they can be interviewed about the reasons why they produced the answers they did. Important prompts for their memories of their responses are the test scripts in the case of reading, writing and possibly listening tests. However, in the case of tests of speaking, useful data is best gathered by having the candidate talk through a video or audio recording of their performance. The questioner should be as undirective as possible, asking general questions like 'Why did you put that answer? Why did you respond that way?' and should only prompt when answers are unclear, or insufficiently specific.

The disadvantage of such retrospections is that candidates may not remember why they answered in a particular way. An alternative is to seek concurrent introspections, where the candidate 'thinks aloud' whilst responding, prompted during periods of silence by an otherwise silent observer. The obvious problem here is that if the test has important consequences it is quite unreasonable to subject test takers to such an investigation. So the informants for this sort of validation will inevitably be people who are not 'taking the test for real', and the process of taking the test for real may be very different from that of taking a test for the purposes of research. In addition, certain sorts of cognition may not be readily available for introspection, especially the more automatic processes that might be associated with 'bottom-up' linguistic processing, with grammar and lexical items or with tests of pronunciation and intonation. Nevertheless, especially for those test types where candidates can be expected to be aware of what they are doing – as in tests of writing ability, for example – such qualitative data collection methods can provide useful insights into what tests are testing.

8.4 External validity

The commonest types of external validity are *concurrent* and *predictive* validity, and the statistic most frequently used is the correlation coefficient (see Chapter 4 for an explanation of correlation). The concept of external validity is perhaps most readily understood through a discussion of concurrent validity.

8.4.1 Concurrent validity

In essence, concurrent validation involves the comparison of the test scores with some other measure for the same candidates taken at roughly the same time as the test. This other measure may be scores from a parallel version of the same test or from some other test; the candidates' self-assessments of their language abilities; or ratings of the candidate on relevant dimensions by teachers, subject specialists or other informants. What is important is that this measure can be expressed numerically (as happens, for example, with rating scales), and that it is not related to the test itself. The result of the comparison is usually expressed as a correlation coefficient, ranging in value from -1.0 to +1.0. Most concurrent validity coefficients range from +.5 to +.7 – higher coefficients are possible for closely related and reliable tests, but unlikely for measures like self-assessments or teacher assessments.

It is important that there should be good reason for believing the results of the external measure. There is little point in comparing students' test scores with their performance on some measure which is known to be unreliable or invalid. Although this may seem logical and obvious, in actual practice it is not so easy to gather believable external data. Take the case of test data: a classic concurrent validation project would involve comparing scores on the test in question with scores on some other test known to be valid and reliable. However, if that other test exists, why would one bother to produce a new test against which to compare it? Why not simply use the original test? There are two answers to this. The first is that the other test may not be easily available. It may be too expensive, or too long for practical use, or it may be a secure test which can be made available only for the purposes of validation but not for regular use by the institution. In this case, an alternative test – the test being validated – is needed. The second answer is that once a new exam has been validated, examination boards often need to bring out regular new versions. (The construction of such equivalent forms of a test is discussed briefly in Chapter 4.) If students take both the new version and a previously validated version, and if the ensuing correlation index between the two sets of scores is high, say above .90, then the new version can be described as having concurrent validity.

However, it is often the case that no test which is known to be valid and reliable is available for the purposes of concurrent validation, yet one does wish to know how the experimental test compares with other tests that are known and used in that particular context, even though their reliability and validity are unknown. In such cases, one is obliged to treat the results of any correlation of the experimental test with the other test very cautiously indeed. Certainly one would not expect the two tests not to correlate at all, since they presumably both test language. Yet one might not expect a high correlation between the two, partly because they are presumably testing different aspects of language ability, and partly because of the possible unreliability and uncertain validity of the other test. In such circumstances, careful judgement is needed!

As well as comparing test results with other test scores, it is frequently useful to compare them with other measures of the students' abilities. One useful measure is teachers' rankings. If the teachers have all taught the same groups of students for some considerable time, they should have a good idea of the students' levels of proficiency and may be able to rank them in order according to some aspect of their language ability. As long as the skill to be rated is comparatively easy to rate, for example 'oral fluency', then the teacher's rankings may give a fair idea of the levels of ability of all the students in the class, but some linguistic areas, such as the receptive skills of reading and listening, may be almost impossible to rate. Since teachers are themselves not necessarily consistent and free from bias, the rankings will always be more valid and reliable if at least two teachers rank a group of students.

Another method of carrying out validation studies is to correlate the students' scores with teachers' ratings of their performance. For example, language teachers might be asked to fill in this form:

How would you assess each student on a scale of 1 to 5 for each of the following skills: grammar, writing, speaking, overall language proficiency?

Student	Grammar	Writing	Speaking	Lang. Proficiency
01				
02				
03				

etc.

The 1 to 5 scale might be a very simple one such as:

1.	Weak
2.	Fairly good
3.	Good
4.	Very good
5.	Like a native speaker

or a more complex one with individual descriptors for each of the levels for each of the skills. (For more about such descriptors see Chapter 5.)

The above kind of form can also be used for self-assessment, though it must be remembered that students may not be as accustomed to rating their language ability as the teachers are. Overleaf are two examples of part of a self-assessment questionnaire.

Example 1:

The following are areas of possible language problems you might have if you were studying French in France. Please indicate whether you think you would have serious difficulties 'very often', 'often', 'sometimes', 'rarely' or 'never'; or whether you think 'this will not apply' because you would not be using French for this purpose whilst in France. Please circle the number in the column which corresponds to your answer:

I expect to have serious problems:	very often	often	some-times	rarely	never	does not apply
Listening to and understanding lectures						
Listening to and understanding the media (TV, radio)						
Understanding people in shops, in public places						
etc.						

Example 2:

How do you assess your ability to use French in the following areas? Please circle the number which describes your ability best.

READING

Not nearly well enough to survive		Just well enough to survive		Very well		With near-native competence
1	2	3	4	5	6	7

8.4.2 Predictive validity

As the name suggests, this type of validity differs from concurrent validity in that instead of collecting the external measures at the same time as the administration of the experimental test, the external measures will only be gathered some time after the test has been given.

Predictive validation is most common with proficiency tests: tests which are intended to predict how well somebody will perform in the future. The simplest form of predictive validation is to give students a test, and then at some appropriate point in the future give them another test of the ability the initial test was intended to predict. A common use for a proficiency test like IELTS or the TOEFL is to identify students who might be at risk when studying in an English-medium setting because of weaknesses in their English. Predictive validation would involve giving students the IELTS test before they leave their home country for overseas study, and then, once they have all arrived in the host study setting and had time to settle down, giving them a test of their use of English in that study setting. A high correlation between the two scores would indicate a high degree of predictive validity for the IELTS test.

Unfortunately, life is never so simple. Firstly, it is unlikely that all students taking the IELTS test would be able to travel to the overseas study setting: some would be excluded because of poor test performance. This is known as the 'truncated sample problem': you can only use a part of the original test population in the validation – in this case, those who can be used will be the better students. The effect of using truncated samples is not well known for such tests, but it is likely to reduce the spread of students' scores, and to depress the predictive validity coefficient. Had all the students been allowed to enter English-medium education instead of only the best students, the correlation between the two tests would have been higher. Secondly, it is likely that in our hypothetical example, the language proficiency of our students might have improved between the first and the second occasions, especially once they had arrived in the host country. This would also have the effect of depressing the predictive validity coefficient. Thirdly, as with concurrent validity, it is unlikely that a suitable external measure of the students' ability to use English in the study setting would be available, unless it were another version of the original test.

Indeed, this latter problem bedevils many predictive validity studies: what can one take as a good measure of the skill one is trying to predict? Some validation studies of proficiency tests use the class of degree or Grade Point Average (GPA) that the students get at the end of their studies. However, not only are such studies obviously using truncated samples, the results of any correlations are obscured by the fact that the class of degree/GPA reflects not only language ability, but also academic abilities, subject knowledge, perseverance, study skills, adaptability to the host culture and context, and many other variables.

It is possible to use other measures than the class of degree/GPA. One might attempt, for example, to gather the opinions of those who come into regular contact with the students. The test validator might ask subject tutors to rate the students who have taken the test on their language abilities: their writing ability, their oral communicative abilities, and so on. Here again, though, there may be only a truncated sample available. There will also be the problem that many tutors are simply unable to give a useful opinion about their students' language abilities until perhaps the end of the first term, by which time the students will have had ample opportunity to improve their language (see Criper and Davies 1988 and Wall, Clapham and Alderson 1994). The resulting correlations are very difficult to interpret.

Another example of a predictive validation study might be the validation of a test of language competence for student teachers of that language. In this example, such students have to pass the test before they are allowed to enter the Teaching Practice component of their course, during which they will need a high level of foreign language competence. Predictive validation of the test involves following up those students who pass the test, and getting their pupils, their fellow teachers and their teacher-observers to rate them for their language ability in the classroom. The predictive validity of the test would be the correlation between the test results and the ratings of their language ability in class.

In all such circumstances we would not expect high correlations between the test and the external measure. In fact, in predictive validity studies, it is common for test developers and researchers to be satisfied when they have achieved a coefficient as low as +.3! Nevertheless, the difficulty of conducting predictive validation studies does not absolve test developers from the responsibility of gathering data to show that their tests possess a degree of validity for the purposes for which they are intended and used.

Sometimes the demarcation between concurrent and predictive validation is very slight. For example, after giving students a placement test, testers may seek to confirm the test's validity by asking the teachers into whose classes the students are placed whether their students are in the correct class. Teachers would generally be asked for their comments during the first week of class, before the students had had time to improve, so the validation could be considered to be both concurrent and predictive.

In many circumstances where tests are developed, it is impractical if not impossible to gather external data on test candidates. It may be that the testing institution has no control over or access to students once they have taken the test; it may be that no relevant criteria are imaginable, given the diversity of reasons for which students take the test; or it may simply be that no resources are available for special validation studies. In such cases it may still be useful to conduct a study of the test itself, in order to see how the various components interrelate and thereby to throw some light on what the test is testing. This will be discussed below under construct validity.

8.5 Construct validity

We have left the discussion of construct validity to last, partly because it is the most difficult concept to explain, and partly because some testers believe that it is a superordinate form of validity to which internal and external validity contribute. Ebel and Frisbie 1991 give the following explanation of construct validity:

> The term *construct* refers to a psychological construct, a theoretical conceptualisation about an aspect of human behaviour that cannot be measured or observed directly. Examples of constructs are intelligence, achievement motivation, anxiety, achievement, attitude, dominance, and reading comprehension. Construct validation is the process of gathering evidence to support the contention that a given test indeed measures the psychological construct the makers intend it to measure. The goal is to determine the meaning of scores from the test, to assure that the scores mean what we expect them to mean.

(page 108)

A shorter explanation is provided by Gronlund 1985, who describes construct validation as measuring 'How well test performance can be interpreted as a meaningful measure of some characteristic or quality' (page 58).

8.5.1 Comparison with theory

To some test theorists, construct validity is a form of test validation which essentially involves assessing to what extent the test is successfully based upon its underlying theory. Note that in this approach the theory itself is not called into question: it is taken for granted. The issue is whether the test is a successful operationalisation of the theory. In effect, this form of construct validation proceeds much as does content validation: experts are selected, given some definition of the underlying theory, and asked to make judgements after an inspection of the test as to its construct validity.

8.5.2 Internal correlations

As we mentioned above, one way of assessing the construct validity of a test is to correlate the different test components with each other. Since the reason for having different test components is that they all measure something different and therefore contribute to the overall picture of language ability attempted by the test, we should expect these correlations to be fairly low – possibly in the order of +.3 – +.5. If two components correlate very highly with each other, say +.9, we might wonder whether the two subtests are indeed testing different traits or skills, or whether they are testing essentially the same thing. If the latter is the case, we might choose to drop one of the two. The correlations between each subtest and the whole test, on the other hand, might be expected, at least according to classical test theory, to be higher – possibly around +.7 or more – since the overall score is taken to be a more general measure of language ability than each individual component score. Obviously if the individual component score is included in the total score for the test, then the correlation will be partly between the test component and itself, which will artificially inflate the correlation. For this reason it is common in internal correlation studies to correlate the test components with the test total *minus* the component in question.

TABLE 9.1 INTER-SUBTEST CORRELATION MATRIX

	Reading	Proficiency	Writing	Oral	Total	Total minus self
Reading	-	.53	.27	.44	.73	.50
Proficiency	.53	-	.43	.66	.84	.72
Writing	.27	.43	-	.45	.66	.46
Oral	.44	.66	.45	-	.86	.66
Total	.73	.84	.66	.86	-	-

n = 2,443

Data taken from Alderson, Wall and Clapham 1986.

In the above correlation matrix the highest correlation is between the Proficiency subtest, which consisted of a series of cloze and c-tests, and the Oral subtest (.66). The correlation is above what might be hoped for if the tests are genuinely testing different skills, but the overlap is not so great that the test writers might wish to drop one of the two subtests. All the subtests except for Writing have correlations with the total test of above .7. The fact that the Writing correlation is on the low side (.66) may be accounted for by the fact that this subtest proved to be unreliable, and correlations between unreliable tests lead to low correlation coefficients as the results are partly due to chance. The correlations of Proficiency and Oral with the Total are over .8. This shows that both these components have a strong effect on the final total score. When each of these is correlated with the total score minus itself, the correlations are reduced to .72 and .66. These are still the strongest correlations between the subtests and the total, and show how important these two subtests are in the test battery.

A somewhat more refined version of this construct validation procedure is to make theoretical predictions about the relationships among test components in the light of the requirements of the underlying theory, and then to compare these predictions with the correlation coefficients.

8.5.3 Comparisons with students' biodata and psychological characteristics

Another form of construct validation which is commonly undertaken is to compare test performance with biodata and other data gathered from students at the time they took the test. The intention is to detect bias in the test for or against groups of students defined by these biodata characteristics – gender, age, first language, number of years studying the language, and so on. The prediction would be that a valid test would be more difficult for students who had been studying the language for a shorter period of time, or whose first language was less closely related to the language of the test than other students, and so on.

An alternative might be to compare performance on the test with theoretically relevant psychological measures. One might wish to validate an aptitude test, for example, by comparing performance on one component, which is to test grammatical sensitivity, with some measure of inductive language learning ability which was theoretically thought to be related.

Note that these validation procedures are similar to the internal and external validities we have discussed above. The difference is that the rationale for the selection of the relevant aspects of the students' history or psychological characteristics is derived from theory.

8.5.4 Multitrait-multimethod analysis and convergent-divergent validation

More complex procedures for construct validation involve somewhat sophisticated uses of statistics and are beyond the scope of this book.

The interested reader is referred to Kerlinger 1973 and Wood 1991 for more detailed explanations. It is nevertheless probably useful to outline two of these approaches here.

What Bachman 1990 calls the 'classic approach to designing correlational studies for construct validation' is the *multitrait-multimethod matrix (MTMM)* described by Campbell and Fiske 1959. This consists of a combination of internal and external validation procedures. The theory is that tests that are related to each other will show higher intercorrelations (convergent validity) than tests that are not related to each other (divergent validity). Students are given the experimental test at the same time as other tests, some of whose properties are already known (as in concurrent validation). Wood 1991 gives a very clear explanation of multitrait-multimethod analysis, and variants on this procedure can be seen in multitrait-multimethod studies such as those by Bachman and Palmer 1981, 1982.

8.5.5   Factor analysis

Another approach is some form of *factor analysis*. What factor analysis does is to take a matrix of correlation coefficients, which is typically too complex to understand by superficial study, and to reduce the complexity of such a matrix to more manageable proportions by statistical means. The result of such reduction is normally a small number of factors. The different tests being compared in the original correlation matrix will relate in different ways to (technically known as 'loading on') the various factors.

There are two main varieties: one is exploratory factor analysis (EFA) and the other is confirmatory factor analysis (CFA). In the former, EFA, one simply explores the data to try and make sense of the factors that emerge: this is usually done by looking at which tests relate most closely to which factors and labelling the factors accordingly. In the latter, CFA, the researcher predicts which tests or components will relate to which others and how, and then carries out tests of 'goodness of fit' of the predictions with the data. The reason that these two factor analytic approaches belong to the class of construct validation procedures is that the factors that emerge are explained or predicted on the basis of theory – in this case one's applied linguistic theory of what should relate to what.

8.6   Reliability and validity

The relationship between reliability (see Chapters 1, 4 and 6) and validity is in principle a simple one, but in practice rather complex and not well understood.

In principle, a test cannot be valid unless it is reliable. If a test does not measure something consistently, it follows that it cannot always be measuring it accurately. On the other hand, it is quite possible for a test to be reliable but invalid. A test can, for example, consistently give the same results, although it is not measuring what it is supposed to. Therefore, although reliability is needed for validity, it alone is not sufficient. The problem for most language testers is that in order to maximise reliability it is often necessary to reduce validity. Thus multiple-choice tests can be made highly reliable, especially if they contain enough items, yet some testers would argue that performance on a multiple-choice test is not a highly valid measure of one's ability to use language in real life. To take a rather extreme example, it is possible to construct a written multiple-choice test of pronunciation which is highly reliable but which fails to identify students whose actual pronunciation is good or bad (see Buck 1989). On the other hand it is possible to conduct an oral test of pronunciation which is highly valid, but which may be difficult to mark reliably. Some people would argue that reliability must be sacrificed to achieve validity. Yet we cannot have validity without reliability. In practice, neither reliability nor validity are absolutes: there are degrees of both, and it is commonplace to speak of a trade-off between the two – you maximise one at the expense of the other. Which you choose to maximise will depend upon the test's purpose and the consequences for individuals of gaining an inaccurate result.

The analysis of correlations between subtests provides a good example of the contrary pressures of reliability and validity. We said above that it was generally best to have low correlations between subtests since each subtest was presumably intended to test a different skill or trait. However, what we did not mention was that the lower these intercorrelations, the less homogeneous the items in the whole test, and therefore the lower the correlations between individual items, and the lower the internal consistency reliability index of the whole test. So a high measure of construct validity may entail low internal consistency.

However, if a test contains items which are not homogeneous, does this mean that the test is genuinely unreliable? It may have a low internal consistency index because it is measuring different traits in the same test, but it may be measuring these traits consistently. If this is the case, the internal consistency index does not seem to be a suitable test of reliability. However, since it gives an indication of whether one or more than one traits are being measured, it may, perversely, be a useful measure of validity. Here then is an example of a reliability index which can be used as an index of validity. This raises two issues. The first is that the concepts of reliability and validity are not always as distinct as we might suppose. The second is that when we calculate a particular reliability index we need to know what that index is telling us so that we can know whether it is appropriate for our purposes. In the case of tests with an intentional spread of heterogeneous items therefore, where we might expect a low internal consistency index, we might argue that the internal consistency index should only be calculated for the separate subtests, and that for the whole test battery it is better to use the parallel forms method of checking reliability as described in Chapter 4.3 and 4.5. With that method it does not matter how many traits are being tested, as long as each complete test tests the same thing. If the two tests correlate highly, then the test is reliable.

However, here again we have a problem distinguishing between reliability and validity. In order to know that the second test is genuinely parallel with the first, we have to correlate the results of the two tests, thus carrying out a concurrent validation of the second test. What then is the difference between this correlation, which is supposedly checking concurrent validity, and the parallel forms correlation, which is supposedly checking reliability? The answer is that there is no difference: it is impossible in this case to distinguish between validity and reliability. (For further discussion see Alderson 1991 and Swain 1993.)

The above blurring between validity and reliability may lead the tester to wonder whether it is worth calculating reliability after all. Let us hasten to say that it is. Whether a particular process is concerned with reliability or validity does not ultimately matter: what is important is that we are aware of the issues involved. Since a test cannot be valid without being reliable, it is essential that tests are checked in as many ways as possible to ensure that they are reliable, and if some of those ways might be considered to be checking validity rather than reliability, at least they are adding to our knowledge of the test. What matters eventually is whether the test yields a score which can be shown to be a fair and accurate reflection of the candidate's ability.

8.7 Survey of EFL Examination Boards: Questionnaire

At the beginning of this chapter we introduced validity by saying that it was the most important question of all in language testing. Not only do we need to ensure that the material included in a test is appropriate for the purpose for which it is intended, but we need to check whether the results are accurate. Is the test passing and failing the right students? In his book, *Assessment and Testing*, Wood has doubts about the UK examination boards' validation procedures, and says:

> If an examining board were to be asked point blank about the validities of its offerings, or, more to the point, what steps it takes to validate the grades it awards, what might it say?

(Wood 1991: 147)

We are now in a position to make some attempt at answering that question.

QUESTION 25: *In addition to the above procedures for face and content validation* (see Chapter 3, Questions 16–19), *are any of the following types of validity a) applicable b) estimated or calculated?*

Five boards either did not answer this question or just wrote an explanatory note. Of those who responded, the answers were as follows:

	Applicable		Estimated	
i) concurrent validity	Yes	6	Yes	6
ii) predictive validity	Yes	4	Yes	2
iii) construct validity	Yes	4	Yes	4

One board provided no responses but added the comment: 'We would require further information on the meaning of these questions and the purpose in asking them'. Another board, also failing to provide detailed responses, nevertheless said:

> The senior examiners might have expectations about the performance of candidates on individual questions, on the components they are specifically responsible for and the test as a whole. Any such assumptions are tested against the actual statistics of the examination prior to decisions being taken on the award of grades. The awarding process also considers individual cases where there are major variations in performance on the different elements of the test.

Yet another board replied that this question was not applicable, since theirs was an oral test. This, of course, is nonsense.

No details were requested, nor in most cases given, as to how these validities were estimated or calculated, but LCCI responded that the validities are estimated 'in impressionistic and anecdotal ways, not mathematically, yet'.

One board did give brief details. On concurrent validity it said 'As data becomes available we conduct comparability studies with TOEFL and UCLES, and comparability with our own [other test for overseas students] is a standard feature of our award procedure at the upper levels.' With respect to construct validity, the board replied, 'The tests are graded in six levels with specific skills tested in each' and noted that predictive validity studies were 'planned, but numbers are as yet too small to provide reliable statistics'. Another board replied that some validities were estimated but not for all exams; however, 'companies and universities using the exams seem happy'. This would seem to refer to face validity.

One detailed response was given by one board as follows:

i) *Concurrent validity*. In a sense concurrent validity is applicable. In fact there have been several pieces of research comparing [the exams] with 'face-to-face' interviews. Most recently there is an ongoing Ph.D. study [student named] to compare performances by candidates in one of our more recent [exams] with results obtained from oral interviews.

ii) *Predictive validity*. A number of organisations use [the exams] to predict ability of individuals to perform in the workplace. For example [x company] require personnel to pass [the exam] before they are allowed to work on international exchanges. Similarly, promotion to 'international' clerical grades in [y company] requires a pass in [the exam] and all teachers in [z country] are also required to demonstrate this same level of oral proficiency. We have never statistically estimated the validity of the exam as a predictor but assume that, as these organisations appear to have been satisfied with the results over many years (12 in the case of [y]), the exam must have the predictive validity we would expect.

Five of the UCLES subject officers did not answer this question so it was difficult to get an overall picture of what happened with UCLES exams. However, from a survey of those who did respond it seems that there was wide variation from exam to exam, and from paper to paper. The Writing/Composition papers in three of the exams and one Use of English paper were checked for concurrent and construct validation, but there were no validation studies of the corresponding Reading, Listening and Speaking papers. Four of the other exams were not systematically validated, but one of these, IELTS, did undergo special validation studies.

From the above answers it seems that some of the boards are not familiar with the methods of assessing validation which are described in this chapter, and that in at least one case a board is not familiar with our use of the term 'validity'. This does not mean, of course, that validity is not being assessed under some other guise, but it does show a lack of awareness of standard terms and procedures in educational measurement.

QUESTION *26: Are special validity studies conducted on your examinations? If Yes, please attach details.*

Five boards said such studies were carried out, although for at least one board this must be doubted as the response explained that, 'Moderating sessions are held throughout the year attended by Assessors'.

In the case of another board, these validity studies were said to take place 'upon review of the scheme', but no further details were given.

The AEB referred to Weir 1983.

One board said that no special studies were conducted but nevertheless said, 'Some Ph.D. studies have used [the exams] as the basis.' It also claimed, 'The English-Speaking Union has validated the examinations.' It should be stressed that this ESU approval does not amount to test validation in the sense we use the term in this chapter.

One board's response was 'a number of projects are under way'.

The only board to provide us with some account of validity studies was the LCCI who, whilst stating that the studies were 'confidential to the Board', said that 'some findings may be published' and attached an article as an example.

QUESTION *27: If different versions of your examination are given each year, are measures taken to ensure that they are equivalent?*

The board's answers were: Yes – 9; No – 1; Not applicable – 2.

When asked to describe the measures taken, various responses were forthcoming.

Two of the boards made use of the statistical analysis of results (one of these specified Rasch analysis) and the rest depended on the views of editing or moderating committees. Five of the boards stressed the fact that the same setters and moderators were used for all test versions, or that all tests for a year were moderated at a single session.

One board gave a more detailed response:

> The paper structure is similar for all examinations at the same level. Grade levels are fixed points. Apart from the post-examination internal standardisation checks, our experienced examiners would notice if any section in a paper was easier or more difficult than in previous papers.

QUESTION *28: Is more than one form of any examination paper given in any examination period? If Yes, what steps are taken to ensure that each form is equivalent in difficulty?*

The board's answers were: Yes – 5; No – 5.

The steps taken to ensure equivalence of difficulty across forms were largely the same as those detailed above in response to Question 27.

The three exceptions were:

1. By standardisation and assessment criteria.
2. This is covered by the moderating procedure. Should any discrepancies appear in performances of candidates it would be dealt with in deciding the grade boundaries at the award meeting.
3. [The Board] operates an 'on-demand' system, so that normally centres may choose the time and date for holding exams. Vetting panel ensures comparability and appropriacy of items. Level of difficulty determined by format of exams.

It seems from the answers to Questions 27 and 28 that most of the boards do not carry out statistical checks on the equivalence of their exams. On the whole they trust their moderating and editing committees to be able to set equivalent exams and to identify any sections which are too easy or too difficult.

8.8 Survey Of EFL Examination Boards: Documentation

The only documents we were sent which related to validity were a confidential report from UCLES which discussed different ways of carrying out validation studies, and an LCCI document produced in March 1989 called *Policy and Practice for Assessment: A Guide for Examiners and Assessors*. This pamphlet gives details of the policies and practices which should guide the Institute's testing activities. It describes what the Institute does and why it does it. A section of the document is devoted to issues of reliability and validity.

8.9 Discussion

We saw in Chapter 3 that most of the boards spend a lot of time and care constructing their test items and concentrating on issues relating to face and content validity. However, with one or two exceptions, it appears from the results of our survey that they do not check whether their exams are valid in practice. In the same way that many of the boards trust individual items to work well without any pretesting, so they appear to trust their exams to be valid without any empirical confirmation.

It is worth quoting Wood's comments on the validation procedures of UK examining boards. Note that these comments referred to UK exams boards in general and not just to EFL ones.

The examining boards have been lucky not to have been engaged in the validity argument. Unlike reliability, validity does not lend itself to sensational reporting. Nevertheless, the extent of the boards' neglect of validity is plain to see once attention is focused. Whenever boards make claims that they are measuring the ability to make clear reasoned judgements, or the ability to form conclusions (both examples from IGCSE Economics), they have a responsibility to at least attempt a validation of the measures ... . The boards know so little about what they are assessing that if, for instance, it were to be said that teachers (?tests) assess ability (intelligence) rather than achievement, the boards would be in no position to defend themselves.

(Wood 1991: 151)

From our discussion of validity it must be clear that validating tests, and in particular carrying out external methods of validation, is time-consuming and difficult. However, we cannot take a test's validity on trust. We must do our best to check that a test is really testing what it is supposed to and that it is testing it in an accurate way.

8.10 Checklist

'Types' of Validity	Procedures for Evaluation
Internal Validity	
Face Validity	Questionnaires to, interviews with candidates, administrators and other users.
Content Validity	a) Compare test content with specifications/syllabus.
	b) Questionnaires to, interviews with 'experts' such as teachers, subject specialists, applied linguists.
	c) Expert judges rate test items and texts according to precise list of criteria.
Response Validity	Students introspect on their test-taking procedures, either concurrently or retrospectively.
External Validity	
Concurrent Validity	a) Correlate students' test scores with their scores on other tests.
	b) Correlate students' test scores with teachers' rankings.

	c) Correlate students' test scores with other measures of ability such as students' or teachers' ratings.
Predictive Validity	a) Correlate students' test scores with their scores on tests taken some time later.
	b) Correlate students' test scores with success in final exams.
	c) Correlate students' test scores with other measures of their ability taken some time later, such as subject teachers' assessments, language teachers' assessments.
	d) Correlate students' scores with success of later placement.

Construct Validity

a) Correlate each subtest with other subtests.
b) Correlate each subtest with total test.
c) Correlate each subtest with total minus self.
d) Compare students' test scores with students' biodata and psychological characteristics.
e) Multitrait-multimethod studies.
f) Factor analysis.

Bibliography

Alderson, J.C. 1988b. New Procedures for Validating Proficiency Tests of ESP? Theory and Practice. *Language Testing* 5(2): 220–232.

Alderson, J.C. 1990. Testing Reading Comprehension Skills (Part Two): Getting Students to Talk about Taking a Reading Test (A Pilot Study). *Reading in a Foreign Language* 7(1): 465–502.

Alderson, J.C. 1991. Dis-sporting Life. In J.C. Alderson and B. North. (eds.), *Language Testing in the 1990s*. London: Macmillan.

Alderson, J.C. 1993. Judgements in Language Testing. In D. Douglas and C. Chapelle, *A New Decade of Language Testing Research*. Alexandria, Virginia: TESOL.

Alderson, J.C. and Y. Lukmani. 1989. Cognition and Levels of Comprehension as Embodied in Test Questions. *Reading in a Foreign Language* 5(2): 253–270.

Alderson, J.C. and B. North (eds.). 1991. *Language Testing in the 1990s*. London: Macmillan.

Alderson, J.C., D. Wall and C.M. Clapham. 1986. *An Evaluation of the National Certificate in English*. Centre for Research in Language Education, Lancaster University.

American Psychological Association. 1985. *Standards for Educational and Psychological Testing*. New York: American Psychological Association.

Bachman, L.F. 1990. *Fundamental Considerations in Language Testing*. Oxford: Oxford University Press.

Bachman, L.F., A.Kunnan, S.Vanniariajan and B.Lynch. 1988. Task and Ability Analysis as a Basis for Examining Content and Construct Comparability in Two EFL Proficiency Test Batteries. *Language Testing* 5: 128–160.

Bachman, L.F. and A.S. Palmer. 1981. A Multitrait-Multimethod Investigation into the Construct Validity of Six Tests of Listening and Reading. In A.S. Palmer, P.J.M. Groot and G.A. Trosper (eds.), *The Construct Validation of Tests of Communicative Competence*. Washington, DC: TESOL.

Bachman, L.F. and A.S. Palmer. 1982. The Construct Validation of Some Components of Communicative Proficiency. *TESOL Quarterly* 16(4): 449–465.

Buck, G. 1989. Written Tests of Pronunciation: Do They Work? *English Language Teaching Journal* 41: 50–56.

Campbell, D.T. and D.W. Fiske. 1959. Convergent and Discriminant Validation by the Multitrait-Multimethod Matrix. *Psychological Bulletin* 56: 81–105.

Carroll, B.J. 1980. *Testing Communicative Performance*. London: Pergamon.

Carroll, B.J. 1985. Second Language Performance Testing for University and Professional Contexts. In P.C. Hauptman, R. LeBlanc and M.B. Wesche (eds.), *Second Language Performance Testing*. Ottawa: University of Ottawa Press.

Clapham, C.M. 1992. The Effect of Academic Discipline on Reading Test Performance. Paper given at the Language Testing Research Colloquium, Princeton, NJ.

Cohen, A.D. 1984. On Taking Tests: What the Students Report. *Language Testing* 1(1): 70–81.

Criper, C. and A. Davies. 1988. *ELTS Validation Project Report, ELTS Research Report 1(i)*. London and Cambridge: The British Council and University of Cambridge Local Examinations Syndicate.

Ebel, R.L and D.A. Frisbie. 1991. *Essentials of Educational Measurement*. Englewood Cliffs, NJ: Prentice-Hall.

Faerch, C. and G. Kasper. 1987. *Introspection in Second Language Research*. Clevedon: Multilingual Matters.

Gronlund, N.E. 1985. *Measurement and Evaluation in Teaching*. New York: Macmillan.

Grotjahn, R. 1986. Test validation and cognitive psychology: some methodological considerations. *Language Testing* 3(2): 159–185.

Henning, G. 1987. *A Guide to Language Testing.* Cambridge, Mass.: Newbury House.

Ingram, E. 1977. Basic Concepts in Testing. In J.P.B. Allen and A. Davies (eds.), *Testing and Experimental Methods.* Oxford: Oxford University Press.

Kerlinger, F.N. 1973. *Foundations of Behavioral Research.* New York: Holt, Rinehart and Winston.

Morrow, K. 1979. Communicative Language Testing: Revolution or Evolution? In C.J. Brumfit and K. Johnson (eds.), *The Communicative Approach to Language Teaching.* Oxford: Oxford University Press.

Morrow, K. 1986. The Evaluation of Tests of Communicative Performance. In M. Portal (ed.), *Innovations in Language Testing.* Windsor, Berks: NFER-Nelson.

Stevenson, D.K. 1985. Authenticity, Validity and a Tea Party. *Language Testing* 2(1): 41–7.

Swain, M. 1993. Second Language Testing and Second Language Acquisition: Is There a Conflict with Traditional Psychometrics? *Language Testing* 10(2): 193–207.

Thorndike, R.L. and E.P. Hagen. 1986. *Measurement and Evaluation in Psychology and Education.* New York: Macmillan.

Wall, D., C.M. Clapham and J.C. Alderson. 1994. Evaluating a Placement Test. *Language Testing* 11(3): 321–343.

Weir, C.J. 1983. *Identifying the Language Problems of Overseas Students in Tertiary Education in the UK.* Ph.D. thesis, University of London.

Wood, R. 1991. *Assessment and Testing: A Survey of Research.* Cambridge: Cambridge University Press.

9 Post-test reports

This chapter discusses why it is important to write reports after a test has been produced and administered. Reports will have a number of different audiences, and the desirable features of reports for each of these audiences are described in some detail.

9.1 The importance of post-test reports

Tests can have important consequences for those who take them, and for those who use the results. It is therefore incumbent upon those who produce the tests to provide all the evidence they can muster for the validity, reliability and meaningfulness of their tests and the results. The issue of accountability is beginning to be discussed in language-testing circles, although no formal standards specific to language tests have yet been developed or agreed by those responsible for developing or researching language tests. Nevertheless, it is clear that pressures will mount for such standards to be developed and for test producers to report on their instruments (see Chapter 11).

In addition, much time and energy are devoted to preparing language tests, and much can be learned from all stages of the testing process. It is therefore important for institutions to keep records of their decisions, their procedures, the analyses that they conduct on test results and the feedback they receive, and to pass information on to the audiences that they consider appropriate.

The most obvious audience constitutes people working within the institution itself: those in charge of designing future versions of the tests and of coordinating related activities (pre-testing, administration, marking, and so on). These people will need detailed information to help them to make sound decisions about the institution's future practice.

Another obvious audience is the teachers who have prepared the current year's candidates and who will be preparing other students to take the test in future. These people will not need technical information so much as summaries of how well their students fared and advice about how to prepare their next group more effectively.

There are also other parties who may need information about tests: amongst these are administrators in other institutions who want to know whether to use the test or to accept its results, and professionals in language testing and related fields, who are interested in learning how different testing bodies deal with the classical challenges of validity, reliability and practicality.

Each institution must decide for itself which audiences it wishes to address and then consider the types of information that would be most useful for these audiences to receive. However, the issue of accountability is important, and we would argue that certain minimum information ought to be made publicly available for all interested parties.

In the sections which follow we shall discuss the kinds of information that each audience will be most interested in, and then we shall review the post-test reports we have received from examination boards to see whether and how they provide information for these audiences.

9.2 Post-test reports for the institution itself

A post-test report written for the testing body itself fills two functions:
1. It serves as a historical record of the test, stating how various aspects of the current test worked out in practice.
2. It serves as a guide for future test development, containing recommendations for improving aspects of the current test which did not work out well.

There are several types of information that an institution needs to collect and analyse in order to decide whether a test was satisfactory. The testing body should report the relevant statistics and its interpretation of the figures. It should also summarise what has been learnt from analysing notes taken during key procedures, examining feedback collected from important participants in the testing process and studying the candidates' performance.

9.2.1 Statistical information

It may not be possible for an institution to collect all the information it would like from all its candidates, especially if there are a very large number of them, but every effort should be made to collect data from at least a sample of the population. It is always wise to consult an educational statistician to determine an adequate sample size for a particular population, as well as to discuss the best method for choosing the sample.

The most important data to gather are the item results for each objective item and the marks given for each subjective section. With these it will be possible accurately to reconstruct total scores for sections of tests and for the complete test.

It is also important to collect the marks given by all the markers who participate in an inter-rater reliability study of the sort described in Chapter 6.

The analyses that should be reported are the following:

1. Descriptive statistics for the whole test and each of its components: histogram, mean, mode, median, range and standard deviation.
2. Item analysis for each objective item: facility value and discrimination index.
3. Correlations between the components, and correlations between each component and the total minus that component.
4. Reliability of each objective section.
5. Reliability of marking for each subjective section.

Details of how to carry out the first four analyses can be found in Chapter 4, and details of the fifth can be found in Chapter 6. The results should indicate whether different parts of the test were behaving as they should and if not, where the major problems seem to be. This statistical information can be combined with the types of information described below to determine whether sections of the test which appear problematic were intrinsically faulty or whether there were other factors, such as inadequate candidate preparation or a badly handled administration, that produced unexpected results.

Explanations of any problems should be given, along with recommendations about how to avoid such problems in future.

9.2.2 Results of observations

Observers should be present during the administration of the test, the training programme for examiners and the marking sessions. The observers should be given a list of specific features to look for when observing each type of procedure, and these should be printed out clearly on an observation instrument. The following are three of the questions that might appear on an observation instrument for test administration:

1. Invigilator checks candidates' identity cards.   Yes   No

    Problems: _____

2. Invigilator reads instructions twice.   Yes   No

Problems: _____

3. Invigilator can be heard by all.   Yes   No

Problems: _____

A summary should be written indicating whether the administration, training, marking, etc. went well and describing problems that might have influenced candidates' results either favourably or negatively. Examples of problems that might affect the outcome are:

> The invigilator does not prevent candidates from talking to each other during a written test. (The candidates may be exchanging information and/or disturbing the concentration of those around them.)
>
> The teacher who is dictating a passage to the candidates badly mispronounces several words. (The candidates cannot make sense of the passage and therefore misunderstand other well-pronounced words.)
>
> After the training meeting the Chief Examiner does not send the examiners a revised version of the rating scales for writing. (The examiners end up using the original rating scale, which contains 'fuzzy' concepts, unclear wording, etc., making it difficult for them to mark consistently.)
>
> During the marking of writing the examiners are allowed to write comments on the candidates' scripts. (The examiners who are to give the second marks for the scripts find themselves influenced by the first markers' comments.)

9.2.3 Results of feedback

Feedback should be collected from administrators, candidates, and examiners regularly, using questionnaires which ask about specific features of the test. For example:

1. Did you understand the instructions for
   Writing Task 1?   Yes   No

2. Was the word length about right?   Yes   No

Summaries of this feedback should be included in the report, along with recommendations about how to improve the procedures in future. Examples of the kinds of insight that can be gained through this feedback include:

The invigilators' instructions stated that the reading test was to last 30 minutes, while the instructions for the candidates stated that it was to last 35 minutes. (There was confusion during the last five minutes of the test as invigilators and candidates tried to sort out whose instructions were right.)

The test designer meant the test to cover the entire textbook, but most of the classes preparing for the test had got no further than the penultimate chapter. (This would not invalidate the test, but it would explain the candidates' poor performance on some of the items.)

The examiners did not like the rule stating that candidates who wrote at least six words would get at least a 1 on a rating scale of 5. (This might explain why there were many more 0 scores than expected.)

9.2.4 Analysis of candidates' scripts

This can be done either as an independent operation, by team leaders or the Chief Examiner, or as part of collecting feedback from examiners. The purpose of the analysis is to find out what kinds of problem candidates had with certain items or tasks. If, for example, an item analysis (see Chapter 4) reveals that a particular open-ended reading item is performing badly, it is worth going through the scripts of a large number of candidates to find out if there are any patterns in the 'incorrect' responses that would throw light on the source of the problem. It is not unusual for an analysis of candidate scripts to reveal problems in an item or task that might have escaped the attention of test designers and moderators alike. Examples of such problems are:

> The writing task asks the candidates to write a set of rules. Those who write good rules naturally use simple syntax, e.g. 'Wipe all spills'. Unfortunately, the rating scale does not allow anyone to receive a high score unless they use complex sentences. The consequence is that even the best writers obtain low scores.
>
> Many candidates answer an item which requires simple arithmetic incorrectly. The fact that so many give the same incorrect answer leads the analyst to realise that the source text contains an ambiguous sentence, which can legitimately be interpreted in a way that was not foreseen by the test designer.

An analysis of scripts will also reveal the problems of candidates who simply do not have the competence that is required to perform well. In these cases it may not be the test design which is at fault.

9.2.5 Analysis of candidate characteristics and the detection of bias

The institution may be interested in collecting background data from all of the candidates, in order to compare the performances of different groups of people. This type of comparison, which may be done by gender, region, first language, age, and so on, sometimes reveals bias in certain test items or tasks. For example, the analysis may reveal that young candidates perform worse than other candidates on sections of the test which assume background knowledge beyond their range of experience. Similarly, it may be found that candidates from a certain language background tend to have more trouble with certain item types than candidates from other language backgrounds. If the testing body makes discoveries of this sort, it will have to decide whether to continue using the same types of test or to change the tests to fit the candidates.

These decisions will depend on many factors. For example, if a testing body claims that a test is appropriate for all age ranges, then it might reconsider its use of items which can only be satisfactorily answered by older people. If, however, a test has always been promoted as one which is only appropriate for older people, then the fact that younger candidates perform worse should not be a matter of concern. In the case of a certain item type proving more difficult for candidates from a particular language background than for others, the testing body would need to consider whether the item type was the only way to test a certain type of knowledge, and whether this knowledge was an indispensable feature of the test. If so, then the testers and the group that had problems would have to accept that the test was 'fair' and that the group was just bound to have more problems. However, it might also be the case that another way could be found which tested the same type of knowledge but did not disadvantage one group over others.

9.2.6 Comparison with statistics from previous versions of the test

It is important for the institution to know how any one version of a test compares with previous versions: Was the test of equal difficulty? Was it as reliable as in previous years? Were the cut-off points the same? Was the distribution of scores similar? Although testers aim to produce tests which are of equivalent difficulty, and may devise pretesting and moderation procedures to ensure that this happens, any of the factors mentioned in the preceding sections, or others which are external to the test (political problems, for example), may produce unexpected results.

9.3 Post-test reports for teachers who prepare students for the test

The second obvious audience for a post-test report is made up of the teachers who have prepared students for the current version of the test and who will be preparing new students for future versions. As noted in Section 1, these teachers do not need technical information so much as summaries of the types of problem that candidates experienced on different parts of the test and advice about how to prepare candidates more effectively in future. Note that although we are referring to teachers in this section, there is no reason why this information should not also be available to students, either directly or through the teachers.

Teachers who are also responsible for administering tests will want to know whether there were administrative problems which affected candidate outcomes, and whether they (and their colleagues) need to pay more attention to certain administrative matters.

The types of information which teachers will want or need to understand are described in the following sections.

9.3.1 Statistical information concerning the test population and its performance on the test as a whole and the individual components.

This sort of information is not vital for teachers or students preparing for the test, but it is useful because it will give the students a better sense of how they fit in with the rest of the test population and of how their own performance compares with others'.

The information that would prove interesting for each test would be the following:

How many candidates were there for the test or for each level of the test? What were their characteristics – gender, nationality, first language, age, etc.?

What was the grade distribution – how many passes, credit passes and distinctions were there for each test or level of test?

What were the mean scores and standard deviations for each section of the test?

How are these figures different from those of the previous year?

The simplest way to give this type of information is in tables, with brief comments to help the readers to interpret what they are reading. These comments should address questions such as why the pass rate for this version is higher or lower than for the previous version, or why the proportion of candidates getting a certain grade did not change even though the test seemed more difficult than the previous version.

9.3.2 The marking key for objective items and the rating scales for subjective sections

It is not always obvious to teachers how test questions should be answered, nor how skills such as writing and speaking are marked. Since one common way of preparing students for tests is by using past papers, it is important for teachers to know whether answers that their students propose would have been considered 'acceptable' by the testing body.

It is also useful for testing bodies to reproduce samples of writing which represent different points on the rating scale, so that students as well as teachers can discuss what makes one piece of writing more effective than another.

9.3.3 The testers' discussion of each component of the test: what was being tested, typical problems and advice for how to prepare more effectively in future

This discussion should be written after taking into account all of the analyses mentioned in sections 9.2.1 to 9.2.6 above. It is of vital importance to teachers and students, and should make up the bulk of the report.

The testers should first make it clear what was being tested in each section.

Next they should indicate how candidates performed on each component and should note the types of problem which proved most difficult for the population or certain segments of the population. It is important to go into some detail here, but it is also important that general points should emerge from the detail. If the testers can see that the problems that candidates had with a specific item are related to problems they had with other items, then they should signal this clearly, partly because teachers may not see the connections (if they do not have access to the specifications for each item they may not be aware of what is being tested), but also because they may otherwise concentrate on teaching the specific forms that gave difficulty this time around rather than the broader categories of language which are likely to appear again in future versions of the test.

Lastly, the testers should give advice about the language and skills that candidates should focus on in future, or about techniques that would be useful for candidates to learn in order to improve their performance.

9.3.4   Acknowledgement of problems in the test itself

It is important for institutions to acknowledge when they have discovered problems in their tests. This often occurs after item analysis and the kinds of problem that might arise include ambiguous instructions, inclusion of language or skills not dealt with in the syllabus, etc. The fact that a testing body has made a mistake will not make a bad impression on the teachers or students if the testers make it clear that they treated the candidates fairly in the end.

9.3.5   Advice to teachers about administering the test

The term 'administration' covers a wide range of activities, from the registration of candidates to the delivery of their final marks, but the activities that teachers are most likely to be involved in are those which occur as the candidates are taking the test. Problems which commonly occur during listening tests include poor positioning of sound equipment, poor acoustics in the testing room or interference caused by noise in corridors or nearby rooms. Problems can also occur during speaking tests, especially (but not exclusively) if the tests involve more than one candidate at a time. Some problems arise because the teachers have not done their preparatory work well: they may not have made the candidates sufficiently aware of the procedures that need to be followed, or they may not have put them in groups or pairs that were compatible. Other problems arise, however, because the teachers lose track of time, give candidates excessive help, fail to observe security rules, etc. Sometimes, unfortunately, the teachers are not really aware of the proper procedures, especially if they have not received training in this area.

The post-test report can be an effective way of reminding teachers of these problems and of what they need to do to prevent further problems in future.

9.3.6   Information about forthcoming changes in the test or in testing procedures

Testing bodies may have good reasons for changing the overall shape of their tests, adjusting the weighting or modifying the language or skills content. The post-test report is a logical place for notifying teachers of the changes that will occur since it is the natural place for teachers to look for guidance when they are preparing new students for future versions of the test.

9.4 Post-test reports for other audiences

There are at least two further audiences for post-test reports: administrators who need to select a test or decide whether to accept the results of a test, and other professionals who wish to understand how institutions translate the principles of testing into practice.

The administrators that we have in mind may be employed in a number of places: schools, institutes of further education, business or industry. They may be in charge of selecting the tests that their students or employees will study for, or they may have to accept or reject potential students or employees on the basis of their test scores. In both cases the administrators will be interested in the same types of question:

> Does this test cover the types of language and skill that we are interested in?
> Is it suitable for the types of student/employee we are dealing with?
> What were the results of the test?
> How do our students' results compare with those of the rest of the population?
> Is the test valid?
> Is it reliable?

The other professionals that we have in mind may be teachers, testers or researchers, working in language education or in related fields. They will have different reasons for wanting to explore beneath the surface of the test they are interested in, but one reason which is fairly common is that they are looking for models to follow as they set up their own testing systems. The types of question they will need to ask are often detailed and sometimes technical:

> What methods have been used to validate the tests?
> What were the results of the validation studies?
> What methods have been used to determine the reliability of the test?
> What were the results of the reliability studies?
> What research has been done into or using this test?

In some countries, institutions which produce tests for external users are expected to provide a test manual, which contains information about the purpose of the test, the population it is intended for, its design and development, validation and reliability studies, and research in progress. Those who are interested in finding out whether a test is appropriate for their purposes or knowing what the test scores are meant to signify, refer first to the manual. The UK testing system does not use manuals as extensively as other systems (indeed, manuals are virtually non-existent), so those who need information on the validity and reliability of a test must look elsewhere. One possible place might be a post-test report. This report would not need to contain as much detail as reports for internal purposes, and would not have to analyse/evaluate candidates' performances in the way that reports for teachers do. It need not be excessively long, since its main purpose would be to inform its readers of the facts, not to serve as evidence for policy decisions or as teacher/learner training material.

9.5 Survey of EFL Examination Boards: Questionnaire

QUESTION 44: *Do Chief Examiners write reports? If so, are these made available a) to teachers, b) to students, c) on a restricted basis only?*

In this question we asked about Chief Examiners because we assumed that these were the people who would be in charge of gathering together all the information for what we refer to in this chapter as 'post-test reports'.

Of the twelve boards that responded, three reported that they produced reports that were for internal purposes only.

One board reported that it would begin producing a Chief Examiner's report the following year, which it intended to distribute to teachers in examining centres. These reports would be available to students in the centres.

The remaining eight boards responded that they already produced CE Reports which they either routinely or sometimes distributed to teachers; however, one of these boards seemed to be referring to the reports that they produce for their secondary school exams in other subjects, not their exams in EFL. This board sent us a copy of their reports for A level English and the Performing Arts: though the information therein was very thorough and probably useful for the audience it was intended for, it was not relevant to our survey.

9.6 Survey of EFL Examination Boards: Documentation

9.6.1 Post-test reports for the boards themselves

Unfortunately we were not sent internal reports produced by any of the EFL boards, so we are not able to comment on the functions these reports fill within the boards nor on the form they take. We do not know whether the boards keep records of the statistical properties of their tests, their observations of various procedures, the feedback they receive, their analyses of candidates' scripts, analyses to detect differing performances between groups of candidates, or test bias. We know that some boards keep track of candidates' performances from previous years because we have seen this information in reports for teachers; however, we know little more about the data that the boards analyse for themselves or about how they react in response to their analyses.

9.6.2 Post-test reports for teachers who prepare students for the test

Three boards sent us post-test reports for examinations they administered in either 1989 or 1990:

The JMB sent us a copy of their *Examiners' Reports 1990*, which covered the March 1990 and November 1990 versions of the UETESOL.

The Oxford Delegacy sent us their *Annual Report*, which covered the November 1989, March 1990 and May 1990 versions of the Oxford Examinations in English as a Foreign Language.

The Pitman Examinations Institute sent us their *Examinations Report 1989*, which included their English for Speakers of Other Languages examinations for that year.

The JMB and Oxford Delegacy reports were similar in that each board presented detailed comments about the exams in question. We have selected several examples from each of these boards to illustrate points we wish to make (see below).

The Pitman post-test report of its ESOL exam is not very detailed, probably because this exam is only one of approximately two dozen which are reported on in the same booklet.

We did not receive copies of post-test reports from any other boards and therefore cannot comment on their nature or effectiveness.

The purpose of the following sections is to review the types of information that would be useful for teachers who are preparing students for tests, and to present extracts from the post-test reports that we have received, to see how different boards attempt to cater for the teachers' needs.

STATISTICAL INFORMATION

In Section 9.2 we stated that teachers would be interested in four types of statistical information. We list here the questions we asked there, along with the information that was presented by either the JMB or the Oxford Delegacy.

1. How many candidates were there for the test or each level of the test? What were their characteristics – gender, nationality, first language, age, etc.?

The Oxford Delegacy report presents this information as follows:

TABLE 9.1 CANDIDATE ENTRY FOR OXFORD EXAMINATIONS, BY YEAR AND BY COUNTRY (PAGE 3)

The Oxford Examinations in English as a Foreign Language

Higher		Preliminary	
1988	2630	1988	6538
1989	3073	1989	6988

Entry figures by country

	Higher		Preliminary	
	1989	1988	1989	1988
Algeria	38	26	105	106
Argentina	25	57	277	268
Belgium	0	2	1	0
Brazil	579	435	219	138
Chile	2	36	95	0
etc.				

Here we can see that there are more entries for the Preliminary examination than for the Higher, and that the figures for each exam increased by about 400 over the course of the year being analysed. We can also see which parts of the world the examinations are most popular in and whether their popularity is increasing or decreasing. These figures will give the teachers and their students some notion of whether the exam is well known or important in their own part of the world, which might help them to decide whether to take it or not.

The boards provided no further details of their candidates.

2. What was the grade distribution – how many passes, credit passes and distinctions were there for each exam or level of exam?

None of the reports presented the number of candidates at each level; however, the JMB report presented the percentage of candidates achieving a given grade for each of the five skills tested (page 2).

3. What were the mean scores and standard deviations for each section of the test?

This information can be found in the JMB report, located just before a discussion of each individual section. This is illustrated in the following extract:

Section 3 Reading
(Maximum mark: 30, mean: 16.03, standard deviation: 5.52)

The two passages both produced a good spread of marks. Weak and moderate candidates tended to do adequately to well on the simple factual questions but performed badly on those requiring a broader understanding of the text. The two summary paragraphs were well done by only the best candidates ...

(Extract from an analysis of Section 3 of the UETESOL exam, March 1990, page 5)

The idea of presenting the statistical information at the beginning of the discussion of each test section is a good one as it helps readers to see the relationship between the figures and the information that follows.

4. How are these figures different from those of the previous year?

The Oxford Delegacy report presents tables with pass rates for four different versions of two examinations (page 2). What the table reveals is that the March 1990 version of both exams had a much lower pass rate than the other three versions. These figures could be taken to mean that the March 1990 exams were 'harder' than other versions. A revelation of this sort might be unsettling for the teachers who entered their candidates for the March versions; however, the board, in its introduction to the report, states that the low pass rate may be due to the nature of the population taking the test rather than to the test itself. We believe that providing information of this sort for teachers is positive; however, it is also important to know what analyses the board undertook to determine whether it was the population or the test questions which made the exam difficult.

THE MARKING SCHEMES FOR OBJECTIVE ITEMS AND THE RATING SCALES FOR SUBJECTIVE SECTIONS

The second function of these reports is to provide the correct response and the rating scales for writing and speaking. The JMB report was the only one we received which provided the marking schemes that were used by the examiners, along with amendments that had been made at standardisation meetings.

None of the reports we received provided the rating scale for writing. We know that at least one board, the Oxford Delegacy, presents a standard rating scale (which is used for all types of writing at every session of the exam), sample scripts and examiners' comments in another publication. However, it would still be useful to provide the rating scale in the post-test report so that all the information is available when teachers are reading the comments on the candidates' main problems.

THE TESTERS' DISCUSSION OF EACH COMPONENT OF THE TEST: WHAT WAS BEING TESTED, TYPICAL PROBLEMS, AND ADVICE FOR HOW TO PREPARE MORE EFFECTIVELY IN FUTURE

The third function of a report is to help teachers and students to understand what is being tested in each section of the paper. The JMB report gives several explanations of this sort: for example, this is an account of what is required in the writing section:

> In the first question of this section examiners are looking particularly for accurate command of simple sentence structures. To achieve a passing mark candidates must show a functional command of those verb forms, prepositional phrases, etc., which the actual question requires. In the second question the emphasis is on more macro elements such as organisation, coherence, development of ideas, argument, etc., though language is obviously an important factor ... (page 3)

It is especially useful for the board to explain the purpose behind new item types. JMB provides this explanation for an editing task which had not been used before:

> This type of question has been introduced to try to encourage better editing of final versions of written work. When a piece of writing has been revised to ensure that ideas and meaning are clearly and logically presented there are usually errors of concord, verb tense, prepositional use, spelling, etc. It is errors of this nature that have been left in or introduced into short sections of writing for this question type. In the real world the number or position of such items is not known by writers correcting their own work. However, for the purpose of the

examination at this time, there will always be some indication given to candidates when this type of question is included.

(page 5)

After explaining the purpose of each section the board should indicate the kinds of problem the candidates had for particular questions. This example comes from the Oxford Delegacy report:

> In Questions 3 to 6 on Paper 1, candidates often misunderstood the difference between writing notes and writing in note form. They should be aware of the difference – a 'note' should be brief and to the point, but should be written in complete sentences; 'note form' omits articles, some verbs, etc. and should only be used when specifically asked for – very rarely at Preliminary Level.

(page 5)

Here the board not only describes the problem that the candidates had, but also attempts to clarify the concept for teachers. Though not everyone would agree with the distinction that the board has given, it is clear that this is what the examiners will expect in future.

The JMB also provides clear criticism of candidate behaviour, albeit after acknowledging that there had been improvement in some aspects of performance over previous years:

> In this question it was noticeable that comments regarding the importance of well-organised and laid-out answers had been noted. In contrast to previous years it was encouraging that the vast majority of candidates provided introductions, paragraphed their answers and wrote some concluding statement.
>
> Unfortunately what came in between was often disappointing. Most candidates still do not know how to handle the reporting of and commenting on data which this question required. When the report is to accompany the data then the repetition of those data is not what a reader looks for. The reader is looking for the writer to interpret and comment on the data. That means noting any patterns or trends, picking out anomalies and selecting particularly interesting points ...

(page 4)

The implications of explicit criticism are often obvious but it is still useful when the boards spell out clearly the types of tuition the teachers should provide or the types of revision that the students should engage in.

The JMB report provides several interesting examples of how this can be done. In the case of the candidates who 'do not know how to handle the reporting of and commenting on data' (see above), they advise:

The language required for commenting on numerical or graphical data needs to be more explicitly taught ...

(page 4)

Later in the same report the board lists useful textbooks which the teacher could use to help candidates with these problems. This information is especially valuable to teachers who are not yet very experienced in preparing candidates for this exam.

ACKNOWLEDGEMENT OF PROBLEMS IN THE TEST ITSELF

The fourth function that post-test reports can fill is to let teachers and students know if there have been any problems in the test itself, and how the boards have coped with them. An example of fair treatment can be seen in the Oxford Delegacy report, where the board presents its evaluation of a particular item:

The only difficulty in May was with choice (b). The word 'appointment' was misinterpreted in many cases. As this is rather a difficult word at Preliminary level, candidates were not marked down if they misunderstood.

(page 4)

In the same report the board discusses the difficulty level of an entire section of the exam, which was harder than in other years:

Candidates found Paper 2 difficult in November, and due allowance was made for this in the examining and awarding processes.

(page 7)

The JMB also acknowledges its problems: in this example it admits that a particular paper was perhaps not as balanced as it could have been:

This section was more difficult than had been anticipated and so marks were adjusted accordingly ... . This particular paper had rather a heavy bias towards grammatical versus lexical items and this may have contributed towards the level of difficulty. Future papers are likely to be more balanced and vocabulary development through texts, dictionary work and a variety of activities is seen as important.

(page 12)

Admissions of this sort can save teachers and students time and trouble. In the examples presented above the problems were not so serious, but teachers might have been confused if they were using past papers for revision purposes and found them to be more difficult than the syllabus led them to believe. In other cases, though, it is even more important that institutions indicate when they have had problems, for example, when they have not edited instructions properly or when they have not noticed that certain items cannot be answered given the texts which the students are presented with. When this kind of mistake occurs, it can cause a great deal of frustration. We believe that the admission of error can help teachers and students a great deal and can enhance a board's reputation if the board makes clear that it has not penalised candidates for faults which are not of their own making.

ADVICE TO CENTRES ABOUT ADMINISTRATIVE MATTERS

The fifth function of the post-test report is to give advice about administrative matters, especially in listening and speaking tests.

The only example we could find of this in the EFL reports that we received was this paragraph from the JMB report, which stressed the need for good accommodation for speaking tests:

> The best accommodation for the test is the fairly intimate room where the candidate is not overwhelmed by size and distance, and where voices do not echo, which results in poor reproduction on the tape-recorder. If there is a neighbouring room available for waiting candidates, this is so much more pleasant than sitting in a corridor where there is a regular movement of the student population ...

(page 16)

However, we have found several good examples of this kind of advice in post-test reports from other subjects, most notably foreign languages. The following advice comes from a report on a Spanish speaking test and illustrates the types of administrative advice the boards could be providing:

> Although in general the standard of recording was good there were still some problems affecting the conduct of the tests.
>
> (i)   Instances of excessive background noise continue to give cause for concern. It is worth pointing out that the examiner can only mark what can be heard. Classes assembling outside the examination room, people interrupting the test and poor positioning of microphones were all factors affecting the audibility of candidates.
>
> (ii)   There were occasions when teachers departed from the given responses in Basic Level role-plays which led to confusion for candidates.
>
> (iii) There was insufficient preparation by some teachers for their part in Role-play 4 and evidence that some teachers do not understand that there are three tasks to be completed by the candidates. It must be appreciated that solving the problems for the candidates, failing to present the problems, introducing additional tasks, and

excessive prompting do not help the candidates.

(Northern Examining Association, Spanish: *Report on the 1990
Examination*, pages 5–6)

This board went on to list three more ways in which the teachers could improve their administration of role-plays. Although some of the advice might seem obvious to an outsider, it is equally obvious that the teachers did not understand or pay enough attention to the rules they were supposed to follow. The board has quite appropriately tried to remind teachers of how to do their job properly in order to help their own students.

INFORMATION ABOUT CHANGES IN THE EXAM OR EXAMINING PROCEDURES

We found many examples of this in the JMB report. The UETESOL exam had just undergone a major revision during the year that was being reported on, but it was clear that more changes were likely to occur in future versions of the exam. The board was careful to signal these possible changes to teachers and students, to give them time to adjust to new demands. This extract from the report concerns the listening section of the test:

It is hoped that teachers will continue to train their candidates to listen to a variety of aural information, in wide ranging contexts, so that they will be prepared for the lectures, the seminars, the individual tutorials which they will encounter in higher and further education, the context and style of which are increasingly reflected in the Listening Test.

(page 7)

9.6.3 *Post-test reports for other audiences*

Reports of the sort we described in Section 9.4 are not produced by the EFL boards. We had assumed that some of the information that administrators or other professionals would be interested in might be available somewhere in the many documents that we received from the boards, but the only information we found were statements about who the tests were intended for (in publicity material and syllabuses), the types of languages and skills that were tested, and distributions of candidate scores.

There was no information about the validity or reliability of any test in the information we received. We were disappointed that technical information of this sort either did not exist or was not available to us, and that we cannot point to any of the EFL boards as being a model for the distribution of information of this kind.

9.7 Discussion

Post-test reports are important for the reasons we discussed at the beginning of this chapter. Yet the evidence we have is that adequate reports on the performance of language tests – at least for EFL – are few and far between. We have quoted at some length from those reports we received because they provide good examples of what sorts of information ought to be available for different audiences and how that information might be presented. However, such reports are all too rare, and this is very much to be regretted. It may be that there has to date been little pressure upon those who produce tests to provide evidence of the validity and reliability of their instruments, but as we said at the beginning of the chapter, this is likely to change, and that can only be a change for the better. It may also be that there is little pressure from teachers for information about student performance because much of the candidature for the exams is from overseas, and thus is less able to apply effective pressure on examination boards. This is in contrast with UK-based teachers in the secondary school system who are able to press boards to provide adequate information to help those who prepare for the examinations. Since UK exam boards pride themselves on the relation between teaching and testing, it is further to be regretted that so few provide anything like adequate information for students and teachers of EFL.

The general thrust of publications like the *Code of Fair Testing Practices in Education* and the *APA/AERA/NCME Standards* (see Chapter 11) is to ensure that test users and other interested parties receive the fullest information possible about the test they are using. Such information is best provided in test manuals and test reports of the sort we have been advocating.

The *APA/AERA/NCME Standards* devotes a whole section (Section 5) to describing what technical manuals and user's guides should contain. The detail of the eleven Standards on this topic is preceded by the statement: 'Publishers should provide enough information for a qualified user or a reviewer of a test to evaluate the appropriateness and technical adequacy of the test' (page 35). UK exam boards should do the same.

9.8 Checklist

Institutions should first determine what obligations exist – legal as well as moral – to provide reports on the performance of their tests. This will vary from context to context.

The audiences receiving reports should be considered: What do they need to know? What would it be helpful for them to know?

Statistical information should be provided relative to the audiences' needs.

Are the results of observations of the examination to be included?

Is feedback available from students/examiners/administrators?

Have the scripts themselves been analysed to see what light they can throw on strengths and weaknesses of the exam and the candidates?

Is there evidence of bias in the test?

How does this test compare with previous versions?

How can teachers best prepare students for the test, or students prepare themselves?

What do examiners consider to be good performances and weak performances, and why? What criteria are used to evaluate performance?

What problems were there in the current test?

What changes will be forthcoming in the near future?

What language/skills does the test cover, and what are a candidate's results good for?

Is the test valid?

Is the test reliable?

10 Developing and improving tests

This chapter discusses how tests can be modified and improved in the light of their performance and of research and feedback. It addresses the questions of why and how tests should be kept up to date, and stresses the need for continuous monitoring of a test during its lifetime.

10.1 Test monitoring

10.1.1 Ongoing analysis: test content, administration, training and marking

It will be apparent from Chapter 8 that establishing the validity of a test is no quick or easy matter. This means that tests are frequently put into operation – used routinely for the purposes for which they are designed – without their validity having been fully established. Responsible test developers will have taken all possible steps to ensure that their instrument is as reliable and valid as it can be, given the time and resources available. However, problems with a test or associated procedures may only emerge once the test has been in operation for some time. This is as true for examinations which are only administered once, but whose pattern is reproduced year after year, as it is for secure tests which are administered on multiple occasions.

In some circumstances, it is simply not possible to continue revising a new test until every item, task, scale or subtest functions perfectly: what typically happens is that a draft test is pretested once and then modified, but is not then submitted to further trialling before implementation. Thus test developers may not actually know how well the modified items, tasks or rubrics perform until the live administration takes place.

On such occasions, it may be possible to analyse the results of the test and to remove poor items before calculating scores. However, it is more likely that post-administration analyses will only be conducted once test results have been issued. In this case, although the current scores cannot be adjusted, the results of the analyses need to be considered before a new version of the test is begun. This will allow adjustments to be made to the specifications of the test, or to training or administrative procedures.

In fact, we recommend that tests should be monitored on a routine and regular basis. Item and subtest analyses should be conducted after each administration, descriptive statistics should be calculated (including the normal reliability indices), and raters should be monitored for the reliability of their ratings (see Chapters 4, 5 and 6 for details of how such analyses should be done). We have suggested in Chapter 8 that post-test reports ought to contain information that will enable a test to be modified in the future if necessary. Essentially, such procedures are similar to those that should be followed in item and test trialling.

However, other problems may emerge during the routine administration of a test that are not easily identified by such standard analyses. To illustrate, we discuss one example we were involved in: a new test of the ability to listen to lectures. This test was developed using video tape: students were expected to watch a video of a lecture whilst listening to the spoken text and then record their answers on an answer sheet. The test was trialled in the normal way, seemed acceptable, and was put into service. However, subsequent observation of routine test administrations revealed that many students were not actually watching the video monitors: rather, they were reading their answer sheets whilst listening to the soundtrack and responding on the basis of what they heard, not what they saw. Item analyses had not revealed any problems with the test, but it appeared from the observations that the video image might actually be redundant. Two small studies were therefore set up: the first compared a group's performance on the video listening test with its performance on the same test using only the soundtrack. There was no difference in performance. The second study asked the same students which version of the test they preferred. They unanimously voted for the test with soundtrack only: they felt that taking the video test was too complicated, since they were required not only to read the questions, listen to the tape and write their answers, but they also had to keep looking up at the TV monitor and then back down at their answer sheet. Ignoring the image reduced the complexity of the task without affecting the measure of their listening ability. We subsequently scrapped the video component!

The first point this example illustrates is that had we not routinely observed the administration of the test, we would not have stumbled upon the problem. Thus, routine observations of test administration are strongly advised as a further monitoring procedure. The second point is that we needed to set up a special small-scale study to investigate the problem that had been observed: routine procedures were not sufficient on their own to help us understand the problem. Testing organisations need to be prepared to set up (possibly only small-scale) special studies when experience or feedback suggests there might be a need.

One problem that may occur is that procedures that are recommended by the test developers may not actually be implemented by those responsible for the test, or they may be quietly dropped after the test has been put into operation. Routine checks on procedures being followed should identify such situations. To illustrate, a new language test had been developed, and part of the task of the development project was to develop procedures for the training, certification and monitoring of examiners of tests of writing and speaking. It was felt to be especially important that such ratings were conducted reliably, because the test was administered in a number of different countries and ratings might be made by only one examiner. The developers produced a training package for examiners, which included the usual video-taped performances and writing samples, and guidance on how to rate, together with instructions on how to conduct the training workshops at which the materials would be used. They also developed a procedure for calculating the reliability of the ratings done by trainees at the end of the workshop, which would enable the authorities to certify a trainee as having reached the required standard. In addition, procedures were developed and agreed for the routine collection of samples of recorded performances of candidates on the speaking test, together with samples of candidates' writing, which would be sent to a central point for re-rating. This monitoring would be done on a regular basis, and those raters who 'stepped out of line' (rated too leniently or harshly) would be notified and either retrained or dismissed.

After trials, the test was put into operation along with the recommended procedures, but the latter were quickly abandoned as being 'unnecessary'. Training workshops were largely replaced by 'self-training' – examiners simply read the training packages and watched the videos, and it was assumed they were as a result able to rate reliably. No routine checks were conducted on the reliability of the ratings. The test developers' proposals to ensure reliability were frustrated by the imperfect implementation of procedures. In such cases there is probably a need for external monitoring of implementation. The availability of post-test reports, as described in Chapter 9, would offer an opportunity for such monitoring.

A related problem occurs when tests are used over a number of years in unchanged form. Examiners begin to feel confident in their use of the rating scales, and the training given to examiners, which is initially adequate, may become more lax and perfunctory as examiners feel they are sufficiently experienced in delivering the test. However, experience does not always equate with reliability, and routine checks on examiner agreement, especially where true double-marking does not occur, are essential to ensure that standards are being maintained and that the training and standardisation of examiners remain satisfactory.

10.1.2 Comments from test users

Another important aspect of test monitoring that should not be overlooked is the gathering of feedback from test users. The candidates can provide test developers with very valuable insights: what they think about the test items, test methods, the clarity of instructions, the timing of the various sections, the relevance of the content in the light of their learning experiences or their purposes for learning the language, the relationship between how they perceive their language abilities and their performance on the test in question, and so on. Such information may be routinely gathered via questionnaires administered immediately after the test has been taken, or in specially designed studies. The advantage of gathering information regularly rather than specially is that one may thereby pick up important information more rapidly.

Similarly, feedback should be sought from examiners on a regular basis and, as suggested in Chapter 9, incorporated into Examiners' Reports. Among other things, this would enable monitoring of changes in difficulty levels or even of changes in the ability of candidates.

Feedback should also be collected from language teachers, especially for tests that are related to language curricula. Where possible, it is useful to gather information not only on the match between the test's content and method and the curriculum, but also on whether the test is influencing how teachers teach. Are there ways in which teachers are preparing students for the test that might be undesirable and that might change if adjustments were made to test design, or if guidance were available to teachers on suitable preparation activities? (See Wall and Alderson 1993 for a discussion of this issue, but note also that teachers may not be the most reliable/open source of information on test preparation activities: direct observation of classrooms may reveal unsuspected and unadmitted practices!)

It is equally important to gather feedback from other consumers of test scores: admissions officers, employers, education authorities and the like. The key question is to what extent such informants feel that the test is doing the job for which it was designed. Such information is in any case (especially, but not only, for proficiency tests) needed for test validation (Chapter 8), particularly where predictive validity is relevant, and one needs to know that the right candidates are being selected on the basis of information provided by the test. As discussed earlier, it is typically very difficult to investigate rejected candidates, but it is certainly possible to monitor the nature of the population being admitted – to higher education, employment, the professions, etc. – and to see whether changes in that population are occurring over time. The opinions of test users will be important sources of information here, but it may be necessary to supplement these with more objective measures of the population.

10.1.3 Characteristics of the test population

A related aspect of test monitoring that is useful is to establish the characteristics of the test population (not just those who succeed on the test). It is quite likely that over time the population will change: geographical origin, linguistic background, gender, educational level, level of attainment and ability, and so on. For such purposes, the routine administration of a questionnaire which gathers biographical information on candidates is of considerable value. In addition, special studies can be mounted to look at characteristics of the test population in more depth, for example, their motivation, reasons for taking the test, their language learning history, communication strategies and the like. The results of such a study might lead to insights into the test and a possible need for modification. Studies of test bias are increasingly common and potentially important for language tests. Is a test gender- or ethnically-biased? Do candidates from certain regions or socio-economic backgrounds do better than other candidates? There may, however, be difficulty in interpreting the results or deciding what action to take. In one study Lynch, Davidson and Henning 1988 discovered that parts of UCLA's (University of California at Los Angeles) English as a Second Language Placement Test were biased against Korean-speaking learners of English and in favour of Spanish-speaking learners. On reflection, though, it seems clear that this is because English itself is so biased: because of linguistic affinity, it is easier for Spanish speakers to learn English than for Korean speakers. Such a bias would suggest test validity rather than invalidity.

Finally, it is important to monitor the standards – the levels of achievement and ability – of the test population. If, over time, standards appear to be changing, then there may be a need to investigate the causes and adjust the test. It may be that with increased familiarity and coaching the test is genuinely becoming easier, or it could be that with improved language teaching the ability of the population is increasing. In either case, it may prove necessary to adjust the test. Alternatively it may be decided that such changes in difficulty or ability should be reflected in increased success rates on the test. Much, as ever, will depend upon the purposes for which the test is given, but if the performance of the population is not monitored, important information will be missed.

10.2 The influence of new developments on the need and opportunity for test revision

10.2.1 New techniques of analysis

The need for improvements in a test or associated procedures may only become evident as new methods of analysis are introduced. For example, the development of multi-trait, multi-method methodologies for the investigation of convergent-divergent validity (see Chapter 8; Bachman and Palmer 1981 and Campbell and Fiske 1959) spawned a number of studies of test validity that helped advance our understanding of how language proficiency might best be tested. The advent of confirmatory factor analysis as a new tool alongside exploratory factor analysis led to similar developments. This is particularly the case where computer software is developed which enables new statistical analyses to be conducted. A striking recent example of this is the development and availability of FACETS (Linacre and Wright 1992). This program enables the analysis of the performance of different examiners on varying tasks, under different operating conditions and with different sorts of candidates. It is possible to explore the extent to which particular examiners are operating inconsistently or idiosyncratically, or where rating scales need to be adjusted or tasks modified in order to arrive at more consistent or valid scores. Before the availability of such software, checks on examiner variability were possible, but were relatively crude. It is now possible to explore the rating process and the factors that influence scores in much more depth and with greater understanding. In such circumstances it is conceivable that tests which once appeared to be performing satisfactorily might, on reinspection with improved tools, prove to be problematic and to need modification.

A similar situation has developed in recent years as language-testing researchers have become more interested in and familiar with more 'qualitative' research techniques, which can be used for investigating a test's validity. One example of such techniques is the use of introspective reports from test takers and examiners of test performance, for example, so-called 'think-aloud' protocols and retrospective accounts of test-taking processes (see Chapter 8). Such qualitative data can reveal surprising insights into what students and examiners are thinking when dealing with test tasks, which may well conflict with what test developers believe students or examiners 'ought to do' when responding to test items or performances. Insofar as such data provide evidence of content (in)validity, those responsible for tests should make every effort to gather information on the process of taking existing instruments and make suitable adjustments to items, rubrics, test method, rating scales or other facets of test design as appropriate.

The clear message is that test administrators and developers as well as researchers need to be familiar with current developments in tools of analysis, in order to be in a position to apply them to existing measures as well as to tests that might be developed in the future.

10.2.2 Changes in technology

Such developments may seem arcane and remote from the average test developer and user – although the pace of development is such that we believe this is no longer the case. However, more mundane developments may well offer opportunities for test modification that were not possible previously, and that would be recognised by the most cynical test writer. One obvious example of this is the advent of cheap and good quality audio-cassette recorders. The availability of such technology makes it possible to standardise the delivery, for example, of dictation tests, and to record the performance of candidates on speaking tests for later rating by trained raters. It even makes it possible, as happens with the AET test and the Test of Spoken English (TSE), to administer oral tests on a group basis, in language laboratories. This makes oral testing a more feasible procedure than might have otherwise been the case. Such technology also means that students can be tested for their ability to understand a range of spoken texts which could not easily have been tested before: radio discussions, commentaries on public events, telephone answering machines, announcements in airports and at railway stations, and so on.

Indeed, one might argue that the possibility of using audio recordings has increased the availability of listening tests, and has led to an increased emphasis on the teaching of listening. One might even argue that cassette recorders, together with more affordable means of reproduction of written texts (photocopiers, for example) have influenced or even initiated the debate about the desirability of the use of authentic language data in tests generally.

Similarly, the advent of video technology makes possible a range of texts and test formats that were previously unthinkable (although our earlier example of the development of a video lecture listening test illustrates that such possibilities may not represent genuine improvement in test validity). It also improves the training of the examiners of oral tests. Currently, interactive video technology offers intriguing possibilities for test innovation.

The availability of personal computers has already led to a number of interesting (and less interesting) developments in computer-based language testing (see Alderson 1986, 1988a and Alderson and Windeatt 1991 for extended discussions of the potential impact of such developments). Adaptive testing, where the computer decides which next item to present in the light of a candidate's performance on previous items, is likely to make radical changes to the ways tests are delivered and scores derived.

Even simple changes like the availability of electricity in schools where none was available previously are likely to provide major opportunities for innovation and development in language tests at a school or even class level.

The message is clear: test developers need to be open to general developments that offer opportunities for changes in test content and test method.

10.3 New thinking

One thing is obvious from the past thirty years of language teaching and testing, and of linguistics and applied linguistics, and that is that ideas are constantly changing about the nature of language and language proficiency, language learning and language teaching, and about the best ways to test language learning and linguistic proficiency.

From focusing upon language as a formal system, linguistics has become more aware of other dimensions of language: the nature of meaning, the relationship between sentences and the context, variation in language by user and by use, and so on. Linguistics has broadened to include sociolinguistic aspects of communication, linguistic competence has been redefined in terms of communicative competence (Hymes 1972), and models of language proficiency have broadened from grammatical competence to involve textual competence, illocutionary competence and sociolinguistic competence (see Bachman 1990).

Similarly in language teaching, the goal of instruction and learning has broadened to encompass not only linguistic structures and lexis, but functions and notions, learning and communication strategies, culturally appropriate behaviour and more. In its turn the communicative revolution has become orthodoxy, and is increasingly challenged by advocates of the importance of learners acquiring an awareness of language – knowledge about language – and a semi-reinstatement of the importance of grammar, broadly defined, in any definition of instructional aims and objectives.

Language testing is not isolated from such developments, and the 1980s saw major changes in test content and, to some extent, in test method, to reflect these new concerns and ideas. Discrete-point testing gave way, at least in some quarters, to more task-based tests, more integrative techniques and a greater emphasis on performance testing. Multiple-choice tests were complemented by techniques like the cloze procedure, C-tests, short-answer questions and more open-ended elicitation procedures, and objective testing yielded some ground to more subjective yet arguably more valid ways of assessing language proficiency.

It is unlikely that we have seen the end of changes in ways of describing language and language proficiency, or of deciding upon what language to teach and how to teach it. Insofar as language testing should embody a view of language, and a view of language learning and teaching, then language tests will also continue to change to reflect changes in theory and practice elsewhere. Thus test developers will always need to be open to new ideas about what it is important and relevant to test, and how those abilities and that content should be measured.

Thus as language curricula and textbooks change, so the tests based on them will also need to adjust in order to retain curricular (content) validity. As new ways are developed of teaching listening abilities, for example, or of teaching grammar in some meaningful, communicative fashion, so language tests will need to adjust to take account of such developments. This is not to assert that language testing is dependent upon language teaching and must respond to every whim of pedagogic fashion; indeed, some tests will need to be kept quite independent of any curriculum in order to achieve their purpose. Language test developers operate under special sorts of constraints that do not apply equally to textbook writers and curriculum developers (tests are samples, they must typically be capable of being administered in a relatively short space of time, they cannot provide much support for weaker learners, and so on) and they must clearly temper any desire or pressure to follow fashion with considerations of practicality, as well as of reliability and validity. Nevertheless, it is hard to conceive of any testing situation where test developers can afford to remain resolutely immune from the influence of outside developments and still have their tests acceptable to the professional community of teachers, applied linguists and other testers. Thus there is a constant need for ways of updating and modifying tests to take account of such outside developments.

One common way in which tests are changed is by major review every so many years, as illustrated in the following quotation from Alderson 1986:

> After considering developments in English as a Foreign Language (EFL) at least, I conclude that a test has a fairly well established life cycle of 12 to 15 years. Once born, a test needs time and careful nurturing to develop, to attract more and more attention and testees, to establish credibility as an instrument for a particular purpose, to become recognized as valid and reliable – something which we in the UK measure more by public opinion and prestige than by empirical data. This period seems to take between three and five years.
>
> Once established, the test is then regarded as acceptable for a reasonable period of time. During this period it might be accepted by a variety of institutions, referred to in the testing and later the teaching literature. It might be taken by large numbers of students, often forming the goal of their instruction and aspirations. This period might last anywhere between five and eight years.
>
> Towards the end of this period, however, signs of senescence appear in the shape of increasing criticism of the test's influence on teaching and on students' ambitions and lives. The usual claim is that the test is exerting a restrictive influence on the teaching, in that it is preventing teachers from teaching in desirable or fashionable ways.
>
> Pressure may then build up within the test-producing body itself (typically in Britain an examination board) for a change in test specifications, content or format. These pressures for change, as we will see, come less from carefully gathered evidence of the test's inability to meet its originally specified purposes than from intuited feelings on the part of interested parties that the test is somehow slipping behind developments in thinking in applied linguistics and teaching. In a more general sense, it may be that the test no longer fulfills its original function.
>
> Change may be instituted by academic applied linguists, in the form of research, often guided by committees and working parties ... or by the examination board itself, through its existing or recently widened network of teacher-testers ... or it may be brought about by direct rather than invited teacher involvement on the lines of the graded test movement in the UK. Whoever the agent of change, however, rebirth is then inevitable, usually after a gestation period of two to three years. And so we have another innovation: another baby test. However, the baby may have a very close resemblance to the parent, or it may look very different indeed from its predecessor.
>
> Yet it is legitimate to ask: what was the real need for a new test?

> Where was the evidence, rather than the opinion, that the old test was
> ineffective, past its prime, ready to pass on to greener pastures? What,
> in particular, did the users of the test – the students, the sponsors, the
> receiving institutions – feel or know about the need for rebirth?

(pages 96–97)

Another way of changing tests, however, is to devise ways of
constantly innovating in test content and method. This entails
continuous changes to test formats, rather than relatively irregular far-
reaching reviews as are implied in the model of test innovation
suggested above. Since any test, even an achievement test based on a
specific syllabus, is inevitably only a sample of what could have been
tested, continuous modification of test design is justified on the grounds
of improving the extent to which the test reflects the syllabus. If the test
format remains fixed for a period of time, it may have the effect of
narrowing the curriculum: not only will the test be confined to those
elements that are thought testable or convenient, but the teaching in
preparation for the test is likely to become restricted to the sorts of
activities and abilities that are tested. To avoid such a narrowing, as
well as to improve content validity, some testing bodies deliberately
adopt a policy of constant innovation each year. For each test
administration some part of the test is changed: a new test method
might be introduced, a different balance of components tried out; new
skills or competencies might be measured; changes in rubrics, task types
or elicitation procedures may be brought in. The purpose of such
innovation is precisely to avoid any fossilisation of the test, with the
predicted undesirable consequences.

10.4 The real world

There are, of course, other considerations than developments in theory
that lead test developers to change their tests. Practical matters are
often of great importance. The cost of producing a test is often a
significant factor in constraining what can be achieved: the degree of
complexity involved in a particular test design, the amount of training
needed for examiners, the number of different pieces of paper, the
amount of time needed for test administration, the number of
examiners required. Similarly, increased financial pressure may lead a
testing body to adjust the nature of its test and its administration in
order to reduce its costs. Increased demands on school examination
timetables may mean that less time is available for a language test than
previously, and compromises might need to be made in test design.
Conversely (though less usually) more time may become available,

and constraints of resources, trained personnel, and so on may be removed, so that tests can develop into something more innovative, reflective of the syllabus and of trends in applied linguistics and language teaching. Pressures from competing testing bodies, too, either within the same country or internationally, are likely to bring about calls to innovate rather than to simplify or to reduce costs.

Many countries have one central authority with the sole responsibility for producing examinations, and experience shows that such state monopolies tend to be conservative in their approach to innovation. However, in other settings, as is the case for UK EFL examinations, for example, 'market forces' tend to bring about competitive innovation in test design in the hope of acquiring a larger market share. Similarly, where testing bodies are competing internationally for the same market (as is the case, for example, with ETS' TOEFL and UCLES' IELTS tests), we might expect test design to change as each institution attempts to gain the advantage. Thus market research and comparisons with rival 'products' might be expected to be important in some settings and to act as a driving force for test development.

10.5 Survey of EFL Examination Boards: Questionnaire

The questionnaire contained several questions intended to discover to what extent UK boards engaged in regular revision and development of their tests. In addition, we sought to determine the extent to which boards were satisfied with their existing tests and test production procedures, in order to estimate to what extent such boards might feel the need to change their tests in the future.

QUESTION 46: *Is feedback on your examinations gathered?*

Only one board reported not gathering feedback on its examinations. How feedback was gathered and from whom varied, however. Some boards gathered feedback informally from teachers, at conferences and seminars and from 'the grapevine'. One or two gathered feedback regularly, using 'Invigilators' Report Forms' or 'Reports from Assessors' or questionnaires to 'schools, centres, teachers and examiners' (not, note, to students). One board replied that feedback was gathered 'informally from personal contact with centres' and another that 'it is our intention to send questionnaires to centres periodically, at approximately three-year intervals'. UCLES' practice varies, but at least one respondent mentioned a 'Candidate Information Sheet' to be filled in by all candidates.

QUESTION 47: *Do routine procedures exist to ensure that your examinations are revised in the light of feedback?*

Interestingly, three boards said that such procedures did not exist. One UCLES respondent said that working parties discussed the matter at six-monthly intervals.

QUESTION 48: *How often, on average, are your EFL examinations revised?*

The frequency of revision of EFL exams varied, from 'in small-ish ways, constantly' to 'about every two years', with one board saying, 'Minor revisions every few years. Major revisions only occasionally. A major revision is in progress now.' Two boards referred to revisions in 1989 and 1990 respectively.

QUESTION 50: *Do you have any plans to make changes in the procedures you follow, as described above?*

Half the boards said they did have such plans, and half said they did not. Reference was made to one major revision still under way, but in no cases were details forthcoming.

The final few questions attempted to gauge how satisfied the boards were with their tests and the extent to which they felt that they were 'superior' to tests available elsewhere. Although strictly speaking these responses do not relate to test monitoring or improvement, they do give some idea of whether UK EFL examining boards feel, at least publicly, that their tests are in need of improvement.

QUESTION 51: *It is said that the strength of British examinations lies in their relationship to language teaching. Do you agree? Can you describe how this relationship can be demonstrated in the case of your examination?*

No board disagreed with this assertion, although one board said that it had no opinion, since 'The strength of our schemes lies in clear performance descriptors. We do not dictate teaching materials'.

Of those who replied, 'Somewhat', one said, 'There are other strengths and teaching is a shaky foundation on which to rely as fashions change so frequently.' The majority replied with a clear Yes and three claimed that their examinations had beneficial washback effects. However, we have no knowledge of any studies of this matter. The commonest claim was that closeness to teaching was ensured by involving teachers as examiners and by testing communicative skills.

QUESTION 52: *It is also said that 'psychometric' or 'American' criteria and procedures are irrelevant to British examinations. Do you agree? If you agree, what criteria and/or procedures are irrelevant to your examinations?*

A large majority of boards disagreed with this assertion, although several felt that such 'procedures' only applied to the objective sections of their examinations. Two boards, however, added qualifications to their disagreement, which we feel it is worth citing in full:

> A combination of British linguistic realism and American psychometrics is, I believe, highly desirable and technically possible, provided one assumes examiners are not blackguards and, within certain tolerances, tend to converge on their judgements of language and candidates ... psychometric processing is never complete enough to allay all suspicions and will not convince teachers if (it is) in conflict with commonsense, empirical evidence which they can understand easily at first sight.

and:

> Their application would significantly increase the cost of a price-sensitive product.

QUESTION 53: *What, in your opinion, are the strengths of your examinations?*

This question elicited a variety of responses, ranging from 'flexibility of delivery', 'available on demand', 'practical realistic tasks', examinations 'available at a number of different levels', to the less modest 'reliability, complete fairness, validity and sound administrative procedures'. Range of text and task types, authenticity, links with teaching and asserted washback effects were the most frequently claimed strengths.

QUESTION 54: *What, if any, are the weaknesses of your examinations?*

Not surprisingly, responses to this question were briefer! Four boards claimed they had no weaknesses, and one maintained that its sole weakness was that its exams were 'not yet taken in the USA or Canada'! However, one or two gave more thoughtful responses, referring, for example, to the difficulty of standardising impressionistic judgements. The lack of testing of oral production was mentioned by two boards, and of interactive skills by a third.

Not all readers will be reassured by one reply: 'Should a weakness be discovered this would be immediately rectified'.

Responses from UCLES were more credible, being refreshingly frank. One respondent made three points:

a) We need to make greater efforts in ensuring the reliability of examiners in certificating and re-certificating them. b) We need to establish to a far greater extent that exam versions are equivalent in terms of reliability and content. c) Subjectively marked writing tasks should all be double-marked routinely.

A second respondent identified two weaknesses as being 'lack of training of exam personnel and cumbersome administration', and a third respondent, referring to a relatively newly-introduced test, mentioned the 'lack of formal procedures for ongoing validation and equating of the test'.

10.6 Discussion

It would appear from these results that the boards are generally satisfied with their tests, and yet are engaged in a process of regular revision of them. What is less clear is the extent to which this revision is the result of systematic data collection, and to what extent it reflects intuitive reactions to perceptions of 'the field' and 'the market'. Our position is that informal feedback 'from the grapevine' is an unreliable basis on which to base satisfaction with one's test, or even test revisions. Nevertheless, some responses gave some reassurance that problems are being identified and steps taken to remedy them.

The claimed close relationship with language teaching was perhaps predictable, but must be regarded somewhat sceptically, since language teaching practice varies considerably. Assertions about beneficial washback effects are common, but unsubstantiated and, as Alderson and Wall 1993 have pointed out, this is an area which would benefit from considerable research. Given the claimed close link between teaching and testing, it may well be the case that tests could be improved through a close examination of test preparation practices.

10.7 Checklist

What routine monitoring procedures are in place?
    item analysis and test reliability
    calculation of reliability of marking
    observation of test administration

observation of training and standardisation procedures
observation of marking and monitoring
comparisons of levels of achievement over time
collection of data on test population characteristics:
        gender
        country or region of origin
        mother tongue
        language learning history
        reasons for taking the test
        ability levels
        etc.
feedback from test users:
        candidates
        examiners
        teachers
        other test users, such as admissions officers
Are monitoring procedures being conducted adequately?
Are any special studies needed?
        item and test bias
        candidate motivation, reasons for taking the test, achievement
        in other areas
        etc.
Are new methods of analysis – statistical or qualitative – available
which might reveal fresh insights into the test?
What technology is available that might lead to improvements?
        audio recorders
        language laboratories
        photocopiers
        electricity
        video
        interactive video
        computers
        optical scanners
        handwriting recognition systems
        light pens
        etc.
Is the view of language contained in the test outdated?
Does the test reflect current thinking and practice in language teaching?
What effect does the test have on teaching? Can this be improved?
Can the test be updated on a routine basis, rather than occasionally?
Can the cost of the test be reduced without affecting validity and
reliability?
Can the test be simplified without affecting validity and reliability?

What are rival tests like? Can your test improve on what they do? Does market research reveal a need for change? Are there gaps in the market?

Bibliography

Alderson, J.C. 1986a. In Leech and Candlin (eds.), *Computers in English Language Education and Research.* London: Longman.

Alderson, J.C. 1986b. Innovations in Language Testing? In M. Portal (ed.), *Innovations in Language Testing.* 93–105. Windsor, Berks.: NFER-Nelson.

Alderson, J.C. 1988a. Innovations in Language Testing: Can the Microcomputer Help? Special issue of *Language Testing Update.*

Alderson, J.C. and S.W. Windeatt. 1991. In J.C. Alderson and B. North (eds.), *Language Testing in the 1990s: The Communicative Legacy.* New York: Macmillan.

Alderson, J.C. and D. Wall, 1993. Does Washback Exist? *Applied Linguistics* 14(2): 115–129.

Bachman, L.F. 1990. *Fundamental Considerations in Language Testing.* Oxford: Oxford University Press.

Bachman, L.F. and A.S. Palmer. 1981. A Multitrait-Multimethod Investigation into the Construct Validity of Six Tests of Listening and Reading. In A.S. Palmer, P.J.M. Groot and G.A. Trosper (eds.), *The Construct Validation of Tests of Communicative Competence.* Washington, DC: TESOL.

Campbell, D.T. and D.W. Fiske. 1959. Convergent and Discriminant Validation by the Multitrait-Multimethod Matrix. *Psychological Bulletin* 56: 81–105.

Hymes, D.H. 1972. On Communicative Competence. In J.B. Pride and J. Holmes (eds.), *Sociolinguistics* 269–93. Harmondsworth: Penguin.

Linacre, J.M. and B.D. Wright. 1992. FACETS: Many-Facet Rasch Measurement. Chicago: MESA Press.

Lynch, B., F. Davidson and G. Henning. 1988. Person dimensionality in language test validation. *Language Testing* 5(2): 206–219.

Wall, D. and J.C. Alderson, 1993. Examining Washback. *Language Testing* 10(1): 41–69.

11 Standards in language testing: the state of the art

In this final chapter we review the principles and standards we have sought to establish and illustrate in the volume so far. Each chapter has dealt with a different stage in the test construction and evaluation process, and has described what we consider to be 'desirable practice' in language testing. At the same time we have tried to illustrate current practice in one particular geographical region – the United Kingdom – for one set of tests: those of English as a Foreign or Second Language. Had we described testing practice in other parts of the world, or in other languages in the UK, we would doubtless have painted a different picture – perhaps brighter, perhaps not so bright as the one which has been painted in these pages. There are many factors which influence what happens in the testing process – practical, financial and political. Different test designers might start off with the same idea but end up with very different instruments and procedures because of the constraints of the contexts they are working in. Heaton 1988: 24 uses the term 'compromise' to describe the give-and-take which is always present in the test construction process. If such compromises are inevitable, then we need to make sure that they are as principled as possible. Having a clear idea of what best practice looks like will help testers to see which elements they can afford to sacrifice and which they must retain in spite of the costs. This is where the idea of 'standards' comes into its own.

11.1 What are standards?

In testing, *standards* can have two different meanings, only one of which will be adopted in this chapter. The first meaning has to do with levels of achievement. This is most commonly used to refer to examination candidates, as in the expression 'Standards have fallen ...', and we have used the term with this meaning in previous chapters.

The second meaning of 'standards' relates to the notion of 'principles'. Pollitt 1990 sees 'standards' as a way of measuring an institution's adherence to 'principles':

'Principles' partition the testing domain horizontally, into the various issues that concern us. 'Standards' define it vertically, stating (for example) how much 'reliability' is to be demanded (or) how well or fully the test construction process should be described.

(page 1)

For Pollitt it is relatively easy to get agreement on 'principles', whereas 'standards' are 'slippery' and may lead to an excess of caution or a stifling of creative developments.

Whilst we see the logic of this distinction, we recognise that for much of the testing world 'standards' and 'principles' refer to the same idea: a basis for evaluating testing practices. This may be because of the influence of the *Standards for Educational and Psychological Testing*, which we describe below, and similar documents which use 'standards' in their titles. We wish to build on what we consider to be a widespread use of the term, and also to encourage a sense of continuity with important work already carried out in this area. We therefore also use 'standards' in this second sense, to mean an agreed set of guidelines which should be consulted and, as far as possible, heeded in the construction or the evaluation of a test. In the UK and European contexts, the term 'code of practice' seems to be preferred to 'standards', and we include an account of two such codes of practice in this chapter.

Recent years have seen considerable discussion about the need for standards, and about whether language testing should have special standards of its own. The International Language Testing Association (ILTA) is currently investigating the standards which already exist for educational tests and other measures, in order to initiate a discussion about a possible development of policy towards these standards or the compilation of a new set which would be more discipline-specific. In this chapter we set out our own views about standards in general and about several particular sets of standards which might serve as useful starting points for work to be done in future.

In the following sections we describe six different sets of standards. We have chosen these standards because we believe that they represent interesting approaches to the problem of defining good practice, and because each set contributes something new to our picture of what standards should look like. We are nevertheless aware that by choosing standards which have been written in English we may be leaving out of the discussion valuable sets of guidelines which may have been produced in other languages. ILTA's survey may soon provide information about the efforts in other languages to ensure the quality of tests and examinations.

In what follows, we present the background, purpose and overall organisation of each of these six sets of standards, and a commentary on the value of their contribution to the field of testing. We then incorporate ideas from all of the sets into a discussion of the questions that should be asked in future debates on the desirability of further standards.

Note that the date which is given in brackets at the beginning of each description is the date of the latest edition of the document being presented. None of the documents is more than ten years old; this does not mean, however, that all of the developments have occurred in the last decade. Indeed, several of the documents are the result of years of reflection and revision. It is also important to note that some of the documents acknowledge the inspiration of others. There has been a great deal of cross-fertilisation in this area so far, and this is likely to continue in the future.

11.2 *Standards for Educational and Psychological Testing* (1985)

11.2.1 Background

Perhaps the best known set of standards is the *Standards for Educational and Psychological Testing*, which are sometimes referred to as the 'APA Standards'. These standards were published in 1985 by The American Educational Research Association (AERA), The American Psychological Association (APA) and the National Council on Measurement in Education (NCME). The APA and the AERA had separately published 'technical recommendations' for tests in the mid-1950s, and they, along with the NCME, built on this work to publish their first joint set of standards in 1966. This was revised in 1974 and again in 1985. The 1985 version takes account of the many changes that were occurring in testing in the 1970s – including technical advances, new uses for tests and 'growing social concerns over the role of testing in achieving social goals' (page 5). We understand that there will be a further revision later in this decade.

11.2.2 Purpose

The Standards document is quite explicit about its purpose:

> The purpose of publishing the Standards is to provide criteria for the evaluation of tests, testing practices, and the effects of test use ... .
> (They) can provide a frame of reference to assure that relevant issues

are addressed ... . All professional test developers, sponsors, publishers, and users should make reasonable efforts to observe the Standards and to encourage others to do so.

(page 2)

The presumption must be that there are some tests which do not offer the quality the public would expect of them: the Standards can be used as a basis for identifying which tests do and which do not live up to their promise. The document recognises that 'the use of standards in litigation is inevitable' (page 2); however, they are intended to offer guidance for judgements in such cases, not prescriptions. Indeed, it is interesting to note recent debates with the AERA about how, or whether, the Standards should be 'enforced'. The Revision Committee clearly saw them as essentially voluntary, but with a degree of moral obligation.

The Preface to the Standards document gives a detailed account of how the Revision Committee saw the Standards operating:

The Standards should:

1. Address issues of test use in a variety of applications.

2. Be a statement of technical standards for sound professional practice and not a social action prescription.

3. Make it possible to determine the technical adequacy of a test, the appropriateness and propriety of specific applications, and the reasonableness of inferences based on the test results.

4. Require that test developers, publishers, and users collect and make available sufficient information to enable a qualified reviewer to determine whether applicable standards were met.

5. Embody a strong ethical imperative, though it was understood that the Standards itself would not contain enforcement mechanisms.

6. Recognize that all standards will not be uniformly applicable across a wide range of instruments and uses.

7. Be presented at a level that would enable a wide range of people who work with tests or test results to use the Standards.

8. Not inhibit experimentation in the development, use, and interpretation of tests.

9. Reflect the current levels of consensus of recognized experts.

(page v)

11.2.3 Targets

The Standards apply to tests, which are defined in the document as follows:

> Tests include standardized ability (aptitude and achievement) instruments, diagnostic and evaluative devices, interest inventories, personality inventories and projective instruments ... . In the Standards three broad categories of test instruments are covered: constructed performance tasks, questionnaires, and to a lesser extent, structured behaviour samples.
>
> (pages 3–4)

However, the Standards apply not only to testing instruments but also, and importantly in the 1985 revision, to test use, to particular applications and to administrative procedures. They are intended to be comprehensive, addressing 'major current uses of tests, technical issues relating to a broad range of social and legal concerns, and the varied needs of all the participants in the testing process' (page viii).

11.2.4 Overall organisation

The Standards document is subdivided as follows:

Part I: Technical Standards for Test Construction and Evaluation

> This contains chapters on Validity; Reliability; Test Development and Revision; Scaling, Norming, Score Comparability and Equating; and Test Publication: Technical Manuals and User's Guides.

Part II: Professional Standards for Test Use

> This contains chapters on General Principles of Test Use; Clinical Testing; Educational Testing and Psychological Testing in the Schools; Test Use in Counselling; Employment Testing; Professional and Occupational Licensure and Certification; and Programme Evaluation.

Part III: Standards for Particular Applications

> This covers Testing Linguistic Minorities; and Testing People Who Have Handicapping Conditions.

Part IV: Standards for Administrative Procedures

> This covers Test Administration, Scoring and Reporting; and Protecting the Rights of Test-Takers.

There is an overview at the beginning of each chapter, which provides a context for interpreting the standards therein. There is also a seven-page glossary of technical terms used in the document and an index to direct testers to the sections they are most interested in.

11.2.5 Distinctive characteristics

The Standards are made up of three different sorts of recommendations: primary, secondary and conditional standards. Primary standards should be:

> met by all tests before their operational use and in all test uses, unless a sound professional reason is available to show why it is not necessary, or technically feasible, to do so in a particular case. Test developers and users, and where appropriate sponsors, are expected to be able to explain why any primary standards have not been met.
>
> (page 2)

An example of a primary standard is Standard 1.1:

> Evidence of validity should be presented for the major types of inferences for which the use of a test is recommended. A rationale should be provided to support the particular mix of evidence presented for the intended uses.
>
> (page 13)

Secondary standards, on the other hand, are desirable but may be 'beyond reasonable expectation in many situations' (page 3). Such standards describe procedures that are beneficial but may be very difficult to implement when there are limited resources. An example of a secondary standard is Standard 2.10:

> Standard errors of measurement should be reported at critical score levels. Where cut-scores are specified for selection or classification, the standard errors of measurement should be reported for score levels at or near the cut-score.
>
> (page 22)

The third category of standards, which is labelled 'conditional', may either be primary or secondary, depending on the particular test which is under scrutiny. Here the test developer needs to use an element of judgement, balancing practical considerations with factors such as the number of candidates who will be taking the test. If the test has only a few candidates and the stakes involved are not very great, then it may not be worthwhile for a test developer to strive to meet a conditional standard. An example of such a standard is Standard 5.1:

A technical manual should be made available to prospective test users at the time a test is published or released for operational use.

(page 35)

Although it would be useful for test sponsors, administrators and others to refer to such a manual, it might be unreasonable to expect the test developer to produce one for every version of the test, especially if several versions are administered every year. This does not mean that there should not be any documents to answer the prospective users' queries, but that these documents might take the form of brief reports rather than formally published booklets.

In addition to making a distinction between essential standards and ones which may be waived if circumstances warrant, the document also provides an explanatory comment for some of the standards. This comment will either contain background information, a justification, an illustration or a paraphrase of the words in the standard: it is meant to provide an aid to understanding, not another principle to be taken into consideration.

11.2.6 Commentary

It will be apparent from the above that the Standards are comprehensive. Though they appear daunting at first glance, with 16 sections and 181 separate guidelines, once the reader is familiar with the organisation of the statements and has read the overviews and the commentary, they are not difficult to understand. There are, however, two issues that we wish to discuss.

The first is that it is not clear why the secondary standards are considered to be more 'dispensable' than the primary standards. About ten per cent of all the guidelines fall into the 'secondary' category, which means that testers do not need to heed them if they feel that they are not practical and that they do not have to explain why they have not heeded them. Of course, if testers concentrated on meeting all of the primary standards, then their practices would be so sound and well-documented that missing out the secondary standards might not even be noticed; however, it is difficult to see the rationale for deciding which standards could be left out.

The second issue has to do with the educational setting where tests are used. In the United States there is a strong dependence on the use of standardised tests, and it was worries about the problems that might result from such testing that prompted the development of the Standards in the first place. In other settings, standardised tests may be much rarer and present less cause for concern about possible abuse and misuse.

Nevertheless, familiarity with the Standards is useful for any language tester or language teacher, programme evaluator or language researcher who needs to develop or use language tests, and we make no apology for having dealt with this particular set of standards in some detail.

11.3 *Code of Fair Testing Practices in Education (1988)*

11.3.1 *Background*

During the early part of the 1980s, during the time that the Standards for Educational and Psychological Testing were in their final stages of revision, the APA became concerned about the amount of criticism that was being directed towards testing practices in the United States, and about the volume of legislation and litigation that related to tests and test use. Although the revised edition of the Standards was to take into account the changing role of tests in society, some members of the APA felt that it would be useful to focus more sharply on how to improve testing practices. A conference was held in 1984, which brought together representatives from the APA, the AERA, the NCME, the Canadian Psychological Association and 23 test publishers. The Joint Committee on Testing Practices (JCTP) was formed, as was a working group to look into the possibility of creating a code of practice for testers. The result of their work was the *Code of Fair Testing Practices in Education* (Diamond and Fremer 1989: passim).

11.3.2 *Purpose*

The purpose of the Code is 'to state the major obligations to test takers of professionals who develop or use educational tests' (JCTP 1980: 1). It is not the intention of the Code to modify or add to the 1985 Standards document, but rather to highlight certain issues that were addressed therein, particularly those pertaining to the proper use of tests in education. Like the Standards, the Code is mainly concerned with professionally-developed tests, including those designed by commercial publishers, rather than with small-scale tests developed by schools or teachers. It is written in language that is meant to be understandable to the general public; in fact, the introductory material states that it is to be 'meaningful to test takers and/or their parents or guardians' (page 2).

11.3.3 Targets

The Code specifies guidelines for test developers and test users. It sees test developers as 'people who actually construct tests as well as those who set policies for particular testing programs', and test users as 'people who select tests, commission test development services, or make decisions on the basis of test scores' (page 1). It recognises that these roles can sometimes overlap, as would be the case, say, if a Ministry of Education decided to develop a new examination to complement a new national teaching syllabus, and then used the results from the exam to judge the effectiveness of the syllabus.

11.3.4 Overall organisation

The Code presents the obligations of test developers and test users in four major areas:

A	Developing/Selecting Appropriate Tests
B	Interpreting Scores
C	Striving for Fairness
D	Informing Test Takers

In Sections A–C these responsibilities are presented in parallel columns: every statement directed to a test developer is matched by a complementary statement to a test user. The test developer is generally asked to provide information to the test user (definitions, descriptions, explanations, evidence, sample of tests and related forms, clear and accurate score reports, and warnings), and the test user is asked to consider all of this information before deciding which test will be most appropriate for the test-taking population. The test developer should also revise test materials to avoid bias to any subset of the population, and the test user should evaluate the procedures used and the results obtained by the test developers and use the best materials or procedures that the test developer provides to ensure that the test is fair for everyone.

Section A contains eight guidelines for test developers and users, Section B five, and Section C three. Some of the guidelines from Section A are printed overleaf, to show how they are laid out and how the developers' and users' guidelines correspond to one another.

Test developers should:

1. define what each test measures and what the test should be used for. Describe the population(s) for which the test is appropriate.

2. accurately represent the characteristics, usefulness, and limitations of tests for their intended purposes.

3. explain relevant measurement concepts as necessary for clarity at the level of detail that is appropriate for the intended audience(s).

4. describe the process of test development. Explain how the content and skills to be tested were selected.

5. provide evidence that the test meets its intended purpose(s).

Test users should:

1. first define the purpose for testing and the population to be tested. Then, select a test for that purpose and that population based on a thorough review of the available information.

2. investigate potentially useful sources of information, in addition to test scores, to corroborate the information provided by tests.

3. read the materials provided by test developers and avoid using tests for which unclear or incomplete information is provided.

4. become familiar with how and when the test was developed and tried out.

5. read independent evaluations of a test and of possible alternative measures. Look for evidence required to support the claims of test developers.

In Section D there are five guidelines. However, in this section test developers and test users have the same obligations, which have to do with providing test takers with the information they need in order to decide whether to take the test in the first place, become familiar with the coverage of the test, obtain copies of the completed test, have tests re-marked, register complaints, and so on.

11.3.5 Commentary

The *Code of Fair Testing Practices in Education* seeks to reinforce many of the principles that first appeared in the APA/AERA/NCME Standards, but it limits itself to tests in education. Although it lays down principles for test developers, it is really aimed at test users and test takers, to inform them of the kinds of information that they are entitled to before and after the administration of a test. The layout of the principles is quite user-friendly and the language is free from technical terms. Like the Standards, the Code uses the modal 'should' instead of the more forceful 'must'; however, it makes a strong statement about the moral obligations of test developers and test users when they agree to observe the Code:

> Organisations, institutions, and individuals who endorse the Code commit themselves to safeguarding the rights of test takers by following the principles listed.

(page 2)

Unlike the Standards document, the *Code of Fair Testing Practices in Education* gives equal weighting to all its guidelines: there is no discussion about how some standards may be desirable but not practical in the real world. This may be because the Code is meant to operate at a fairly general level, whereas the Standards document makes recommendations which are much more technical and much more detailed.

11.3.6 The ALTE Code of Practice

The JCTP Code has had an impact on language testing, in that it is the basis for the *ALTE Code of Practice* (1994). ALTE is the Association of Language Testers in Europe, a group of providers of language examinations. Languages tested by members of this association include Catalan, Danish, Dutch, English, French, German, Italian, Portuguese and Spanish. The association aims, amongst other things, to:

> ... establish common standards for all stages of the language testing process: that is, for test development, question and item writing, test administration, marking and grading, reporting of test results, test analysis and reporting of findings.

(page 2)

The Code of Practice has been adopted by ALTE 'in order to make explicit the standards they aim to meet, and to acknowledge the obligations under which they operate' (page 3).

The Code is closely modelled on the JCTP Code, using much of the same wording. It is addressed to examination developers, users and takers, and covers the same areas as the JCTP. However, the modality of the Code is interesting. With respect to examination developers, the Code says, for each section: 'In practice, this means that members of ALTE will guarantee to do the following: ...' (ibid., passim).

This new code for language testers is to be welcomed, and it will be interesting to see how it is implemented and monitored in practice.

11.4 *ETS Standards for Quality and Fairness* (1987)

11.4.1 *Background*

In 1981 the Educational Testing Service in the United States adopted the *ETS Standards for Quality and Fairness*. The aim of this document was to make explicit the principles, policies and procedural guidelines that ETS intended to follow in its desire to ensure 'openness in testing, public accountability, quality, and fairness' (page iii). The ETS Standards document was amongst the policy statements examined by the AERA/APA/NCME Standards Revision Committee in the early 1980s as they attempted to update their own standards and make them more sensitive to the changing educational context in the US. Several years later ETS repaid the compliment, examining the revised Standards document as it attempted to rewrite its own document. By doing so ETS hoped to stay 'in the forefront of measurement and the latest thinking of the profession' (page iv).

11.4.2 *Purpose*

The ETS Standards are meant to ensure quality services and products within a particular organisation. They contain explicit criteria for judging the performance of testing professionals, at the level of principles, policies and procedural guidelines. ETS makes it clear, however, that the Standards have been written with ETS in mind; they might not be applicable to other testing bodies or individuals.

11.4.3 *Overall organisation*

The ETS Standards document is divided into seven different sections: Accountability, Confidentiality of Data, Quality Control for Accuracy and Timeliness, Research and Development, Tests and Measurement, Test Use and Public Information. The first three sections contain statements which are relevant to all ETS's activities, while the remaining four are relevant to specific areas of interest. Each section contains a statement of the principles to which ETS intends to adhere and the policies by which it intends to abide. These are followed by detailed procedural guidelines, which state precisely what action needs to be taken to ensure high-quality tests and services.

About a third of the document is devoted to the area of Tests and Measurement. This section contains detailed guidelines relating to validity, test development, test administration, reliability, scale definition, equating and score interpretation. We reproduce the final five entries under 'Test Development', to give some idea of their level of detail:

10. Evaluate the performance of each test edition by:

    carrying out timely and appropriate item and test analyses, including analyses for reliability, intercorrelation of sections or parts, and speededness; and

    comparing the test's characteristics to its psychometric specifications.

11. Review periodically the adequacy of fit of item response models and the sample used for estimating item parameters, when item response theory procedures are used to develop, score, or equate the test.

12. Review test content and test specifications periodically to assure their continuing relevance and appropriateness to the domain being tested.

13. Review periodically all active test editions developed in prior years and their descriptions in publications to assure the continued appropriateness of both content and language for the present test-taking population and the subject-matter domain.

14. Analyse major changes in test specifications to assure that they are followed by appropriate consideration of the implications for score comparability and to determine whether test name changes or other cautions to test users about comparisons with earlier tests are necessary.

(page 12)

11.4.4 *Distinctive characteristics*

There are two characteristics which set the ETS Standards apart from the other standards we are presenting: the fact that they represent 'corporate policy' and the fact that there is a regulatory mechanism built into the ETS organisational structure which ensures that the standards will be heeded.

In the Introduction to the ETS Standards, it is acknowledged that the Standards 'reflect and adopt' the AERA/APA/NCME Standards. However, ETS also makes it clear that their standards have been designed to suit their own particular professional context: '... the Standards may not be useful to organisations whose practices, programs, or services differ from those of ETS' (page vi).

ETS itself is the first judge of whether it has interpreted the policies and followed the procedural guidelines satisfactorily; however, the organisation also submits itself to an elaborate and rigorous auditing procedure in which independent external reviewers evaluate whether ETS's performance in various areas measures up to its own Standards. The auditing team report to the ETS Office of Corporate Quality Assurance, which summarises both the auditing report and the action that ETS personnel have taken in response to the report. This summary is submitted to individuals and committees at the top of the organisational hierarchy.

ETS also invites a 'Visiting Committee' to evaluate its performance in relation to the Standards. This committee is made up of 'distinguished educational leaders, experts in testing, and representatives of organisations that have been critical of ETS in the past' (page iii). This committee also prepares a report for ETS, which is published by the organisation and is released to the media and any members of the public who request a copy.

It is clear that in the ETS context the term 'standards' carries more than a moral connotation: since there is a regulatory mechanism built into the organisation's policy, the Standards resemble rules more than guidelines. However, the rules are not mechanical. There is room for interpretation (e.g. 'ETS will construct tests that are sufficiently reliable for their intended use(s)'), and testers are given the opportunity to explain how they have interpreted certain statements and why they have not been able to follow certain procedures.

11.4.5 Commentary

The ETS Standards are clear and comprehensible: they were written for testing professionals rather than the general public, but the organisation and wording of the standards are easy to follow. The document includes a 7-page glossary to clarify the key terms used in the procedural guidelines.

The coverage of the Standards is also thorough. ETS has dealt with the technical quality of tests and its responsibilities toward test users and test takers; in addition, ETS has addressed issues having to do with accessibility of information for researchers and the general public.

However, the most interesting feature of the Standards is not the wording or the coverage, but rather the fact that they were written to be complied with. Since non-compliance, if not explained convincingly, can lead to serious consequences (including programme curtailment), ETS professionals must consider very carefully all the steps they follow when preparing a product for their public, and they cannot allow themselves or their colleagues to slip into complacency. It is not clear whether such scrutiny would be possible or even desirable amongst testers at large. This is one of the many issues which needs to be considered in future debates on standards.

11.5 *Standards for Educational Testing Methods (1986)*

11.5.1 *Background*

Nevo and Shohamy wrote in 1986 of an adaptation they had made of the *Standards for Evaluation of Educational Programs, Projects and Materials* (1981). These Standards had been developed over a number of years by the Joint Committee on Standards for Educational Evaluation, made up of members from the AERA, the APA, the NCME and nine other organisations. They were designed in order to give guidance to professionals involved in the evaluation of educational programmes, and it was hoped that the establishment of a common set of principles would help to upgrade the practice of educational evaluation (page 5).

The Joint Committee developed a set of 30 Standards, divided into four headings: Utility Standards, Feasibility Standards, Propriety Standards and Accuracy Standards. They devoted a chapter to each of the Standards, containing a formal statement of the Standard, an overview explaining why it was important, guidelines to help researchers to achieve the Standard, a list of possible pitfalls, a set of caveats, and an authentic case history illustrating the problems that researchers in the past had faced when they were not aware of or did not apply the Standard. The case history is accompanied by advice to help future researchers avoid the same problems.

Nevo and Shohamy attempted to extend these Standards to testing methods. From the Joint Committee's original 30 Standards they produced a list of 23 that they believed were suitable for testing methods. This was accomplished by eliminating some of the original Standards, combining others, and adding one or two new ones. Like the Joint Committee, they divided their Standards into four sections. They arranged these sections in a different order, but left the Standards within each section in roughly the same order as the original document. All of the Standards were re-worded so that they would apply to test methods rather than to evaluation programmes.

Nevo and Shohamy were not content with the mere formulation of the Standards: they decided to try them out on relevant professionals. They asked two groups to study the Standards and use them to rank four alternative testing methods which were being considered for a new national matriculation examination. The first group consisted of the policy-makers who were supposed to make the final decision about which of the testing methods would be included in the new exam; the second group consisted of testing experts attending a language-testing

249

conference. They also designed a sample test which contained all four of the testing methods under consideration. This was administered to 1,000 students, to find out not only how the tests performed in the real world but also to provide a basis for assessing whether several of the new testing Standards could be used to evaluate such testing methods.

11.5.2 Overall organisation

The resulting *Standards for Educational Testing Methods* were organised as follows:

1. *Utility Standards*

   The Utility Standards are intended 'to ensure that a testing method will serve the practical information needs of given audiences'.

   The issues addressed in this section are Audience Identification, Tester Credibility, Information Scope, Justified Criteria, Report Clarity, Report Dissemination, Report Timeliness and Evaluation Impact.

2. *Accuracy Standards*

   The Accuracy Standards are intended 'to ensure that a testing method will reveal and convey technically adequate information on the educational achievements of those that are being tested'.

   The issues presented in this section are Valid Measurement, Reliable Measurement, Testing Conditions, Data Analysis and Objective Reporting.

3. *Feasibility Standards*

   Feasibility Standards are intended 'to ensure that a testing method will be realistic, prudent and frugal'.

   The issues presented in this section are Practical Procedures, Political Viability and Cost Effectiveness.

4. *Fairness Standards*

   These are intended 'to ensure that a testing method is conducted legally, ethically, and with due regard to the welfare of tested individuals as well as those affected by test results'.

   The issues presented here are Accepted Criteria, Rights of Human Subjects, Public's Right to Know, Conflict of Interest, Social Values and Balanced Reporting.

   (page 151)

11.5.3 Commentary

Although Nevo and Shohamy's proposals deal with some technical aspects of testing (e.g. B–1, Valid Measurement: 'Testing is conducted by instruments and procedures providing valid information for a given use'; and B–2, Reliable Measurement: 'Testing is conducted by instruments and procedures providing reliable information for a given use.'), they show a stronger interest in the context of the testing situation and how the public views the test itself; the reports; and the effect of the test on the candidates, education and society. The political viability of a test (C–2: 'Testing is planned and conducted with anticipation of the different positions of various interest groups, so that their cooperation may be obtained.') is an issue which does not appear in other sets of testing standards. In the Joint Committee's original document this Standard was presented thus:

> The evaluation should be planned and conducted with anticipation of
> the different positions of various interest groups, so that their
> cooperation may be obtained, and that possible attempts by any of
> these groups to curtail evaluation operations or to bias or misapply the
> results can be averted or counteracted.
>
> (page 56)

It is interesting that Nevo and Shohamy have left out the second part of the original Standard, in which it is clearly recognised that educational evaluations can be used as political weapons, and that evaluators need to be aware of all of the possible ways in which their evaluations can be misused so that they can pre-empt any wrong-doing. Both the AERA/APA/NCME Standards and the Code of Fair Testing Practices have sections concerning the possible misuse of tests, but it is not clear whether they refer to misuse as the result of ignorance or carelessness or whether they recognise that there are parties who might deliberately misuse information in the way that is implied in the Standard above. The question for the future is whether the dangers that exist for educational evaluators also exist for test developers and users, and whether testing standards should include guidelines to help those involved in testing to cope with the problems of *Realpolitik*.

As for the applicability of the new set of standards to testing methods, Nevo and Shohamy conclude that their Standards could be adopted and could be used 'as a framework to analyse and assess the merits of alternative testing methods' (page 157). They state that they consider their study as 'only a partial attempt to study the whole scope of the Standards', and encourage other researchers to undertake more systematic research in this area.

11.6 *SEAC's Mandatory Code of Practice* (1993)

11.6.1 Background

The Schools Examination and Assessment Council (SEAC) was established by the UK Government in the 1980s to oversee standards and procedures in examination development within the context of the National Curriculum for primary and secondary schools in England and Wales. It has since been somewhat reorganised and renamed Schools Curriculum and Assessment Authority (SCAA).

At the age of 16 in England and Wales, secondary school pupils take a set of examinations which, for many, are their school-leaving examinations (known as the General Certificate of Secondary Education – GCSE). Such examinations are developed by a number of different examining groups or boards, and over time a large number of different syllabuses, examinations and examining practices have evolved.

With the advent of the National Curriculum, it was felt necessary to rationalise this plurality of syllabuses and systems, and to regulate how examining groups prepared and validated their examinations. In the late 1980s, the Secretary of State for Education requested SEAC to prepare a Code of Practice for the future conduct of the GCSE examining process in England and Wales. 'Compliance with the Code will be a requirement for the approval of GCSE qualifications and associated syllabuses under Section 5 of the 1988 Education Reform Act.' (SEAC, Preface)

11.6.2 Purpose

The Code is intended to guarantee 'quality and consistency in the examining process across all examining groups offering GCSE. It will ensure that grading standards will be constant in each subject across different examining bodies and different syllabuses and from year to year' (loc. cit.).

11.6.3 Organisation

The Code of Practice is divided into six sections, as follows:

1. *Responsibilities of Examining Groups and Examining Group Personnel*

   This defines the roles of the group's governing council, its Chief Executive, examining group officers, Chairman of Examiners, Chief Examiner, principal examiners, revisers, assessors, assistant examiners and principal and assistant moderators.

2. *Setting of Question Papers and Provisional Mark Schemes for Terminal Examinations and End-of-Module Tests*

This deals with how examining groups should ensure that question papers and mark schemes cover the assessment objectives and that standards are maintained across different syllabuses. It includes detail on how the editing and revising process should be conducted.

3. *Standardisation of Marking: Terminal Examinations and End-of-Module Tests*

This seeks to ensure reliability of marking by stipulating marking team membership and training, the standardisation process, and the monitoring of marking, as well as eventual mark adjustment in the light of problems with individual examiners.

4. *Coursework Assessment and Moderation*

This covers the external monitoring of standards of assessment of coursework across examining centres or schools. It details the need for teacher training and supervision of the setting of coursework tasks as well the standardisation of marking and the moderation of marks across centres.

5. *Setting of Grade/Level Boundaries*

This deals with procedures aimed at ensuring that grade/level standards are maintained across time and over different syllabuses. It stipulates what information should be taken into account in determining grade/level boundaries, and how grade/level boundaries must be set and reviewed.

6. *The Assessment of Spelling, Punctuation and Grammar*

This reflects the Government's concern that levels of spelling, punctuation and grammar must be maintained or improved, and defines the proportion of marks that must be given for performance in these areas, regardless of the subject matter being examined. This applies to examinations, end-of-module tests and coursework.

11.6.4 Commentary

Perhaps the most noteworthy feature of this Code of Practice is that it is mandatory, that is, legally enforceable. How the Code will operate is still unknown: how it will be implemented and monitored, and quite what sanctions will be taken if an examining group should fail to comply with one or more of the requirements. It will be most interesting to observe developments over time.

The second point to note is that the Code is intended to relate to tests/examinations that are achievement-oriented, whose syllabuses act as teaching syllabuses in the schools and whose content is defined by law through the National Curriculum. Thus the Code applies equally to coursework and end-of-module assessment as it does to examinations.

Since English as a Foreign Language is not part of the National Curriculum, EFL tests are unaffected by the Code, although English as a Mother Tongue will be affected, as will modern foreign languages. Whether those examination boards that produce EFL examinations will decide voluntarily to adhere to the Code remains to be seen, but we would want to scrutinise closely the motives of any examination board that decided not to extend this Code (which is said to be based on 'the very best examining practice') to include non-regulated subjects like EFL.

Finally, it is interesting to note that the UK Government has seen fit to attempt to legislate the assessment of one part of English language use, whilst ignoring many other aspects. Five percent of marks for each written component of any examination (except for multiple-choice papers and examinations written in a foreign language) must be allocated to spelling, punctuation and grammar according to three so-called performance criteria: Threshold, Intermediate and High. Whether any internationally agreed set of standards would dare or even wish to be so prescriptive is a moot point, which we touch upon in the next section.

11.7 What should we be looking for in standards?

We mentioned earlier that we had selected six specific sets of standards because these sets were good examples of the kind of work that has been done in the recent past and because each set of standards adds something new to our understanding of what standards can and need to be. Our commentary at the end of each description discusses what we consider the strong and weak points of each set of standards to be, and we will not repeat those points here. What we will do, however, is to provide a list of questions which we feel should be addressed by any organisation attempting to design its own standards in the future.

Is it necessary to create any more standards? What is wrong with the ones we have got already?

If the answer is that the standards already in existence do not cater for language testing, what is missing that should be there?

If the answer to this question has to do with a particular view of language or methodology, will we reach agreement about which content and methodology are best and will this agreement last for more than a few years, when a new fashion changes our views about what the most appropriate content and methodology should be?

Will any one set of standards be suitable for the range of tests on offer, or will standards which are suitable for one sort of test force all other tests into the same mould (e.g. discrete-point vs. performance-based tests)?

How comprehensive should standards be? Should they be confined to testing instruments and test procedures, or should they concern themselves with test use? Should they go even further and provide guidelines for dealing with political realities and the dubious intentions of some people in our societies?

How detailed should they be? Where is the line between essential detail and triviality?

What sort of language should be used – language that will be understood by testers or language that the general public can understand?

Which languages should they be written in, and who will do the translations?

How idealistic should they be? Should they describe the minimum in good practice or should they describe the maximum?

How prescriptive should and can they be?

Should some standards be more dispensable than others? Is the primary, secondary and conditional distinction useful or is it confusing?

Should standards be enforceable? If so, who will enforce them? If not, how can we be sure that all parties are putting their best into the effort?

Is there a way of 'piloting' the standards, so that we can find out if they are effective?

11.8 State of the art in EFL testing in the UK

In this book we have presented the results of a survey of EFL examination boards in the UK, to illustrate current practice in language testing in one geographical area. We are confident that our survey covered the most significant EFL examinations in the UK and is representative of current UK practice in EFL testing.

The results of the survey show that there are some procedures which all or most boards follow, and others where there is considerably more variation. The most important areas of agreement are: the availability of descriptions of exam content; the criteria used to appoint item/test writers, and the nature of their contractual relationship with the boards; the editing or moderation process; the production of different versions each year; the criteria for the appointment of examiners; the lack of 'objective' or clerical marking; the existence of standardising meetings for examiners; the calculation, if only occasionally, of some estimate of examiner reliability; the production (though they are generally not made available to the public) of Chief Examiners' Reports; and the gathering of feedback on exams, typically from exam centres and, possibly, teachers. Most boards felt that psychometric criteria were indeed relevant to UK examinations, although it was not clear from the survey how they felt that their exams met such criteria.

The most significant areas where practice varies considerably are: item/question pretesting; test validation; procedures to ensure the equivalence of different versions of exams; the training and monitoring of administrators; the double-marking of all scripts; the existence of grade-awarding meetings; the availability of Chief Examiners' Reports; and the calculation and availability of statistics on an examination's performance.

Some of our analyses showed, however, that agreement may, in some cases, be more apparent than real. Thus, for example, although marker reliability may be calculated by most boards, the frequency with which it is calculated, how it is calculated, and what happens to the results, appears to vary considerably. Similarly, although double-marking was said to be carried out by most boards, what was meant by double-marking varied, amounting in several cases to little more than a Chief Examiner doing some spot checking of single markers. Although most boards have standardising meetings for markers, what actually happens in those meetings seems to vary. We would need to conduct a much more detailed inspection of each board's activities to arrive at an accurate account of what actually happens.

Thus, although we do not eschew judgement, it is likely that justified evaluations of the quality of the quality control procedures must await such a detailed inspection. That would only be feasible with the co-operation of the boards, and it would only make sense to conduct it if there were agreement on what should happen when examinations are produced and administered and what an investigator should be looking for. The various standards we have reviewed in this chapter are obvious points of reference.

The results of the survey seem to show that information is generally available on the content of the examinations, but that the nature of this information and the degree of detail contained varies considerably. Guidance specifically addressed to candidates appears to be lacking, and few boards give examples of students' performances on previous examinations. Although the majority of boards claim that a 'needs analysis' exists to justify or guide the development of their exams, the nature of such analyses seems likely to be very variable. Most boards seem to understand the term 'needs analysis' to be equivalent to 'consulting teachers'.

Item writers are generally qualified and experienced teachers of EFL who might be considered to be in touch with current thinking within the teaching profession, and therefore to be potentially capable of incorporating that thinking into the exams. The lack of full-time professional item writers might also be seen as one way of ensuring continued contact with the teaching profession. Test writers receive a reasonable amount of guidance as to test content and test method. Test editing/moderating procedures do exist, although it is difficult to determine how thorough these are. This is likely to vary from board to board, from committee to committee and, particularly, from Chief Examiner to Chief Examiner. Much, in other words, depends upon the quality of the judgements of individuals. In particular, the thoroughness of procedures for checking exam content against the syllabus is unknown. In addition, it is not clear to what extent the editing committees are open to the views of 'critical outsiders'.

The widespread absence of pretesting is a cause for considerable concern, since pretesting can provide corroboration or otherwise of the value of the judgements of the editors, moderators and examiners. At present, it appears that even when it occurs, pretesting is largely confined to objective items, yet most boards do not use objective items. In any case, there is no obvious reason why open-ended or other non-objective test types should not also be subject to the rigour of pretesting.

The absence of evidence from some boards that their exams are validated empirically in any way other than anecdotally is worrying, as is the suggestion that not all boards understand what is meant by validation, validity and reliability. It may well be the case that these exams are valid, but validity should be the subject of investigation, not assertion. Even when validation is said to be done, this is acknowledged by some to be done 'impressionistically and in anecdotal ways', for example by claiming that 'companies and universities seem to be happy'. Some boards claimed they undertook occasional validity studies, but as no details were provided, we must remain sceptical.

The equivalence of different versions of exams was said to be guaranteed through the use of the editing/moderating procedures, by reference to the syllabus, and by the use of the same item writers and editing committees over a period of time. It is certainly possible that where they exist, those grade-awarding procedures that take account of the performance of candidates on previous years' examinations might contribute to a comparability in difficulty over the years, but in any case not all boards engage in such procedures.

Similarly, there is a lack of evidence to date on the reliability of the exams and the reliability of marking. Steps are taken to train and monitor markers, but little systematic attention seems to be paid to establishing whether the training and monitoring procedures have indeed been effective. Again, reliability should be measured, not asserted. It appears that about half the responding boards do calculate statistics on marker performance, but we have not had access to these. True double-marking occurs very rarely.

The examination boards claim that their exams are based upon the best of current EFL teaching and have a beneficial effect upon teaching, but we neither know what the best of current EFL teaching is, nor have we seen any evidence of beneficial washback effect. Once again, unsubstantiated claims are made for the quality of the exams that ought to be subject to critical scrutiny.

Nevertheless, our survey suggests that the various procedures followed by the boards are not necessarily inadequate, and that the boards may well have data available which could attest to the quality – the reliability and validity – of their exams. The results of our survey suggest that more is being done by the various boards than was expected and than is known publicly. The fact is that what information there is is not readily, publicly available, and it took a great deal of effort and time on our part to get as far as we have. This should not be necessary. If evidence is available to support claims of test quality, that evidence ought to be made publicly available. Furthermore, we believe that the information ought to be readily available, and not only after considerable efforts have been made to extract it.

At present, it appears that the different boards involved in EFL testing do different things, with differing degrees of rigour, to monitor the quality of their examinations. The results of this survey imply that there is no agreement on what procedures should be followed by those who produce EFL exams, and no accepted set of standards which those EFL exams should meet.

We believe that the time is ripe for UK examination boards and UK language testers to develop a set of standards which all EFL tests should follow, and to discuss what procedures would be most appropriate to ensure that those standards are met.

11.9 Conclusion

Language testing still lacks any agreed standards by which language tests can be evaluated, compared or selected. The need for such standards is being discussed and work is already in progress which may in due course lead to the development of internationally appropriate standards.

Nevertheless, as we hope this volume has made clear, language-testing theory already has a set of principles which can inform test development and test research. These are broadly subsumed under headings such as validity, reliability, practicality or feasibility, and impact or washback. Language testers also have an array of procedures which are generally thought to be appropriate in the development and administration of tests if those tests are to represent the best of professional practice. This book has sought to explain the principles and describe the procedures. We have also been able to describe the current practice of one set of developers of language tests. That practice varies considerably in its nature, in its detail, and in its quality.

There are, of course, understandable reasons why the development of any one test will not conform to all the best principles and procedures, and it is to be hoped that most test developers are conscious of the continuous need to improve their procedures and products. We hope that this book has indicated not only where these might be improved, but also how that improvement might be achieved, and we look forward to conducting a similar survey in the future, either in the UK or internationally, with reference to English or to other languages. We very much hope that we will find that things have moved on, that there have been improvements, and that the professionalism of language testers, be they within examination boards, commercial companies, ministries or individual schools and colleges, has made progress.

Bibliography

Association of Language Testers in Europe. 1994. *The ALTE Code of Practice*. Cambridge: ALTE.

American Education Research Association, American Psychological Association, and National Council on Measurement in Education. 1985. *Standards for Educational and Psychological Testing.* Washington, DC: American Psychological Association, Inc.

Diamond, E.E. and J. Fremer. 1989. The Joint Committee on Testing Practices and the Code of Fair Testing Practices in Education. *Educational Measurement: Issues and Practice.* Spring issue.

Heaton, J.B. 1988. *Writing English Language Tests.* 2nd edition. London: Longman.

Joint Committee on Standards for Educational Evaluation. 1981. *Standards for Evaluations of Educational Programs, Projects, and Materials.* New York: McGraw Hill.

Joint Committee on Testing Practices. 1988. *Code of Fair Testing Practices in Education.* Washington, DC: American Psychological Association.

Nevo, D. and E. Shohamy. 1986. Evaluation Standards for the Assessment of Alternative Testing Methods: an Application. *Studies in Educational Evaluation* 12: 149–158.

Pollitt, A. 1990. Standards. Notes prepared for a meeting to discuss language testing standards. Cambridge: University of Cambridge Local Examinations Syndicate.

Schools Examination and Assessment Council. 1993. *Mandatory Code of Practice for the GCSE.* London: SEAC.

Appendices

Appendix 1

Examination boards consulted in the questionnaire survey and the tests they produce

Names of Examination Boards

ARELS Examination Trust (AET)
Associated Examining Board (AEB)
City and Guilds of London Institute (C & G)
English Speaking Board (ESB)
Joint Matriculation Board (JMB)
London Chamber of Commerce and Industry Examinations Board (LCCI)
North West Regional Examinations Board (CENTRA)
Pitman Examinations Institute (PEI)
Trinity College London (Trinity)
University of Cambridge Local Examinations Syndicate (UCLES)
University of London Schools Examination Board (ULSEB)
University of Oxford Delegacy of Local Examinations (OUDLES)

Examinations Referred to in Board's Response

ARELS Examination Trust (AET)
ARELS Examinations in Spoken English & Comprehension (3 levels)

Associated Examining Board (AEB)
Test of English for Educational Purposes (TEEP)

City and Guilds of London Institute (C & G)
Communication in Technical English (Overseas) (CTE)
Communication Skills (CS)
English
Wordpower

<u>English Speaking Board</u> (ESB)
English as an Acquired Language (EAL)

<u>Joint Matriculation Board</u> (JMB)
University Entrance Test in English for Speakers of Other Languages (UETESOL)

<u>London Chamber of Commerce and Industry Examinations Board</u> (LCCI)
English for Commerce (3 levels) (EfC)
English for Business (3 levels) (EfB)
Spoken English for Industry and Commerce (4 levels) (SEfIC)

<u>North West Regional Examinations Board</u> (CENTRA)
Tests in English Language Skills (3 levels) (TELS)

<u>Pitman Examinations Institute</u> (PEI)
English for Speakers of Other Languages (5 levels) (ESOL)

<u>Trinity College London</u> (Trinity)
Graded Examinations in Spoken English for Speakers of Other Languages

<u>University of Cambridge Local Examinations Syndicate</u> (UCLES)
Preliminary English Test (PET)
First Certificate in English (FCE)
Certificate in Advanced English (CAE)
Certificate of Proficiency in English (CPE)
Diploma of English Studies (DES)
Certificates in Communicative Skills in English (4 levels) (CCSE)
Certificate in English for International Business and Trade (CEIBT)
Cambridge Examination in English for Language Teachers (CEELT)
International English Language Testing System (IELTS)
International General Certificate of Secondary Education (IGCSE)

<u>University of London Schools Examination Board</u> (ULSEB)
Certificate of Attainment in English: (CAE)
    a) non-language laboratory version levels 1–6
    b) language laboratory version levels 3–6

<u>University of Oxford Delegacy of Local Examinations</u> (OUDLES)
Oxford Preliminary Exam (OPE)
Oxford Higher Exam (OHE)

Appendix 2

Questionnaire and covering letter sent to examination boards

JCA/AIGD

November 1990

Dear Colleague,

As you may remember, the Lancaster Language Testing Research Group is conducting a survey of British ESOL examining boards in an attempt to determine what standards and procedures are followed in the construction, validation and administration of language tests.

We have already benefited from your responses to a letter containing three open-ended questions seeking to elicit the boards' own views of their standards, and the procedure used to establish reliability and validity. In addition, we have gathered data from four other sources:

i) Members of the Research Group have been able to draw upon a range of experience in working with various ESOL examining boards as markers, item and test writers, members of editing or moderating committees and grade awarding meetings, as well as ad hoc working parties and advisory bodies. EFL examining boards with whom we have worked include: the JMB, AEB, UCLES, Institute of Linguists, RSA, PLAB. In addition, several members have experience of teaching students who have been working towards one or more of the exams produced by such examining bodies.

ii) A series of interviews with representatives of several examining boards as part of a separate research project into English examinations overseas. These interviews resulted in a number of reports whose content was subsequently agreed with the examining boards.

iii) Visits to a number of examining boards with participants on courses in language testing over a period of three years.

iv) Reviews of 13 British EFL tests, and the reactions to these reviews of representatives of the responsible boards, which were published in Alderson, Krahnke and Stansfield 1987, *Review of English Language Proficiency Tests*.

We are now seeking to complete the information through a structured questionnaire, which draws in part upon the above sources of information.

We are very aware that you are likely to be very busy, and so we have attempted to restrict the length of time required to complete the questionnaire. However, in the interests of ensuring that we have as complete a dataset as possible, we would be very grateful if you could take some time to answer the enclosed questionnaire.

We shall be presenting a paper (a revised abstract for which will shortly be submitted) on our findings at an international conference in March 1991, and so we hope to be able to gather as much information as possible before then, to ensure that our report is as representative as it can possibly be. In that presentation, we do not propose to mention the names of any individual boards unless this is explicitly requested by the board. If, however, you would prefer any of the information you are able to let us have to remain confidential, then please let us know.

We are very grateful for the cooperation we have enjoyed to date on this project, and would especially thank those boards who have already taken the trouble to respond at length. We hope that the attached questionnaire does not unduly duplicate the information some boards have already passed on. We feel, however, that to avoid possible misinterpretations on our part of the responses we have already received, it would be in the interests of clarity and completeness if you could spare the time to answer all the questions, even if this means some duplication. We believe that the results of this survey will be of considerable use to the profession, and will also help the British examining boards in their attempts to establish the value of their tests in the international marketplace. We are concerned that our results should reflect the quality of British examinations and therefore very much hope that our data can be as complete, accurate and unprejudiced as possible.

We very much hope that you will be able to respond to this questionnaire. If, however, you would prefer us to discuss these matters with you rather than for you to respond in writing, we will be happy to arrange to meet your representatives.

We would be very grateful if you could respond by December 21st. If this is not possible, could you please let us know by when we might expect a response.

Thank you in advance for your cooperation.

Yours sincerely,

J. Charles Alderson
Coordinator
Lancaster Language Testing Research Group

Questionnaire

The aim of this questionnaire is to establish and confirm the practices followed by British ESOL examining boards in constructing, validating, and administering their examinations. It may be that some of the information you are able to supply is confidential or restricted in circulation. Please indicate in your responses to the questions below when this is the case.

It may be the case that you feel unwilling to answer a particular question or that the question is irrelevant. If either applies, please indicate against the question concerned.

You may feel upon completing this questionnaire that there are important aspects of your work that we have not covered, or emphasised sufficiently. Should this be the case, please indicate this, either in a separate letter, or at the end of the questionnaire.

Finally, if practices or procedures are different for the different examinations you produce, could you please indicate the differences where appropriate.

1. Name of Examining Board ....

2. Name of Respondent ....

3. Position within above Board ....

4. For how long have you worked in the above capacity? ....

5. Which examinations are referred to in your responses below?

....

....

....

SYLLABUS

6. Does your board publish a description of
   the content of the examination(s)?   Yes   No

7. If Yes, does this description include any
   of the following?
   a) A statement of the purpose of the   Yes   No
       examination.
   b) A description of the sort of student   Yes   No
       for whom the examination is
       intended.

c)	A description of the level of difficulty of the examination.	Yes	No
d)	A description of a typical performance at each grade level or score.	Yes	No
e)	A description of what a candidate achieving a pass or any given grade or level can be expected to be able to do 'in the real world'.	Yes	No
f)	A description of a/the course of study which students might be expected to follow prior to taking the examination.	Yes	No
g)	A description of the content of the examination with respect to:		
	structures	Yes	No
	vocabulary	Yes	No
	language functions	Yes	No
	topics	Yes	No
	text length	Yes	No
	question types	Yes	No
	weighting of questions	Yes	No
	timing of each paper	Yes	No
	timing of subsections of each paper	Yes	No
h)	A description of the criteria which will be used to evaluate students' performance.	Yes	No
i)	A description of how final scores or grades are derived.	Yes	No
j)	Examples of previous papers.	Yes	No
k)	Examples of students' performances on previous papers.	Yes	No
l)	Anything in addition to the above. Please give details below or separately.	Yes	No

8. Has any form of 'needs analysis' been conducted to help the board decide upon the purpose, content, method, level etc. of of the examination?   Yes   No

If Yes, please attach the description to this questionnaire.

9. Are item or test writers given any further   Yes   No
   information or guidance?

   If Yes, please attach the description to this
   questionnaire.

10. When students register for your
    examination, what information are they
    given about the test's purpose and content?

EXAMINATION CONSTRUCTION

11. What criteria are used in the appointment
    of item/test writers?

12. For what period are item/test writers
    appointed?

13. How far in advance of the date of the
    examination's administration are item
    writers first asked to produce their items?

14. How long are item writers given to produce
    the first draft of an item?

15. Once the first draft has been produced
    by an individual setter, what then
    happens to it?

16. Does a committee meet at any point to   Yes   No
    discuss each paper/test?

    If Yes, what is this committee called?

17. What qualifies people to be members of
    this committee?

18. How long (number of hours/days) does a
    committee take to discuss/edit a complete
    examination?

19. What steps, if any, are taken to ensure that
    the draft examination follows the syllabus
    (if one exists)?

20. What typically happens to the draft
    examination after the above committee
    has deliberated?

21. Are items/questions pre-tested?   Yes   No

    If Yes, how are students selected, and how
    many take each item/question?

22. If items/questions are pre-tested, what
    statistics are calculated on the results?

23. What happens if trial items/questions
    are unsatisfactory?

24. What steps, if any, in addition to the above,
    are taken to monitor the quality of
    individual item/test writers?

VALIDATION

25. In addition to the above procedures for face
    and content validation, are any of the
    following types of validity:

    a) applicable?
    b) estimated or calculated?

	applicable		*estimated*	
i) concurrent validity	Yes	No	Yes	No
ii) predictive validity	Yes	No	Yes	No
iii) construct validity	Yes	No	Yes	No

26. Are special validity studies conducted on
    your examinations?   Yes   No

    If Yes, could you please attach details or a
    copy of relevant reports?

27. If different versions of your examination   Yes   No
    are given each year, are measures taken to
    ensure that they are equivalent?

    If Yes, please attach a description of these
    measures.

28. Is more than one form of any examination   Yes   No
    paper given in any given examination
    period?

    If Yes, what steps are taken to ensure that
    each form is equivalent in difficulty?

ADMINISTRATION

29. Are examination administrators given   Yes   No
    special training?
    If Yes, by whom and how long does this
    training last?

30. Is the administration of the examination   Yes   No
    monitored?
    If Yes, by whom?
    What happens as a result of the monitoring?

MARKING

31. What criteria are used in the appointment
    of markers?

32. For how long (months, years) are markers
    appointed?

33. Are any parts of the examination
    a) objectively marked, e.g. by   Yes   No
       machine or clerically?
    b) marked centrally, i.e. by teams
       working together?   Yes   No
    c) marked locally, by individuals,
       e.g. the test administrator or
       equivalent?   Yes   No

34. Does your examination board hold a   Yes   No
    meeting to standardise markers?
    If Yes, what is this meeting called?
    How long does it typically last?

35. If your examination board holds a
    'standardising meeting', what normally
    happens during this meeting?

36. What steps are taken at the end of the
    standardising meeting to establish the
    degree of agreement among markers?

37. Once marking is under way, are any scripts   Yes   No
    double marked?
    If Yes, what proportion of scripts?

38. What happens in the event of a disagreement
between first and second marker? Please
circle those that apply:
> 1) a third marker is brought in, and the two closest
>   marks used.
> 2) the two marks are averaged.
> 3) the second marker's opinion holds.
> 4) the two markers discuss and reach agreement.
> 5) other (please specify).

39. Are inter-marker correlations routinely   Yes   No
calculated?

   If No, are they ever calculated?   Yes   No

40. Are markers' means and standard   Yes   No
deviations routinely calculated?

41. Are any other procedures routinely   Yes   No
followed to calculate or to check upon
marker reliability?

   If Yes, can you describe these below or
separately or send a copy of relevant reports?

RESULTS

42. Do any further meetings (grade awarding   Yes   No
meetings, examiners' meetings) take place
before results are issued?

   If Yes, what form do these meetings take?

43. Are any special procedures followed to   Yes   No
decide upon pass/fail distinctions or
grade boundaries?

   If Yes, is it possible for you to describe these
procedures, or to send or give references to
relevant publications/reports?

44. Do Chief Examiners write Reports?	Yes	No
If Yes, are these made available		
a) to teachers?	Yes	No
b) to students?	Yes	No
c) on a restricted basis only?	Yes	No
If such reports exist, is it possible for you to send us a copy of one?	Yes	No
If it is not possible to send a copy, can you describe below or separately what such a report typically contains?		
45. Are item/question statistics calculated after the examination has been concluded?	Yes	No
If Yes, which?		
If Yes, what happens to the results?		

EXAMINATION REVISION

46. Is feedback on your examinations gathered?	Yes	No
If Yes, how is this gathered and from whom?		
47. Do routine procedures exist to ensure that your examinations are revised in the light of feedback?	Yes	No
48. How often, on average, are your EFL examinations revised?		
49. Are there any important aspects of your quality control procedures that you feel we have not covered in this questionnaire?	Yes	No
If Yes, please give details below or separately.		
50. Do you have any plans to make changes in the procedures you follow, as described above?	Yes	No
If Yes, please give details, together with an estimation as to when these will be in operation.		

51. It is said that the strength of British   Yes   No   Somewhat
    EFL examinations lies in their
    relationship to language teaching.
    Do you agree?
    Can you describe how this relation-
    ship can be demonstrated in the case
    of your examination?

52. It is also said that 'psychometric' or   Yes   No   Somewhat
    'American' criteria and procedures
    are irrelevant to British examinations.

    Do you agree?

    If you (partially) agree, what criteria
    and/or procedures are irrelevant to

    your examinations?

53. What, in your opinion, are the strengths
    of your examinations?

54. What, if any, are the weaknesses of your
    examinations?

We intend to publish the results   Yes   No
of this survey anonymously. Would you
prefer us to name your board in our
presentation?

Thank you very much indeed for your cooperation.

© Language Testing Research Group
Lancaster University, UK.
1990

(Please note that because of space limitiations in this volume,
no room has been allowed for responses to the questions.)

Appendix 3

E_{1-3} discrimination index (Ebel's D)

1. Rank the students according to their total score.

2. Divide them into three groups, making sure that the top and bottom groups have equal numbers of students.

3. Count how many students in the top group get an item right, and how many in the bottom group.

4. Find the difference between the number of correct answers in the top group (RT) and the number of correct answers in the bottom group (RB). Divide this by the total number of people in the top group (NT):

$$\frac{RT - RB}{NT}$$

For example, for the results shown in Table 4.1:

14 are correct in the top group;
13 are correct in the bottom group.

The total number of students in the top group is 21.

So, to find the D.I. you have

$$\frac{14 - 13}{21} = \frac{1}{21} = .047619$$

Corrected to two decimal places, the D.I. is +.05.

Appendix 4

Distribution statistics

Imagine eight students got the following scores:

12   28   19   15   15   35   14   15

The mean

The mean is the sum of all the scores, divided by the number of students:

$$M = \frac{\Sigma X}{N}$$

M = mean   X = the score

Σ = 'the sum of'   N = the number of students

$$\frac{\Sigma X}{N} = \frac{12 + 28 + 19 + 15 + 15 + 35 + 14 + 15}{8} = \frac{153}{8} = 19.125$$

The mean is therefore 19.13.

The mode

This is the most frequently occurring score. In this case there are three 15s, and only one of each of the other scores. The mode is therefore 15.

The median

The median is the middle score, or the mid-point in the scores. First put the scores in order:

35   28   19   15   15   15   14   12

Then count along to the mid-point of the scores. There are eight students, so the mid-point comes between the fourth and the fifth scores (there are four scores above this point, and four scores below it). Since the fourth and the fifth scores are both 15, the mid-point is 15. The median is therefore 15.

If the scores had been 35–28–19–17–15–15–14–12, the mid-point would have been between 17 and 15, so the median would have been 16.

If there had been an uneven number of scores, the median would have been the middle score. For example, if the scores were 35–28–19–17–15, the median would be 19.

The range

The range is the difference between the top score and the bottom score. The range is: 35 − 12 = 23

The standard deviation

This is the square root of the average squared deviation from the mean of the students' scores.

$$SD = \sqrt{\frac{\sum(X - M)^2}{N - 1}}$$

SD = standard deviation $\sum$ = 'the sum of'

X = the score   M = the mean of the scores

N = number of students

Step 1   List scores under X.

Step 2   List the differences between each score and the mean (19.125) under (X − M).
         Notes:
                 (i) Use the exact mean; do not correct to one or two decimal places.
                 (ii) The numbers under (X − M) should add up to 0.

Step 3   Square all the numbers listed under (X − M) and list under (X − M)².

<u>Step 4</u>   Add up the $(X - M)^2$ column. The resulting total is

$$\sum(X - M)^2.$$

<u>X</u>	<u>(X – M)</u>	<u>(X – M)²</u>
35	15.875	252.02
28	8.875	78.77
19	– .125	.02
15	– 4.125	17.02
15	– 4.125	17.02
15	– 4.125	17.02
14	– 5.125	26.67
12	<u>– 7.125</u>	<u>50.77</u>
	0	$\sum(X - M)^2 = 458.91$

You are now ready to use the formula.

$$SD = \sqrt{\frac{\sum(X - M)^2}{N - 1}} = \sqrt{\frac{458.91}{8 - 1}} = \sqrt{\frac{458.91}{7}}$$

$$= \sqrt{65.56} \quad \text{(Note: 65.56 is the variance (v) which is used in the Kuder Richardson 21 formula in Appendix 7.)}$$

$$SD = 8.1 \text{ (Use a calculator to find the square root.)}$$

Appendix 5

Rank order correlation

The formula is:

$$\text{rho} = 1 - \left(\frac{6 \sum d^2}{N(N^2 - 1)} \right)$$

rho = correlation coefficient d = difference between ranks

$\sum$ = sum of N = number of students

Example

1. List the students' scores on each test as in the table opposite. Make sure both of a student's scores are opposite one another. So, for example, Student A's scores are 20 and 12, and Student G's scores are 13 and 7.

2. Rank students on each test according to their score on that test. For example, Student A came 1st on Test 1 and 3rd on Test 2. Student G is 8th on Test 1 and also 8th on Test 2. (If you have tied scores, give the students the average of the ranks concerned. For example, C and D would have been ranked 3rd and 4th on Test 1, so their average rank is

    $$\frac{3+4}{2} = \frac{7}{2} = 3.5$$

    Students G, H and I would have been 7th, 8th and 9th, so their average rank is 8.)

3. Find the differences between each student's two ranks (d), taking the smaller number from the bigger. The difference between Student A's two ranks is $3 - 1 = 2$.

4. Square these differences.

5.   Add together these squared differences. This gives you $\sum d^2$.

Student	Score on Test 1	Score on Test 2	Rank on Test 1	Rank on Test 2	d	d²
A	20	12	1	3	2	4
B	18	11	2	4	2	4
C	17	8	3.5	7	3.5	12.25
D	17	15	3.5	1	2.5	6.25
E	16	14	5	2	3	9
F	14	6	6	9	3	9
G	13	7	8	8	0	0
H	13	10	8	5	3	9
I	13	9	8	6	2	4
J	9	4	10	10	0	0

$$\sum d^2 = 57.50$$

$$N = 10$$

$$\sum d^2 = 57.50$$

You are now ready to use the formula.

$$\text{rho} = 1 - \left(\frac{6\sum d^2}{N(N^2 - 1)} \right) = 1 - \left(\frac{6 \times 57.50}{10(100 - 1)} \right) = 1 - \left(\frac{345}{990} \right) = 1 - .3484 = .6516$$

Corrected to two decimal places, the correlation is: 0.65.

Appendix 6

Split half reliability

For this, first calculate the rank order correlation (see Appendix 5) between the odd and the even halves of the test, and then use the Spearman Brown correction formula.

1. Divide the test into two halves, with the odd items (Items 1, 3, 5, 7, etc.) in one test, and the even items (Items 2, 4, 6, 8, etc.) in the other.

2. Calculate each student's scores on the odd and even tests.

3. Give each student two ranks, one for the odd test and one for the even.

4. Calculate the rank order correlation between the two sets of ranks.

$$\text{rho} = 1 - \left(\frac{6\Sigma d^2}{N(N^2 - 1)} \right)$$

5. This correlation between the two halves of the test tells you what the reliability would be for a test which is half the length of the complete test. To find out what the reliability is for the complete test, use the Spearman Brown correction formula:

$$r_{tt} = \frac{2r_{hh}}{1 + r_{hh}}$$

r_{tt} = reliability

r_{hh} = the correlation between the two halves of the test

Student	Score on whole test	Score on Odd	Score on Even	Rank Odd	Rank Even	d	d²
A	15	8	7	2.5	3	.5	.25
B	8	6	2	4.5	9	4.5	20.25
C	9	6	3	4.5	7.5	3	9
D	6	2	4	8	5.5	2.5	6.25
E	3	0	3	10	7.5	2.5	6.25
F	10	5	5	6	4	2	4
G	14	4	10	7	1	6	36
H	18	10	8	1	2	1	1
I	2	1	1	9	10	1	1
J	12	8	4	2.5	5.5	3	9

$$\sum d^2 = 93.00$$

$$N = 10 \qquad \sum d^2 = 93$$

$$r_{hh} = 1 - \left(\frac{6\sum d^2}{N(N^2 - 1)} \right) = 1 - \left(\frac{6 \times 93}{10 \times 99} \right) = 1 - \left(\frac{558}{990} \right) = 1 - .56 = .44$$

The correlation between the two halves of the test is .44, so
$r_{hh} = .44$

$$r_{tt} = \frac{2r_{hh}}{1 + r_{hh}} = \frac{2 \times .44}{1 + .44} = .61 \qquad \text{So } r_{tt} = .61$$

The split half reliability index is .61.

Appendix 7

Kuder Richardson 21

The formula is:

$$r_{tt} = \frac{nv - M(n - M)}{(n-1)v}$$

r_{tt} = the reliability index

n = number of items

v = test variance

M = mean score

This example uses the test results given in Appendix 6.

1. The number of items in the test is 20, so: n = 20.

2. The mean score is $\frac{97}{10}$, so: M = 9.7

3. v = 26.9 (To calculate the variance follow steps 1–6 in the standard deviation example in Appendix 4.)

4. nv = 20 x 26.9 = 538

5. n – M = 20 – 9.7 = 10.3

6. M(n–M) = 9.7 x 10.3 = 99.91

7. n – 1 = 20 – 1 = 19

8. (n – 1)v = 19 x 26.9 = 511.1

Replace the symbols in the formula with the numbers:

$$r_{tt} = \frac{nv - M(n - M)}{(n-1)v}$$

$$r_{tt} = \frac{538 - 99.91}{511.1} = \frac{438.09}{511.1} = .857$$

The KR21 reliability index is .86.

The reason that this reliability index is so different from the split half one is probably because the number of students is so small, and because the results are therefore strongly affected by chance. If there had been 100 or even 50 students, the two indices would probably have been very similar, although the split half index might have been slightly lower.

Appendix 8

Statistical packages

ITEMAN *Part of the MicroCAT testing system*

Assessments Systems Corporation,
2233, University Avenue, Suite 400,
St Paul,
Minnesota 55114,
USA.

SPSS *Statistical Package for the Social Sciences*

SPSS Inc.,
444 N. Michigan Avenue,
Chicago,
Illinois 60611,
USA.

SAS *Statistical Package for Data Analysis*

SAS Institute Inc.,
SAS Circle,
Box 8000,
Cary,
North Carolina 27512-8000,
USA.

FACETS *Rasch Measurement Computer Program*

MESA Press,
5835 S. Kimbark Avenue,
Chicago,
Illinois 60637,
USA.

BIGSTEPS   *Rasch Measurement Computer Program*

MESA Press,
5835 S. Kimbark Avenue,
Chicago,
Illinois 60637,
USA.

QUEST   *The Interactive Test Analysis System*

Australian Council for Educational Research,
Radford House,
Frederick Street,
Hawthorn, Victoria 3122,
Australia.

TESTAT   *A Supplementary Module for SYSTAT*

1800 Sherman Avenue,
Evanston,
Illinois 60201-3793,
USA.

BILOG   *One-, Two-, and Three-Parameter Item Response Theory Analysis*

Scientific Software, Inc.,
Mooresville,
Indiana 46158,
USA.

Glossary

Achievement tests – Achievement tests are similar to progress tests, but they are given at the end of the course. The content of both progress and achievement tests is generally based on the course syllabus or the course textbook. (Chapter 2)

Analysis of variance – An analysis of variance essentially compares the distributions (means and standard deviations) of two or more groups to see whether the differences in the means are significant. A t-test is used for the comparison of two groups, and an F-ratio for more than two groups. (Chapter 4)

Analytic scale – An analytic scale is a type of rating scale where a candidate's performance (in, for example, writing) is analysed in terms of various components (e.g. organisation, grammar, spelling), and descriptors are given at different levels for each component. In analytic marking the candidate may receive a higher rating on one component of the performance than on another; it is up to the user to decide whether or how to combine these different ratings to provide an overall mark. (Chapter 5)

Bimodal – A distribution is bimodal if it has two modes. (Chapter 4)

Biserial correlation – See **Discrimination index**.

Concurrent validity – Concurrent validation involves the comparison of the test scores with some other measure for the same candidates taken at roughly the same time as the test. This other measure may consist of scores from a parallel version of the same test, or from some other test, or candidates' self-assessments of their language abilities, or ratings of the candidate by teachers, subject specialists, or other informants. This measure must be expressed numerically (as happens, for example, with rating scales), and must not be related to the test itself. (Chapter 8)

Construct validation – A construct is a key component in a theory. Every theory contains a number of constructs and attempts to define the relationship between the constructs. For example, some theories of reading state that there are many different constructs involved in reading (skimming, scanning, etc.) and that the constructs are different from one another. To measure the construct validity of a test a tester must articulate the theory underlying his or her test and then compare the results with that theory. Construct validation involves assessing how well a test measures the constructs it is based on. (Chapter 2)

What Bachman 1990 calls the 'classic approach to designing correlational studies for construct validation' is the multitrait-multimethod matrix (MTMM) described by Campbell and Fiske 1959. Essentially this consists of a combination of internal and external validation procedures. The theory is that tests that are related to each other will show higher intercorrelations (convergent validity) than tests that are not related to each other (divergent validity). Students are given the experimental test at the same time as other tests, some of whose properties are already known (as in concurrent validation). Wood 1991 gives a very clear explanation of multitrait-multimethod analysis, and variants on this procedure can be seen in multitrait-multimethod studies such as those by Bachman and Palmer, 1981 and 1982. (Chapter 8)

Content validity – Content (or rational) validation depends on a systematic analysis of the test's content to see whether the test contains a representative sample of the relevant language skills. Content validation involves gathering the judgement of 'experts': people whose judgement one is prepared to trust, even if it disagrees with one's own. (Chapter 8)

Correlation coefficient – A correlation coefficient is a numerical figure which represents the extent to which two sets of results agree with each other. There are many different ways of calculating correlation coefficients. The Rank Order correlation and the Pearson Product Moment correlation are explained in Chapter 4, and the formula and a worked example of the Rank Order correlation are given in Appendix 5. (Chapter 4)

Criterion-referenced – If a test is criterion-referenced, students are compared not with one another, but with a level of achievement, or a set of criteria set out in marking descriptors. (Chapter 4) (See **Norm-referenced**)

Descriptors – Descriptors are the statements which define the levels of performance at every point or nearly every point on a rating scale. (Chapter 5)

Diagnostic tests – Diagnostic tests seek to discover those areas in which a student needs further help. They can be fairly general, and show, for example, whether a student needs particular help with one of the four main language skills, or they can be more specific, seeking perhaps to identify weaknesses in a student's use of grammar. (Chapter 2)

Discrimination index (D.I.) – The discrimination index measures the extent to which the results of an individual item correlate with results from the whole test. As well as knowing how difficult an item is, it is important to know how it discriminates, that is how well it distinguishes between students at different levels of ability. If the item is working well we should expect more of the top-scoring students to know the answer than the low-scoring ones. If the strongest students get an item wrong, while the weakest students get it right, there is clearly a problem with the item, and it needs investigating. There are several different methods for calculating an item's discrimination index (E_{1-3} formula, biserial correlation, point biserial correlation), and these are explained in Chapter 4. (Chapter 4)

E_{1-3} **formula** – See **Discrimination index.**

Empirical validity – Empirical validation depends on empirical and statistical evidence as to whether students' marks on the test are similar to their marks on other appropriate measures of their ability such as their scores on other tests, their self-assessments, or their teachers' ratings of their ability. There are two types of empirical validity: concurrent validity and predictive validity. (Chapter 8) (See **Concurrent validity** and **Predictive validity**)

Equivalent tests – Equivalent tests are based on the same specifications, but they may vary as to the number of items, the response types and the content. Examining boards often have a range of test types which may be used in an exam, and they often do not expect or indeed want all of these to be used each time. What is important with equivalent tests is that they each measure the same language skills, and that they correlate highly with one another. (Chapter 4) (See **Parallel tests**)

Examiner – In this book the term 'examiner' indicates the person who is responsible for judging a candidate's performance in a test or examination. We use this term to cover all those who have this responsibility, regardless of whether they mark objective or subjective sections of the test, and regardless of whether they have been involved in the design or administration of the examination. We distinguish between examiner and interlocutor in the testing of speaking: the former refers to the person who assesses the candidates, while the latter refers to a separate person who interacts with the candidate while the examiner assesses the candidate's performance. (Chapter 5)

External validity – External validity relates to studies comparing students' test scores with measures of their ability gleaned from outside the test. External validity is often called criterion validity (see American Psychological Association 1985) because the students' scores are being compared to other criterion measures of their ability. There are two types of external validity: concurrent validity and predictive validity. (Chapter 8) (See **Concurrent validity and Predictive validity**)

Face validity – Face validity refers to the test's 'surface credibility or public acceptability' (Ingram, 1977: 18), and is frequently dismissed by testers as being unscientific and irrelevant. Essentially face validity involves an intuitive judgement about the test's content, by people whose judgement is not necessarily 'expert'. Typically such people include 'lay' people – administrators, non-expert users and students. (Chapter 8)

Facility value (F.V.) – The facility value measures the level of difficulty of an item. It represents the percentage of students answering it correctly. (Chapter 4)

Factor analysis – Factor analysis takes a matrix of correlation coefficients, which is typically too complex to understand by superficial study, and reduces the complexity of such a matrix to more manageable proportions. The result of this reduction is used to identify factors which groups of items have in common. (Chapter 8)

Generalisability theory – Generalisability theory is based on analysis of variance and can estimate the reliability of a whole group of markers at once. (Chapter 6)

Holistic scale – A holistic scale is a type of rating scale where examiners are asked not to pay too much attention to any one aspect of a candidate's performance, but rather to judge its overall effectiveness. They are asked, for example, to judge general writing ability rather than to make separate judgements about a candidate's organisation, grammar, spelling etc. (Chapter 5)

Impression scale – This is a type of holistic scale which allows examiners to make fairly quick judgements of a candidate's performance. (Chapter 5)

Interlocutor – A person (usually a teacher) who interacts with the candidate in a test of speaking, to elicit language, while a separate person called the examiner assesses the candidate's performance. (Chapter 5) (See **Examiner**)

Internal validity – Internal validity relates to studies of the perceived content of a test and its perceived effect. There are several types of internal validity: Face validity, Content validity, Construct validity and Response validity. (Chapter 8) (See **Face validity, Content validity, Construct validity** and **Response validity**)

Inter-rater reliability – Inter-rater reliability refers to the degree of similarity between different examiners: can two or more examiners, without influencing one another, give the same marks to the same set of scripts or oral performances? It would not be realistic to expect all examiners to match one another all the time; however, it is essential that each examiner try to match the standard all the time. Inter-rater reliability is usually measured by means of a correlation coefficient, or through some form of analysis of variance. (Chapter 6) (See **Intra-rater reliability**)

Intra-rater reliability – An examiner is judged to have intra-rater reliability if he or she gives the same marks to the same set of scripts or oral performances on two different occasions. The examiner may still be considered reliable even if some of the marks are different; however, not much variation can be allowed before the reliability becomes questionable. Intra-rater reliability is usually measured by means of a correlation coefficient, or through some form of analysis of variance. (Chapter 6) (See **Inter-rater reliability**)

Item bank – An item bank is a set of pretested items or tasks which have been calibrated according to characteristics such as person ability, item difficulty, and powers of discrimination, and stored in a central file for use when needed. When test constructors are devising a new version of a test, they can select from the bank items which will not only be of a suitable level for the test population, but will also, when assembled together, combine to form a test which is equivalent in difficulty and discrimination to previous tests in the series. (Chapter 4)

Item characteristic curve (ICC) – See **Item Response Theory**.

Item Response Theory (IRT) – Item Response Theory is a measurement system which takes account of both candidate and item characteristics. It is based on probability theory, and shows the probability of a given person getting a particular item right. Candidates' scores and item totals are transformed on to one scale so that they can be related to each other. The relationship between the candidates' item performance and the abilities underlying item performance is described in an item characteristic curve (ICC). There are three main IRT models: the one-parameter (Rasch) model which only takes account of candidate ability and item difficulty; the two-parameter model, which also takes account of item discrimination; and the three-parameter model, which in addition takes account of guessing. (Chapter 4)

Key – A key is the full set of acceptable answers for an objective test. In a key there is only one acceptable answer for each item. (Chapter 5)

Kuder Richardson 20 and 21 (also known as **KR20** and **KR21**) – See **Reliability**.

Kurtosis – Kurtosis refers to the steepness of a test distribution curve. (Chapter 4)

Main trials – See **Pretesting**.

Mark scheme – A mark scheme is similar to a key, in that it contains a set of acceptable answers for an objective test. However, unlike a key, there may be more than one correct answer for each item. (Chapter 5)

Mean – The mean score on a test is what is commonly known as the average; that is, the sum of all the students' scores divided by the number of students. (Chapter 4)

Median – The median is the score obtained by the student who is in the middle of the student rankings. If, for example, five students took a test, and had scores of 9, 7, 6, 2 and 1, the median score would be 6. The median is particularly informative when the tester feels that the mean is in some way not representative of the whole group's level of ability. (Chapter 4)

Mode – The mode is the score which is gained by the largest number of students. (Chapter 4)

Multitrait-multimethod analysis (MTMM) – See **Construct validity.**

Negatively skewed – In a negatively skewed distribution, scores cluster at the top end of the histogram and tail off towards the bottom end. Such a distribution shows that the test was easy for the candidates. (Chapter 4) (See **Positively skewed**)

Norm-referenced – If a test is norm-referenced it aims to place candidates on some sort of ordered scale, so that they can be compared with one another. (Chapter 4) (See **Criterion-referenced**)

Objective testing – Objective testing refers to items such as multiple-choice, true-false, and error-recognition, amongst others, where the candidate is required to produce a response which can be marked as either 'correct' or 'incorrect'. In objective marking the examiner compares the candidate's response to the response or range of responses that the item writer has determined is correct. (Chapter 5) (See **Subjective testing**)

One-parameter model – See **Item Response Theory.**

Parallel form reliability – See **Reliability.**

Parallel tests – Parallel tests are designed to be as similar to each other as possible. They should, therefore, include the same instructions, response types and number of items, and should be based on the same content. They should also, if tried out on the same students, produce the same means and standard deviations. (Chapter 4) (See **Equivalent tests**)

Pearson Product Moment Correlation Coefficient – See **Correlation coefficient.**

Pilot testing – See **Pretesting.**

Placement tests – Placement tests are designed to assess students' levels of language ability so that they can be placed in the appropriate course or class. (Chapter 2)

Point biserial correlation – See **Discrimination index.**

Positively skewed – In a positively skewed distribution, scores cluster at the bottom end of the histogram, and tail off towards the top end. Such a distribution shows that the test was difficult for the candidates. (Chapter 4) (See **Negatively skewed**)

Predictive validity – Predictive validity involves the comparison of test scores with some other measure for the same candidates, taken some time after the test has been given. Predictive validation is most common with proficiency tests: tests which are intended to predict how well somebody will perform in the future. (Chapter 8)

Pretesting – In this book pretesting refers to all trials of an examination that take place before it is launched, or becomes operational or 'live' as some of the boards put it. Most of the pretesting takes place during the 'main trials' but it should be preceded by less formal pretesting which we call pilot testing. Pilot testing may vary in scope from trying out a test on a small group of colleagues to running a trial on say a hundred students, but in all cases the aim is to iron out the main problems before the main trials. (Chapter 4)

Proficiency tests – Proficiency tests are not based on a particular language programme. They are designed to test the ability of students with different language training backgrounds. Some proficiency tests, such as many of those produced by the UK examination boards, are intended to show whether students have reached a given level of general language ability. Others are designed to show whether students have sufficient ability to be able to use a language in some specific area such as medicine, tourism, or academic study. (Chapter 2)

Progress tests – Progress tests are given at various stages throughout a language course to see what the students have learnt. (Chapter 2)

Range – The range is the difference between the top and the bottom scores on a test. (Chapter 4)

Rank Order correlation – See **Correlation coefficient**.

Rasch analysis – See **Item Response Theory**.

Rating scale – A rating scale is most commonly used to mark tests of writing and speaking. This type of scale consists of numbers, letters or other labels (e.g. 'Excellent' or 'Very good'), which may be accompanied by descriptors, statements of the kind of behaviour that each point on the scale refers to. (Chapter 5)

Rational validity – See **Content validity**.

Reliability – Reliability is the extent to which test scores are consistent: if candidates took the test again tomorrow after taking it today, would they get the same result (assuming no change in their ability)? (Chapter 2 and throughout the book.) There are several ways of measuring the reliability of 'objective' tests (test-retest, parallel form, split-half, KR20, KR21 etc.): these are explained in detail in Chapter 4. The reliability of subjective tests is measured by calculating the reliability of the marking. This is done in several ways (inter-rater reliability, intra-rater reliability etc.). (Chapter 6)

Reported scores – A reported score is the score that is reported to candidates, employers or schools. (Chapter 7)

Response validity – Response validation (Henning 1987: 96) refers to a growing range of qualitative techniques where test-takers are asked to report on how they respond to test items. (Chapter 8)

Scaling – Scaling is a procedure which is used by examination boards to adjust the marks that have been given by an examiner who is later found to be 'out of line' with other examiners. Marks may be scaled up if an examiner is found to be too strict in marking, and scaled down if an examiner is too lenient. (Chapter 6)

Significant difference – A significant difference is one which is large enough not to be due solely to chance. The usual test of whether the difference between two means is significant is the t-test. (Chapter 6)

Specifications – A test's specifications provide the official statement about what the test tests and how it tests what it intends to test. The specifications are the blueprint to be followed by test and item writers, and they are also essential in the establishment of the test's construct validity. (Chapter 2) (See **Syllabus**)

Split-half reliability – See **Reliability**.

Standard deviation (S.D.) – The standard deviation is, approximately, the average amount that each student's score deviates (differs) from the mean. If a student has a score of 4, and the mean score is 6, then that student deviates –2 from the mean. Similarly a student with a score of

10 will deviate +4 from the mean. The S.D. reports the average amount that all the scores differ from the mean. (Chapter 4)

Standard setting – In this book standard setting is used to refer to a procedure in which expert judges – trained professionals with relevant expertise – inspect the content of the test, and decide what the likely performance of <u>barely</u> adequate candidates on the test would be. (Chapter 7)

Subjective testing – Subjective testing refers to items or tasks where examiners cannot make judgements which are simply 'correct' or 'incorrect'. Rather, they must assess how well a candidate completes a given task, and for this they need a 'rating scale'. (Chapter 5) (See **Objective testing**)

Syllabus – The syllabus of a test derives from the test's specifications. Although some UK examination boards use specifications and syllabus interchangeably, we see a difference between them. A test specification is a detailed document, and is often for internal purposes only. It is sometimes confidential to the examining body. The syllabus is a public document, often much simplified, which indicates to test users what the test will contain. Whereas the test specification is for the test developers and those who need to evaluate whether a test has met its aim, the syllabus is directed more to teachers and students who wish to prepare for the test, to people who need to make decisions on the basis of test scores, and to publishers who wish to produce materials related to the test. (Chapter 2) (See **Specifications**)

t-test – A t-test is performed to find out whether the difference between two means is significant. (Chapter 6)

Test-retest reliability – See **Reliability**.

Three-parameter model – See **Item Response Theory**.

Transformation – Transformation occurs when test designers wish to give equal weighting to subtests of unequal length. The commonest form of transformation is to convert the sub-test scores into percentage scores, that is divide each sub-test score by the number of items, and multiply by 100. More complex forms of score transformation are possible (standardised scores, z scores and so on). (Chapter 7)

Trialling – See **Pretesting**.

Two-parameter model – See **Item Response Theory.**

Validity – Validity is the extent to which a test measures what it is intended to measure: it relates to the uses made of test scores and the ways in which test scores are interpreted, and is therefore always relative to test purpose. Although the only chapter in the book with a reference to validity in its title is Chapter 8, the concept of validity is central to all the chapters, from Specifications through to Standards.

Weighting – Test designers often believe that some items are more important than others and that such items should therefore carry more weight. Giving extra value to some items is known as weighting. (Chapter 7)

Abbreviations and acronyms

ABEEB	Association of British ESOL Examining Boards
AEB	Associated Examining Board
AERA	American Educational Research Association
AET	ARELS Examination Trust
ALTE	Association of Language Testers in Europe
APA	American Psychological Association
ARELS	Association of Recognised English Language Schools
C & G	City and Guilds of London Institute
CAE	Certificate in Advanced English (UCLES)
CCSE	Certificates in Communicative Skills in English (UCLES)
CEELT	Cambridge Examination in English for Language Teachers (UCLES)
CEIBT	Certificate in English for International Business and Trade (UCLES)
CENTRA	North West Regional Examinations Board
CPE	Certificate of Proficiency in English (UCLES)
CS	Communication Skills (C&G)
CTE	Communication in Technical English (Overseas) (C&G)
CUEFL	Examination in the Communicative Use of English as a Foreign Language
DES	Diploma of English Studies (UCLES)
EAL	English as an Acquired Language (ESB)
EAP	English for Academic Purposes
EfB	English for Business (LCCI)
EfC	English for Commerce (LCCI)
EFL	English as a Foreign Language
ELTS	English Language Testing Service (The British Council)
ESB	English Speaking Board
ESL	English as a Second Language
ESOL	English for Speakers of Other Languages (PEI)
ESP	English for Specific Purposes
ESU	English Speaking Union
ETS	Educational Testing Service
FCE	First Certificate in English (UCLES)
GCSE	General Certificate of Secondary Education
IELTS	International English Language Testing System (UCLES)

IGCSE	International General Certificate of Secondary Education
ILTA	International Language Testing Association
JCTP	Joint Committee on Testing Practices
JMB	Joint Matriculation Board
LCCI	London Chamber of Commerce and Industry Examinations Board
NCME	National Council for Measurement in Education
OHE	Oxford Higher Exam (OUDLES)
OPE	Oxford Preliminary Exam (OUDLES)
Oxford	University of Oxford Delegacy of Local Examinations
PEI	Pitman Examinations Institute
PET	Preliminary English Test (UCLES)
RSA	Royal Society of Arts
SCAA	Schools Curriculum and Assessment Authority
SEAC	Schools Examination and Assessment Council
SEfIC	Spoken English for Industry and Commerce (LCCI)
TEEP	Test of English for Educational Purposes (AEB)
TELS	Tests in English Language Skills (CENTRA)
TESOL	Teaching English to Speakers of Other Languages
TOEFL	Test of English as a Foreign Language (ETS)
Trinity	Trinity College London
TSE	Test of Spoken English (ETS)
TWE	Test of Written English (ETS)
UCLES	University of Cambridge Local Examinations Syndicate
UETESOL	University Entrance Test in English for Speakers of Other Languages (JMB)
ULSEB	University of London Schools Examination Board

Bibliography

Alderson, J.C. 1978. *A Study of the Cloze Procedure with Native and Non-Native Speakers of English*. Unpublished Ph.D. thesis, Edinburgh University.

Alderson, J.C. 1979. The Cloze Procedure and Proficiency in English as a Foreign Language. *TESOL Quarterly* 13(2): 219–227. Reprinted in J.W. Oller, 1983. (ed.), *Issues in Language Testing Research*. Rowley, Mass.: Newbury House.

Alderson, J.C. 1980. Native and Non-native Speaker Performance on Cloze Tests. *Language Learning* 13(1): 59–76.

Alderson, J.C. 1986a. In Leech and Candlin (eds.), *Computers in English Language Education and Research*. London: Longman.

Alderson, J.C. 1986b. Innovations in Language Testing? In M. Portal (ed.), *Innovations in Language Testing*. 93–105. Windsor, Berks.: NFER-Nelson.

Alderson, J.C. 1988a. Innovations in Language Testing: Can the Microcomputer Help? Special issue of *Language Testing Update*.

Alderson, J.C. 1988b. New Procedures for Validating Proficiency Tests of ESP? Theory and Practice. *Language Testing* 5(2): 220–232.

Alderson, J.C. 1990. Testing Reading Comprehension Skills (Part Two): Getting Students to Talk about Taking a Reading Test (A Pilot Study). *Reading in a Foreign Language* 7(1): 465–502.

Alderson, J.C. 1991. Dis-sporting Life. In Alderson J.C. and B. North. (eds.), *Language Testing in the 1990s*. London: Macmillan.

Alderson, J.C. 1993. Judgements in Language Testing. In D. Douglas, and C. Chapelle, *A New Decade of Language Testing*. Alexandria, Virginia: TESOL.

Alderson, J.C. and G. Buck. 1993. Standards in Testing: A Survey of the Practice of UK Examination Boards in EFL Testing. *Language Testing* 10(2): 1–26.

Alderson, J.C. and C.M. Clapham. 1992a. Applied Linguistics and Language Testing: a Case Study of the ELTS Test. *Applied Linguistics* 13: 149–167.

Alderson, J.C. and C.M. Clapham. 1992b. *Examining the ELTS Test: An Account of the First Stage of the ELTS Revision Project*. IELTS Research Report 2. Cambridge: The British Council, University of Cambridge Local Examinations Syndicate and International Development Program of Australian Universities and Colleges.

Alderson, J.C., K. Krahnke and C. Stansfield (eds.). 1987. *Reviews of English Language Proficiency Tests*. Washington, DC: TESOL.

Alderson, J.C. and Y. Lukmani. 1989. Cognition and Levels of Comprehension as Embodied in Test Questions. *Reading in a Foreign Language* 5(2): 253–270.

Alderson, J.C. and B. North (eds.). 1991. *Language Testing in the 1990s*. London: Macmillan.

Alderson, J.C. and D. Wall. 1993. Does Washback Exist? *Applied Linguistics* 14: 115–129.

Alderson, J.C., D. Wall and C.M. Clapham. 1986. *An Evaluation of the National Certificate in English*. Centre for Research in Language Education, Lancaster University.

Alderson, J.C. and S.W. Windeatt. 1991. Computers and Innovation in Language Testing. In J.C. Alderson and B. North (eds.), *Language Testing in the 1990s: The Communicative Legacy*. New York: Macmillan.

Allan, A. 1992. Development and Validation of a Scale to Measure Test-Wiseness in EFL/ESL Reading Test Takers. *Language Testing* 9: 101–123.

American Education Research Association, American Psychological Association, and National Council on Measurement in Education. 1985. *Standards for Educational and Psychological Testing*. Washington, DC: American Psychological Association, Inc.

Anastasi, A. 1988. *Psychological Testing*. London: Macmillan.

Angoff, W. and A.J. Sharon. 1971. A comparison of scores earned on the Test of English as a Foreign Language by native American college students and foreign applicants. *TESOL Quarterly*. 5: 129.

Association of Language Testers in Europe. 1994. *The ALTE Code of Practice*. Cambridge: ALTE.

Bachman, L.F. 1990. *Fundamental Considerations in Language Testing*. Oxford: Oxford University Press.

Bachman, L.F., A. Kunnan, S. Vanniariajan and B. Lynch. 1988. Task and Ability Analysis as a Basis for Examining Content and Construct Comparability in Two EFL Proficiency Test Batteries. *Language Testing* 5: 128–160.

Bachman, L.F. and A.S. Palmer. 1981. A Multitrait-Multimethod Investigation into the Construct Validity of Six Tests of Listening and Reading. In A.S. Palmer, P.J.M. Groot and G.A. Trosper (eds.), *The Construct Validation of Tests of Communicative Competence*. Washington, DC: TESOL.

Bachman, L.F. and A.S. Palmer. 1982. The Construct Validation of Some Components of Communicative Proficiency. *TESOL Quarterly* 16(4): 449–465.

Buck, G. 1989. Written Tests of Pronunciation: Do They Work? *English Language Teaching Journal* 41: 50–56.

Buck, G. 1991. *Expert estimates of test item characteristics.* Paper presented at the Language Testing Research Colloquium, Princeton.

Campbell, D.T. and D.W. Fiske. 1959. Convergent and Discriminant Validation by the Multitrait-Multimethod Matrix. *Psychological Bulletin* 56: 81–105.

Carroll, B.J. 1980. *Testing Communicative Performance.* London: Pergamon.

Carroll, B.J. 1985. Second Language Performance Testing for University and Professional Contexts. In P.C. Hauptman, R. LeBlanc and M.B. Wesche (eds.), *Second Language Performance Testing.* Ottawa: University of Ottawa Press.

Carroll, B.J. and R. West. 1989. *ESU Framework: Performance Scales for English Language Examinations.* London: Longman.

Clapham, C.M. 1992. *The Effect of Academic Discipline on Reading Test Performance.* Paper given at the Language Testing Research Colloquium, Princeton, NJ.

Clapham, C.M. and J.C. Alderson (forthcoming). *Constructing and Trialling the IELTS Test.* IELTS Research Report 3. Cambridge: The British Council, University of Cambridge Local Examinations Syndicate and International Development Program of Australian Universities and Colleges.

Cohen, A.D. 1984. On Taking Tests: What the Students Report. *Language Testing* 1(1): 70–81.

Cohen, A. 1994. *Assessing Language Ability in the Classroom.* 2nd edition. Rowley, Mass.: Newbury House/Heinle and Heinle.

Criper, C. and A. Davies. 1988. *ELTS Validation Project Report,* ELTS Research Report 1(i). London and Cambridge: The British Council and University of Cambridge Local Examinations Syndicate.

Crocker, L. and J. Algina. 1986. *Introduction to Classical and Modern Test Theory.* Chicago, Ill.: Holt Rinehart Winston.

Davidson, F. and B. Lynch. 1993. Criterion-Referenced Language Test Development. A Prologomenon. In A. Huhta, K. Sajavaara and S. Takala (eds.), *Language Testing: New Openings.* Institute for Educational Research, University of Jyvaskyla, Finland.

Davies, A. 1991. *The Native Speaker in Applied Linguistics.* Edinburgh: Edinburgh University Press.

Diamond, E.E. and J. Fremer. 1989. The Joint Committee on Testing Practices and the Code of Fair Testing Practices in Education. *Educational Measurement: Issues and Practice.* Spring issue.

Douglas, D. (ed.). 1990. *English Language Testing in U.S. Colleges and Universities.* Washington, DC: NAFSA.

Ebel, R.L. 1979. *Essentials of Educational Measurement.* 3rd edition. Englewood Cliffs, NJ: Prentice-Hall.

Ebel, R.L. and D.A. Frisbie. 1991. *Essentials of Educational Measurement.* 5th edition. Englewood Cliffs, NJ: Prentice-Hall.

Faerch, C. and G. Kasper. 1987. *Introspection in Second Language Research*. Clevedon: Multilingual Matters.

Gronlund, N.E. 1985. *Measurement and Evaluation in Teaching*. New York: Macmillan.

Grotjahn, R. 1986. Test validation and cognitive psychology: some methodological considerations. *Language Testing* 3(2): 159–185.

Guilford, J.P. and B. Fruchter. 1978. *Fundamental Statistics in Psychology and Education*. Tokyo: McGraw Hill.

Hambleton, R.K., H. Swaminathan and H.J. Rogers. 1991. *Fundamentals of Item Response Theory*. Newbury Park, Calif.: Sage Publications.

Hamilton, J., M. Lopes, T. McNamara and E. Sheridan. 1993. Rating Scales and Native Speaker Performance on a Communicatively Oriented EAP Test. *Melbourne Papers in Language Testing* 2: 1–24.

Heaton, J.B. 1988. *Writing English Language Tests*. 2nd edition. London: Longman.

Henning, G. 1987. *A Guide to Language Testing*. Cambridge, Mass.:Newbury House.

Hudson, T. and B. Lynch. 1984. A Criterion Referenced Measurement Approach to ESL Achievement Testing. *Language Testing* 1: 171–202.

Hughes, A. 1988. Achievement and Proficiency: The Missing Link. In A. Hughes (ed.), *Testing for University Study*, ELT Documents 127. London: Modern English Publications.

Hughes, A. 1989. *Testing for Language Teachers*. Cambridge: Cambridge University Press.

Hutchinson, T. and A. Waters. 1987. *English for Specific Purposes: A Learner Centred Approach*. Cambridge: Cambridge University Press.

Hymes, D.H. 1972. On Communicative Competence. In J.B. Pride and J. Holmes (eds.), *Sociolinguistics, 269–93*. Harmondsworth: Penguin.

Ingram, E. 1977. Basic Concepts in Testing. In J.P.B. Allen and A. Davies (eds.), *Testing and Experimental Methods*. Oxford: Oxford University Press.

Joint Committee on Standards for Educational Evaluation. 1981. *Standards for Evaluations of Educational Programs, Projects, and Materials*. New York: McGraw Hill.

Joint Committee on Testing Practices. 1988. *Code of Fair Testing Practices in Education*. Washington, DC: American Psychological Association.

Kerlinger, F.N. 1973. *Foundations of Behavioral Research*. New York: Holt, Rinehart and Winston.

Klein-Braley, C. 1981. *Empirical Investigation of Cloze Tests*. Doctoral Dissertation, University of Duisburg.

Lado, R. 1961. *Language Testing*. New York: McGraw Hill.

Linacre, J.M. and B.D. Wright. 1992. *FACETS: Many-Facet Rasch Measurement*. Chicago: MESA Press.

Lord, F.M. 1980. *Applications of Item Response Theory to Practical Testing Problems*. Hillsdale, NJ: Lawrence Erlbaum.

Lynch, B., F. Davidson and G. Henning. 1988. Person dimensionality in language test validation. *Language Testing* 5(2): 206–219.

Magnusson, D. 1966. *Test Theory*. Reading, Mass.: Addison Wesley.

Mathews, J.C. 1985. *Examinations: A Commentary*. London: George Allen and Unwin.

Morrow, K. 1979. Communicative Language Testing: Revolution or Evolution? In C.J. Brumfit and K. Johnson (eds.), *The Communicative Approach to Language Teaching*. Oxford: Oxford University Press.

Morrow, K. 1986. The Evaluation of Tests of Communicative Performance. In M. Portal (ed.), *Innovations in Language Testing*. Windsor, Berks: NFER-Nelson.

Munby, J. 1978. *Communicative Syllabus Design*. Cambridge: Cambridge University Press.

Nevo, D. and E. Shohamy. 1986. Evaluation Standards for the Assessment of Alternative Testing Methods : an Application. *Studies in Educational Evaluation* 12: 149–158.

Oller, J. 1979. *Language Tests at School*. London: Longman.

Peirce, B.N. 1992. Demystifying the TOEFL Reading Test. *TESOL Quarterly* 26: 665–689.

Pollitt, A. 1990. *Standards. Notes prepared for a meeting to discuss language testing standards*. Cambridge: University of Cambridge Local Examinations Syndicate.

Popham, W.J. 1990. *Modern Educational Measurement: A Practitioner's Perspective*. 2nd ed. Boston, Mass.: Allyn and Bacon.

Robinson, P. 1980. *ESP (English for Specific Purposes)*. Oxford: Pergamon.

Schools Examination and Assessment Council. 1993. *Mandatory Code of Practice for the GCSE*. London: SEAC.

Stevenson, D.K. 1985. Authenticity, Validity and a Tea Party. *Language Testing* 2(1): 41–7.

Swain, M. 1993. Second Language Testing and Second Language Acquisition: Is There a Conflict with Traditional Psychometrics? *Language Testing* 10(2): 193–207.

Swales, J. 1985. *Episodes in ESP*. Oxford: Pergamon.

Thorndike, R.L. and E.P. Hagen. 1986. *Measurement and Evaluation in Psychology and Education*. New York: Macmillan.

Valette, R.M. 1977. *Modern Language Testing*. 2nd edition. New York: Harcourt Brace Jovanovich.

Wall, D. and Alderson, J.C. 1993. Examining Washback. *Language Testing* 10(1): 41–69.

Wall, D., C.M. Clapham and J.C. Alderson. 1994. Evaluating a Placement Test. *Language Testing* 11(3): 321–343.

Weir, C.J. 1983. *Identifying the Language Problems of Overseas Students in Tertiary Education in the United Kingdom.* Ph.D. thesis, University of London.

Weir, C.J. 1988. *Communicative Language Testing.* University of Exeter.

Weir, C.J. 1990. *Communicative Language Testing.* Englewood Cliffs, NJ: Prentice-Hall Regent.

Wood, R. 1991. *Assessment and Testing: A Survey of Research.* Cambridge: Cambridge University Press.

Wright, B.D. and G.N. Masters. 1982. *Rating Scale Analysis: Rasch Measurement.* Chicago, Ill.: Mesa Press.

Wright, B.D. and M.H. Stone. 1979. *Best Test Design: Rasch Measurement.* Chicago, Ill.: Mesa Press.

Index

Entries marked in *italics* refer to definitions given in the Glossary.

Lightning Source UK Ltd.
Milton Keynes UK
UKOW02f1345091216

289522UK00001B/82/P